RELIGION, LAW, USA

NORTH AMERICAN RELIGIONS

Series Editors: Tracy Fessenden (Religious Studies, Arizona State University), Laura Levitt (Religious Studies, Temple University), and David Harrington Watt (History, Haverford College)

In recent years a cadre of industrious, imaginative, and theoretically sophisticated scholars of religion have focused their attention on North America. As a result the field is far more subtle, expansive, and interdisciplinary than it was just two decades ago. The North American Religions series builds on this transformative momentum. Books in the series move among the discourses of ethnography, cultural analysis, and historical study to shed new light on a wide range of religious experiences, practices, and institutions. They explore topics such as lived religion, popular religious movements, religion and social power, religion and cultural reproduction, and the relationship between secular and religious institutions and practices. The series focuses primarily, but not exclusively, on religion in the United States in the twentieth and twenty-first centuries.

Books in the Series

Religion, Law, USA

Edited by
Joshua Dubler and Isaac Weiner

NEW YORK UNIVERSITY PRESS
New York

NEW YORK UNIVERSITY PRESS
New York
www.nyupress.org

References to Internet websites (URLs) were accurate at the time of writing. Neither the author nor New York University Press is responsible for URLs that may have expired or changed since the manuscript was prepared.

Library of Congress Cataloging-in-Publication Data
Names: Dubler, Joshua, editor. | Weiner, Isaac, editor.
Title: Religion, law, USA / edited by Joshua Dubler and Isaac Weiner.
Description: New York : NYU Press, 2019. | Series: North American religions |
Includes bibliographical references and index.
Identifiers: LCCN 2018042918| ISBN 9781479893362 (cl : alk. paper) |
ISBN 9781479891399 (pb : alk. paper)
Subjects: LCSH: Religion and law—United States. | Freedom of religion—United States. |
Religion and state—United States.
Classification: LCC KF358 .R45 2019 | DDC 342.7308/52—dc23
LC record available at https://lccn.loc.gov/2018042918

New York University Press books are printed on acid-free paper, and their binding materials are chosen for strength and durability. We strive to use environmentally responsible suppliers and materials to the greatest extent possible in publishing our books.

Manufactured in the United States of America

10 9 8 7 6 5 4 3 2 1

Also available as an ebook

CONTENTS

Introduction

Religion, Law, USA

JOSHUA DUBLER AND ISAAC WEINER

It might well seem imprudent for drug-rehabilitation counselors, especially ones with histories of dependency, to use prohibited substances. But what if they take themselves to be religiously obligated to do so? In 1983, Alfred Smith and Galen Black, Oregonian members of the Native American Church, were fired from their counseling jobs at the Douglas County Council on Alcohol and Drug Abuse Prevention and Treatment for violating its substance abuse policy. As part of their church's religious ceremonies, the two men had ingested peyote, a powerful hallucinogen. Denied their subsequent claim for unemployment compensation, Smith and Black sued, alleging that the state was infringing on their religious freedom. Taking peyote was not evidence of "workplace misconduct," they argued, but rather was a sacramental expression of their sincerely held religious beliefs—and thus categorically protected by the US Constitution.

Smith and Black's case would twice reach the US Supreme Court. In what was eventually decided in 1990 as *Employment Division v. Smith*, a sharply divided court ruled against the Native American Church members. Religious motivation, it said, did not exempt people from an otherwise generally applicable law. Writing for the majority, Justice Antonin Scalia dismissed the applicability of the "*Sherbert* test" and its generation-old directive that only a "compelling state interest" justifies placing a "substantial burden" on a religious practice. To date, Scalia reasoned, this test had been applied only to cases involving "hybrid rights," where the right to religious free exercise was asserted in support of another fundamental right, such as the right to free speech or a parent's right to shape their children's education. Absent such hybridity, religious practitioners should expect little relief through litigation. For special exemptions from otherwise neutral laws, religious citizens would have to seek redress through legislative channels and not via the courts.[1]

The *Smith* decision was an outrage and, in cultural terms, a landmark. In the years to follow, liberals and conservatives banded together to pass a plethora of specialized legislative acts, including the Religious Freedom Restoration Act (RFRA), the International Religious Freedom Act (IRFA), and the Religious Land Use and Institutionalized Persons Act (RLUIPA), each of which meant to resecure the federal government's commitment to protecting religious liberty. Many states adopted their own "mini-RFRAs," which afforded religious claims further accommodation. A specialized legal bar arose alongside an array of well-funded political advocacy groups, each committed to preserving and defending the legal rights of religion.[2]

In the academy, meanwhile, *Smith* unleashed a flood of consideration. Legal scholars dissected Scalia's reasoning, questioning whether his decision was consistent with or a departure from thirty years of free exercise clause jurisprudence. They debated the proper standards by which courts should adjudicate petitions for religious exemptions and outlined competing visions for how courts might best safeguard religious rights in the future.[3] These are questions of momentous consequence. However, as we ourselves discovered early in our trainings as scholars of American religion, to wade into these waters is to follow the court's opinion into a rarefied and somewhat exclusionary realm. It is a world of legal experts, disciplined to approach religion and law with particular tools in hand and particular questions in mind. To the uninitiated, this discursive terrain can feel alienating, and to humanists, its argumentation can feel remote from the lives and concerns of people like Alfred Smith and Galen Black.

Scholars of American religion, though indebted to and engaged with these conversations, have charted a somewhat different course in recent years. More and more, we have turned to law as a productive site of inquiry, but we have approached it with our own theoretical preoccupations and disciplinary vocabularies, and from our own methodological vantage points. Now an established and vibrant subfield, academics working at the intersection of American religion and American law have produced influential and innovative works of scholarship. It seems the right time to take stock and consider the value of this collective enterprise. Why, we might ask, has religion and law emerged as a burgeoning area of study now? What has this recent work enabled us to perceive more clearly about religion, about law, and about American society? What, precisely, are we doing and why? It is to think through these questions that we decided to write this book.

Surveying the Terrain

Before we can zero in on a single copse of trees, a special group to be tagged, measured, and evaluated for diseases, we must first consider the forest.

Religion, law, the United States of America: these are concepts of mammoth consequence, categories with complex histories and rich material lives. These ideas populate a range of individual, communal, and civic practices, where, as often as not, they appear in a moralizing register and act as carriers of accentuated feeling and identification. To think through these concepts requires that we consider not solely what they mean but also the trajectories and circumstances that call these meanings to life. Necessarily, then, to do theory is also to do history and ethnography.

RELIGION.[4] As we tend to observe in our classrooms, in our nonprofessional social circles, and in the public square, for most Americans, the category of religion connotes first something associated with a presumed state of interiority. As indicated by its companion terms "belief" and "faith," "religion" is most commonly associated with certain cognitive content. This means that religion is located within an individual, who is presumed to believe in a certain thing in a certain way. When multiple individuals are thought to avow a shared set of doctrines, they are said to belong to a religious community. These religious credos are thought to be distinct from ordinary principles in that they are nonfalsifiable. They are, one might say, "taken on faith."[5] That God sent his only Son, who died on the cross to deliver us from our sins; that God revealed himself on Mount Sinai to an appointed tribal leader; that God revealed himself in the seventh century to an illiterate messenger: the essence of religion is generally presumed to be the avowal of doctrines of this kind. As a general rule, Americans who profess a belief in God and Americans who profess an absence of belief in God tend to agree that this sort of creed is what religion is fundamentally about.

The roots of this American way of conceptualizing religion begin elsewhere and prior. This notion of religion as something doctrinally based, interiorized, and individualistic is indebted to the history and theology of Protestant Christianity, a religious, social, and political movement launched in sixteenth-century Europe. It is fair to say that nothing has been more determinative of the ways that Americans talk about religion than Protestantism, and that this is true even for those many Americans, including the authors of these words, who are not themselves Protestant. In theological terms, the Protestant emphasis on inward faith stood as corrective to what reformers regarded as the excessive ritualism and institutionalized corruption of the Roman Catholic Church. In historical or political terms, channeling religion into a narrowly circumscribed private realm promised a philosophical and pragmatic solution to the "problem" of religious violence, especially in response to the bloody conflicts that followed in the Reformation's wake. Half a millennium later, what and how individual "religious" people believe remains the purported essence of religion.

What then of religious practices—what in a Catholic context one might call "works," in a Jewish context one might call "mitzvoth," or in a Hindu context one might call "yogas"? These genres of practices are conventionally regarded as the material actualization of religious belief, perhaps secondary or ancillary to inward commitment but nonetheless consequential. In combination with a lay theology, then, it is possible to pinpoint in the United States a lay sociology of religion: religious bodily behaviors matter. Sermons, liturgies, catechisms, life-cycle celebrations and festivals: these things are thought to have substantial effects. In religious ritual feelings flow and convictions are confirmed. In ways both quiet and loud, abiding and ephemeral, in religious activity, selves congeal and collectivities cluster. Marching orders are given, and marching orders are received. Whether or not accompanied by something like bona fide faith, religion, it is generally thought, is like a spirit come to earth. It makes bodies move in righteous or curious ways, toward this or that end. That is, religion is frequently credited as being a shaping force in the world.

With the rarest of exceptions, this force is thought to arrive with a charge. Religion is something good or bad; almost never is it seen as neutral. This is weird and interesting. Compare this, for a second, to some of the study of religion's neighboring humanistic disciplines. While a particular introductory history lecture course may be spoken of as exceptionally good, would anyone think to call history *as such* "a good thing"? And while as a tradition of inquiry there is much in anthropology's fraught relationship to colonialism that invites critique, it would raise an eyebrow were a colleague or student to call *culture*—anthropology's organizing concept—"bad." Yet, with religion, such judgments do not seem remotely so odd. According to one common view, religion is a good thing, even an essential thing, for self, community, and nation. In this read, religion is said to engender virtue, to bind families together, and to foster avid citizenship, up to and including the enabling of righteous sacrifice. Without religion, many have long worried, individuals will succumb to vice, families will fracture, and the republic will teeter. If only they could get right with God, many reason, degenerates and communists might also be saved.

For others, meanwhile, religion is a bad thing, and not infrequently a *very* bad thing. In this read, religion is a holdover from primitive times, the delusional refusal to see the world for what it is, a barrier to individual and collective flourishing. Sometimes, people we might describe as "religious" counterpose this kind of bad religion to bona fide faith. The pejorative sense of the English word "ritualistic" captures this negative judgment of ritual behaviors. Mostly, however, the critique of religion (which is to say, of *all* religion) is a secularist position. In certain alien or insurgent forms most especially, religion is cast as a machine for superstition and compulsion, a weapon of patriarchal domination, and a fount of extremist violence. As John Lennon longingly implied in his anthem "Imagine," the abolition of religion would be nothing less than a symptom of peace on earth. Between defenders and detractors, a common ground may be marked out. That is, whether as something to be nurtured or something to be defended against, religion is a powerful force that requires considered management. In this project, it is assumed, law has an important part to play.

LAW.[6] If religion is a force, law is a firmament. Whether as existential threat or possible utopia, a world without religion is possible to imagine. But what would a world without law look like? To edify or entertain, various genres of fiction explore such a possibility, and the result tends to be awfully bloody. This side of *The Road*, however, law is more or less elemental, like water or air. Along with norms—law's less discrete cousin—law is thought to enable governance and to enforce social coherence. Law is a centripetal force. It is gravity, and without it, things would fall apart. This pervasive, deeply reactionary attitude toward law doesn't come up all that much in casual conversation. As an ethnographic matter, law—by which we mean law *as such*—borders on the untheorizable. Canvass a hundred Americans on a random street corner, we figure, and most would have some sort of take on "religion"; solicit their position on "law" and—other than the odd loquacious anarchist or dispensationalist—few would know quite how to respond.

One notable exception to the general attitude of deference shown to the law as such is a widespread bias against law when it is enforced in a manner so literal as to be stupid—that is, when the *spirit* of the law is sacrificed to the *letter* of the law. Consider the following sort of sentiment: "I mean, I don't care what it says in the freaking rule book, nothing you say can convince me that Dez Bryant's catch against the Packers in the 2014 playoffs wasn't a catch."[7] This position (which we share) is commonsense populist, and in a way that rhymes with the English language's polemic against ritualism, a fundamentally Protestant proposition. An astute reader might already note this as a recurring theme.

In contrast to religion, law when it is objectified is generally objectified in the particular. Unless otherwise specified, "religion" is all religions, but "law" is one given body of law. It is here where critical attitudes toward the law generally begin. John Lennon imagined no religion, but the Clash fought *the law* (and the law won). For a notable minority—those who live in certain sectarian religious communities—the "law" could mean divine law. As *halakhah*, as *sharia*, or as God's law, the law is something revealed in scripture, interpreted by scholars, and (unless superseded by Christ's salvific death on the cross) implemented by community elders. In such subcultures, the law can unspool an entire way of life. But in the United States, those who seek to live the law in this way are the minority.

Whether religious or secular, most Americans belong to multiple, overlapping communities, each of which imposes, in formal and informal ways, its own normative demands. In aggregate, however, when Americans speak of the law, they refer to the law of the state. Across the many ways we live, this law is attended by a special force. Federal, state, and local laws govern who is permitted to vote, who can drive and how fast, and what sorts of things one is free to do on one's property without specially secured dispensation. Some laws are seen as bad, and opposing such laws can be a glue that holds communities together.[8] Other laws tend to be disregarded entirely.[9] As a formal matter, the law is recognized as the machine that produces public justice. According to this dominant view, we may fail the law; the law does not fail us. Law enforcement officers who break the law or who act wantonly within the law are painted as bad apples. With proper training, law enforcement is necessarily just. In the United States, this apologetic attitude toward state law is buttressed with an arsenal of national myths and rituals. Via courthouse monuments and grade-school civics lessons, we are instructed that justice is blind. In courtrooms, we rise. At parades and sporting events, we honor those who enforce the law at home and extend the sovereignty of American law abroad.

How precisely these rituals make one feel depends on a slew of factors not limited to race, class, folkways, and family ties. These rituals of deference to the law engender for some feelings of collectivity, of being at home, of being safe, of gratitude. For others, these rituals spark feelings of alienation or even terror. If, for the former group, the law is that which guarantees fairness, for others, whose social positioning may be different, the law is that which enforces unfairness. From this latter critical vantage point, the law protects some and preys upon others. One of the things that makes the present moment in the United States such an interesting one, a moment ripe with new dangers but also new possibilities, is that this dissident perception of the law has rapidly become, for an increasing number of Americans, a species of common sense.

As apologists and dissidents understand equally, the flesh of the law may be reason but its soul is violence.[10] A police officer pulls over a speeding motorist; a suspect is taken into custody; a prisoner has his appeal denied. The object of the law's violence is the body. Even in its coolest forms—jurisdiction and civil procedure—the law can kill, and, routinely, it does. Depending on one's social positioning, the moments in which law articulates itself in lethal violence are grounds for mourning or for celebration.

Not just a set of value-neutral rules meant to facilitate social coexistence, state law constitutes its own distinct culture, structuring social experience and creating meaning through its distinct norms and practices.[11] As is true of religious doctrines, the law propagates a series of consequential fictions that describe and prescribe what it is to live as a human being. The law's human beings are capable of keeping their promises, of being held responsible, of being deterred by punishment. To undo the harm they've done and to ensure that they won't do it again, those who break the law are subjected to penalties. To say that such propositions are considered "uncontroversial" overstates the degree to which they are considered at all.

Not by accident have we repeatedly appealed to religion to make sense of law. In the conceptual field of American popular discourse, the two entities are closely and variously related. As concepts, religion and law share a jealous tendency. Placed in combination, the results are often fractious: a sovereign regime with a legal system backed by scripture suppresses dissent; a charismatic leader, perhaps one in direct communication with God, comes into conflict with secular authorities; a group of religious enthusiasts campaigns to make certain proscriptions the law of the land. The oppressive theocracy, the persecuted prophet, the reformist crusade: in American literature and lore, tropes such as these frequently signal high-stakes conflict. In a different guise, meanwhile, religion—and, in particular, the religious law of Christian scripture—is seen as the precursor to secular law.[12] For some, this story is one of decline. But for others, this putative succession is cited to valorize the law of the state and to imply a covenantal relationship between our special nation and the creator of the world.

THE UNITED STATES OF AMERICA. In the United States, the most heralded site of encounter between religion and law is the regulation of religion within the scope of the Constitution. Any institutionalized tradition is a powerful thing, and American constitutionalism is no mere tradition. Two hundred and thirty years after they were first drafted, the first two clauses in the First Amendment to the Constitution provide the rules by which most public contestation over religion and law takes place and the playing field for the coming conversations. Chances are that many readers know them by heart, and even those of you that don't know them by heart know them nonetheless: "Congress shall make no law respecting an establishment of religion, or prohibiting the free exercise thereof."

It largely took until the twentieth century for justices on the Supreme Court to spell out what precisely these two clauses mean in practice, but it is not false to say that in the US, religion has been, from the very beginning, an object of legal discourse. "Religion" demarcates a discrete sphere, a sphere of special privilege, of inalienable rights for citizens and inviolable restrictions placed on government. An obvious tension is plain from the start. Religion is to be made sacred, but by what authority? By secular law, of course. For this thing "religion" to be protected, it must first be subordinated. Religion may well be privileged by the Constitution, but not before it is also brought to heel. Sovereignty hates to share, and so, while state law can certainly act as religious law's protector, it can also be its killer.[13]

This normative configuration of religion and law has its roots in the entwined historical legacies of the Protestant Reformation and the early modern European wars of religion. The construction of religion as a peculiar object of legal concern arose as a philosophical solution to the "problem" of religious violence and as a pragmatic strategy for managing religious differences. The drafters of the US Constitution were well versed in the writings of Enlightenment thinkers like John Locke, whose political theory of toleration ascribed to religion an inviolable sphere of personal autonomy, free from the coercive power of civic authority, yet only to the degree that it refrains from infringing on the public good.

How well or poorly this somewhat paradoxical directive has been realized has long been a keystone in public discourses about the success or failure of the United States as a political project. Some of the United States' most prominent civic myths—a city on a hill, a light unto the nations, a new Jerusalem—are both religious in origin and *point* to the special protections of religion under American law as positive proof of the United States' exceptionality. Draped in a patriotic spirit, religion, and in particular *religious freedom*, frequently becomes a hallmark of this land of opportunity, liberty, equality, and immigrants who get the job done. For others and at other times, the purported failure to deliver on this sacred promise burnishes an American exception built of other stuff: nativism, white supremacy, plutocracy, imperialist excess, settler colonialism. Our time especially is a heyday of both impulses: the patriotic celebration of American religious freedom and the emphatic negation of the same. Our guess is that it would be hard to find an American community today that does not in one way or another engage in regular conversations—celebratory or polemical, impassioned or by rote—about the fact and relative beneficence of American sovereignty and of the special place of religion as agent or object of this political enterprise. Albeit often at a level of some abstraction, in this regard, scholars of American religion are no exception.

Looking Backward

The earliest accounts of US religious history adopt a tone that is at once defensive and triumphalist. Written in the middle decades of the nineteenth century, primarily by (and about) Protestant Christian clergymen, and intended mostly for European audiences, these works sought to explain the distinctive character of American religious and civic life. They did so by celebrating the "voluntary principle," according to which church and state were formally separated and Americans were purportedly left free to follow the dictates of their own consciences, while at the same time insisting that the United States remained fundamentally, and essentially, a Christian nation. As compared to the continent they had left behind, Americans were both more free and more religious. "Religion is left to the free will of each individual," church historian Philip Schaff wrote in a series of lectures delivered in Berlin in 1854, "and the church has none but moral means of influencing the world." Yet "under such circumstances," he continued, "Christianity, as the free expression of personal conviction and of the national character, has even greater power over the mind, than when enjoined by civil laws and upheld by police regulations."[14] Countering what many in his audience had expected to hear, Schaff attributed American Protestantism's surprising vitality precisely to its formal disestablishment.[15]

Beginning with these earliest historical accounts, scholarly discussions of religion and law could not be disentangled from assertions of what made the United States of America different and special. The separation of church and state was the great American experiment, an ideological and practical project that was both the legacy of its founders' Protestantism and the progenitor of the sprawling and varied shape that Protestantism in the United States was beginning to assume. The secret of how disestablishment favored Protestantism has therefore long been an open one. Writers like Schaff and Robert Baird noted the many ways that American law continued to privilege Protestant moral precepts, whether through enforcement of Sabbath observance, appointment of legislative chaplains, or prohibitions on blasphemy. This was exactly as it should be, they maintained. Far from being inconsistent with the principle of American voluntarism, such observances were, rather, the natural expressions of the American people's fundamentally Christian character. In other words, if religious liberty was what made America special, it was *also* what made it Protestant.

A century later, scholars of American religion were no longer inclined to name Divine Providence as an agential force in US history, but they otherwise colored their accounts with many of the same themes. In the grand synthetic narratives of the 1950s and '60s, which focused still almost exclusively on the stories of white male Protestants, religious liberty and the separation of church and state retained their place as key factors shaping America's exceptional character. These sacred principles were credited with creating the conditions in which Protestant Christianity had both flourished and fragmented. That which the Protestant Reformation had made possible in theory, the United States had realized in practice. In his 1963 collection of essays on "the shaping of Christianity in America," for example, Sidney Mead identifies legal disestablishment and religious freedom, along with the availability of space, as the defining themes of American religious history. American conditions made it impossible to enforce religious orthodoxy, he explained (even citing Philip Schaff as he did so). With the concomitant rise of Christian denominationalism, churches had learned to rely on persuasion rather than coercion. The results of this "lively experiment" might have made Christian life chaotic, Mead concluded, but they were also what made the American story distinct.[16]

By the time Mead wrote, the legal landscape had shifted in dramatic ways. Despite its prominent place in the stories told by religious historians, the First Amendment, to that point, had exerted relatively little direct influence on US history. For most of the nineteenth and early twentieth centuries, regulating religion had largely been a state-level affair. Whatever else it might have meant, the First Amendment was understood to apply only to the federal government ("*Congress* shall make no law . . ."). In a series of cases, however, culminating with two landmark decisions of the 1940s—one involving the proselytizing rights of

Jehovah's Witnesses, the other centered on the constitutionality of public aid for parochial schools—the US Supreme Court gradually came to determine that the First Amendment's protections should also be applied against municipal and state-level action.[17] This meant that by the 1960s, the court had assumed a far more active role in determining the proper scope of religious free exercise and of government involvement in religious matters. In so doing, the court ushered in what historian Sarah Barringer Gordon has described as a "new constitutional world."[18]

Among the territories of this new constitutional world was the academy. For scholars of American law, new questions and imperatives arose. Alongside historical accounts that treated America's distinctive legal arrangements as a necessary precondition for its fractious diversity arose a distinct field of legal scholarship focused on analyzing the new federal jurisprudence.[19] Primarily though not exclusively prescriptive in intent, these law professors' critical assessments of the Supreme Court's varied decisions attempted (unsuccessfully) to identify a consistent set of principles undergirding them.[20] Scholars also revisited the founding period in order to try to excavate what the founders had in mind when it came to the crafting of the First Amendment's religion clauses. Already by the 1960s, much of the agenda that continues to define this subfield had been set: scholars sought to understand the proper relationship between disestablishment and religious free exercise, to define the scope and limits of state neutrality, and to assess how far state actors had to go to accommodate religious commitments.

Alongside these jurisprudential interests, legal scholars began to wrestle with the question of religion's distinctiveness; that is, what is religion, and what about it does or does not warrant special treatment? On the basis of what precisely were beliefs and practices to be included or excluded from the First Amendment's umbrella of protection? How were courts even to know in the first place that what they were dealing with was something we might call religion? The new constitutional world invested these questions with renewed significance as jurists and scholars alike struggled to craft a workable definition. As a widely read 1978 *Harvard Law Review* note put it, the "abundance of recent analysis has enriched our understanding of *how* the religion clauses should be applied; that analysis, however, has failed adequately to define *what* religion is for first amendment purposes."[21]

These definitional questions featured most prominently in a series of Vietnam War–era conscientious-objector cases. What if a would-be objector looking to avoid service grounded his belief in an ideological framework that rejected the existence of a "Supreme Being," as the relevant statutory law required? Did such a conviction merit First Amendment protection? In its fumbling around with questions of this sort, the court found support for its expansive reading of religion in the work of existentialist Protestant theologian Paul Tillich and other liberal religious thinkers. With this prominent exception, however, the court mostly ignored (or demonstrated its ignorance of) the nascent academic field of religious studies.[22] Would concerted engagement with the scholarship of the emergent field of religious studies have made a difference? Perhaps not. What is indisputable is that absent any such guidance, the court's muddled attempts to define religion were widely deemed a failure. Alternately lambasted as either too broad or too restrictive, the court's decisions demonstrated the fundamental unworkability of any fixed definition of religion. Even more, many scholars questioned the constitutionality of the whole enterprise, suggesting that the very task of defining religion for First Amendment purposes ran afoul of its prohibition on religious establishment.

By the 1980s, this definitional project had largely been abandoned. Courts continued to do their thing, but, faced with a fractious and fragmented religious landscape, judges avoided as best they could having to commit themselves on paper to any explicit definition of religion. Scholars of American religion acted similarly, turning away from the grand synthetic narratives that had dominated the field to that point. Buoyed by the dramatic cultural shifts of the 1960s and '70s, including changes to immigration laws, civil rights movements, and political realignments, "diversity" became the new watchword. Suspicion abounded toward any possibility of a single story standing in for the "whole." And as the field grew out from under church history and embraced the methodologies and literatures of its proximate disciplines, including anthropology and sociology most notably, scholars of American religion discovered the law anew. Paul the apostle's polemical insight—that not by the letter of the law do people actually live—here provided a new research agenda. Law and religion ceased to be solely a matter of text and precedent and became instead a matter of norms, narratives, and practices. As constitutional jurisprudence gave way to lived experience, historians and ethnographers of American religion directed their attention away from courtrooms and legislative chambers and toward less formal sites of religious regulation and discipline.[23]

With the Supreme Court's decision in *Smith*, the legal landscape shifted yet again. While the fate of religious freedom in federal courts seemed newly precarious, the *Smith* case reinvigorated it as a potent political discourse. As expressed in and consolidated by the varied legislative and advocacy efforts on its behalf, religious freedom gained a new public salience, allowing it to be mobilized and deployed toward a wide variety of often-contradictory political ends. To date, this process shows little sign of slowing down.

The new politics of religious freedom has rightly elicited ample scholarly scrutiny. Indeed, for a variety of reasons that reflect general goings-on both in the republic and in the field of religious studies, the twenty-first century has witnessed renewed attention to law among scholars of American religion. Questions of definition have returned once again, but now turned inside out. No longer the naïve inquiry, "What is religion?" definitional questions today come from a much more suspicious place: Under what conditions, by what means, and to whose ends have jurists and political actors drawn boundaries around what religion is and is not? Whose interests have been served by the varied ways that religious freedom has been mobilized as a political discourse? Informed by genealogical critiques of religion and of religion's purported opposite, the secular, scholars have interrogated how and why "religion" came to be constructed as a special object of legal concern and the bases on which it continues to warrant distinctive treatment.

Key in this movement has been professor of religion and law Winnifred Fallers Sullivan, who, in her pioneering 2005 work, surveyed the diffusely fragmented and radically disestablished character of American religious life and, on that basis, declared religious freedom "impossible." "In order to enforce laws guaranteeing religious freedom," she explained, "you must first have religion." Yet modern law's need for an "essentialized religion" could not be squared with the messy vagaries of lived experience. In this and subsequent works, Sullivan urged scholars to attend to the marked disjuncture between the discourse of constitutional jurisprudence and the phenomenology of American religious life.[24] Her arguments have inspired a younger generation of scholars, including many of the contributors to this volume, to track the consequences of this pivotal disjuncture across a range of ethnographic sites.

A number of new historical works appeared during this time as well, which revisited earlier periods of American history, focusing especially on the long nineteenth century or the stretch of time between the First Amendment's drafting and its legal incorporation by the mid-twentieth-century Supreme Court. Paying greater attention to the perspectives and experiences of religious minorities and dissenters, these works rejected the progressive narratives of earlier eras, which had interpreted US history as a story of gradually expanding freedom, and offered instead more critical takes on the saga of American religious freedom. Where historians had once emphasized themes of liberty and consensus, they now turned their attention to analyzing Protestant power and hegemony. They showed how American commitments to the separation of church and state were as much the product of anti-Catholic and anti-Mormon animus as of high-minded Enlightenment ideals and how the discourse of religious freedom could be deployed to serve imperialist ends as much as emancipatory ones. In their hands, the American story of religion and law was recast as a series of highly contentious struggles over the uneven distribution of sovereignty, power, and resources rather than as a triumphalist narrative, confirming the nation's venerated exceptionality.[25]

Over the last decade, scholars of American religion have also entered into more robust conversation with scholars of other parts of the world. This has been facilitated, in part, through the work of the law, religion, and culture interest group at the American Academy of Religion, the premier professional association for professional scholars of religion, as well as via a variety of well-funded collaborative research projects. Through these initiatives, historians, anthropologists, political theorists, and others have investigated a range of topics, including the global politics of religious freedom, the relationship between religious and secular law, the varied ways that religious life comes to be regulated and managed under secular democratic governments, and the ways that American assumptions about religion have been incorporated into foreign policy and dealings with other peoples of the world. In significant ways, these comparative enterprises have helped to de-parochialize the study of religion and American law, further undermining long-held assumptions of American exceptionality.[26]

Points of Departure

For today's students of American religions, law is a privileged object, and it is also an archive. Court cases and other legal documents provide extraordinary access to subterranean religious discourses, practices, and histories. These sources occasion powerful insights into how religion has been produced, imagined, and managed and how, under the banner of religion, individuals and communities have accommodated themselves to, endured, and resisted the forces and interests that shape life in America. When approached with our own distinct set of interests and questions and through our own discrete but disciplined practices of reading and reflection, law offers an enormously productive point of entry into a variety of broader conversations in the academic study of religion.

To gesture toward some of these openings, we return to *Smith*. At the top, we described some of the questions law professors posed about the case, but what is *Smith* to a scholar of American religion? A religionist, as one example, might approach the *Smith* decision with a focus "not on the Court as the ultimate authority on the United States Constitution," as scholar of religion Jonathan Z. Smith has put it, "but rather on the Court as the legally authorized interpreter of religion."[27] This means, in part, attending to how the court has come to conceptualize religion in the way that it has and what the implications of its imaginings are for religious practitioners. How has "sincere belief" come to be the standard by which religious legitimacy is to be assessed, and what does this mean for practices like the consumption of peyote? What can we learn from the court's turn to comparison as a strategy for making sense of unfamiliar practices? Is the Native American Church's use of peyote analogous to the Catholic Church's administration of the Eucharist, or is it more like polygamy or female circumcision, each of which the state has placed beyond the boundaries of legal acceptability? Is it an innovative practice, the product of a new religious movement with syncretic origins in the late nineteenth and early twentieth centuries, or an ancient one, tracing a continuous lineage to Indigenous Mexican tradition? How are we to interpret the significance of this ritual and its place in Native American life? In each of these questions, we find hints of broader classificatory dilemmas facing any student of religion, yet they are invested here with the imprimatur and heightened stakes that attend the administration of state authority.

Alternatively, one might analyze the *Smith* case with reference to the contested legacies of religious freedom as an American ideal.[28] Celebrated by many as the defining feature of American exceptionalism, religious freedom has an uneven history, functioning just as often to marginalize minority religious communities as to embrace them. In this telling, Alfred Smith and Galen Black might be said to have joined a long list of litigants—including other Native Americans, Catholics, Mormons, Muslims, and others—who have found US law surprisingly inhospitable if not outright hostile to their distinct ways of life. Whether due to its privileging of belief over practice, individual rights over communal autonomy, or universal claims over ones tied to particular geographic spaces, US law has rendered legible only certain kinds of religious appeals. By attending to this history, we might interrogate how the rhetoric of religious freedom has functioned as much to legitimate particular ways of being religious as to make space for robust forms of difference. We might approach law as a tool by which empowered American agents have distinguished "good" religion from "bad" so as to dispense the former with support and the latter with violence.

Finally, we might locate *Smith* within the history of Indigenous efforts to secure sovereignty or self-governance. How did peyote religion and the Native American Church emerge, in part, as responses to direct acts of governmental suppression? In what ways have Native Americans worked to carve out space free from state regulation and interference? Has the category of "religion" advanced this project or hindered it? Telling this story would require ethnographic attention to the lived experience of Indigenous peoples under the law. How has the legal system served—and how does it continue to serve—as an arena for struggle, resistance, and even revitalization? How have Native American engagements with the law shaped and reshaped the tenets and practices of its community's religious life?[29]

In each of these ways, and others, the Supreme Court's decision in *Employment Division v. Smith* opens itself up not only to jurisprudential analysis but also to other modes of investigation, including historical, ethnographical, and genealogical. Circulating through these disparate readings is a common vocabulary of critical terms, including "belief," "practice," "sincerity," "freedom," "sovereignty," "indigeneity," and "race." To wrestle with the competing meanings and contested legacies of these categories is to enter a complex world of mutual entanglement of law and religion in the United States. It is to consider how religion and law have shaped and informed each other in ways that complicate civic slogans like "separation of church and state." It is to approach religion and law as critical sites for understanding the manifold moods and modes of American life. Such are the concerns of this volume.

This book emerges from an invitation we sent to fourteen prominent and up-and-coming scholars of American religions. Select a term, we wrote, and show us what it reveals about the mutual entanglement of religion and law in America. Hoping for some regularity of rhythm, we encouraged our contributors to ground their explorations in a particular case or event. We then asked them to spin out from this discrete site and consider how their selected category might open itself up to any number of productive paths of inquiry. Finally, we asked them to proceed along one of those paths, guided only by their own scholarly interests. In doing so, we hoped, this volume would be diverse but coherent as it grappled with the broader theoretical concerns of the academic study of religion, writ large.

As befitting a field which, at its best, strives to make the strange familiar and the familiar strange, the resulting chapters include new takes on topics you would expect, such as belief, conscience, and establishment, alongside others that might seem less conventional, like noise, hope, and friend. We readily concede that the selected terms and sites of inquiry are by no means exhaustive. Nevertheless, we believe that the chapters that follow showcase the rich variety of approaches to religion and law currently available within American religious studies. They include attention to the relative (in)commensurability of the practices and categories of legal and religious studies scholarship, to the lived experience of American religionists under the law, and to the secularization through law of theological concepts and principles. We have divided the chapters into four sections, which reflect the volume's overarching concerns: definition, contestation, management, and limits. Winnifred Fallers Sullivan has graciously supplied a concluding reflection.

Perhaps it was the specificity in our prompt, perhaps it was the set of scholars we invited, perhaps it is the historical moment in which we assembled, but the following chapters generally share a statist and Americanist perspective. There is much that is distinctive about the American approach to managing religion, and any abstract or comparative conversation must proceed from a recognition of and engagement with those particularities. Yet we do hope this volume will also be useful for those working on religion and law in other theoretical and historical contexts. We ourselves have learned much from those working in other contexts and at other scales of analysis, and we expect that the questions, concepts, and approaches introduced here can be fruitfully taken up and applied elsewhere.

What the volume's chapters may lack in sweep they compensate for in heat. There is a sense of urgency at work in these pages. We finalize these words in the days following the Supreme Court's decisions gutting public-sector unions and affirming President Trump's Muslim ban and Justice Anthony Kennedy's retirement announcement, which portends new vulnerabilities. The landscape is shifting quickly, and we cannot anticipate where things will stand when this book goes out into the world. Where and how should residents of the United States best pursue justice? What can we reasonably expect of courts of law? What role might religion have to play? To our readers who are grappling with these issues in and beyond the classroom, we hope this book has something to offer.

NOTES

1 Employment Division, Department of Human Resources of Oregon v. Smith, 494 U.S. 872 (1990).

2 Winnifred Fallers Sullivan, "The World That Smith Made," *Immanent Frame* (blog), March 7, 2012, http://blogs.ssrc.org.

3 The legal literature on *Smith* is voluminous. For representative articles written in the immediate wake of the court's decision, see James D. Gordon, "Free Exercise on the Mountaintop," *California Law Review* 79, no. 1 (January 1991): 91–116; Michael W. McConnell, "Free Exercise Revisionism and the Smith Decision," *University of Chicago Law Review* 57, no. 4 (1990): 1109–53; William P. Marshall, "In Defense of Smith and Free Exercise Revisionism," *University of Chicago Law Review* 58, no. 1 (1991): 308–28; James E. Ryan, "Smith and the Religious Freedom

Restoration Act: An Iconoclastic Assessment," *Virginia Law Review* 78, no. 6 (1992): 1407–62; Christopher L. Eisgruber and Lawrence G. Sager, "The Vulnerability of Conscience: The Constitutional Basis for Protecting Religious Conduct," *University of Chicago Law Review* 61, no. 4 (1994): 1245–1315; Kent Greenawalt, "Quo Vadis: The Status and Prospects of 'Tests' under the Religion Clauses," *Supreme Court Review* 1995 (1995): 323–91.

4 For a genealogy, see Jonathan Z. Smith, "Religion, Religions, Religious," in *Critical Terms in Religious Studies*, ed. Mark C. Taylor (Chicago: University of Chicago Press, 1998), 269–84.

5 See, as an example, Brian Leiter, *Why Tolerate Religion?* (Princeton, NJ: Princeton University Press, 2012).

6 See Harold Joseph Berman, *Law and Revolution: The Formation of the Western Legal Tradition* (Cambridge, MA: Harvard University Press, 1983); Peter Fitzpatrick, *The Mythology of Modern Law* (New York: Routledge, 1992); Paul W. Kahn, *The Cultural Study of Law: Reconstructing Legal Scholarship* (Chicago: University of Chicago Press, 1999).

7 NFL, *Cowboys vs. Packers: Dez Bryant's Non Catch*, YouTube, September 25, 2015, www.youtube.com/watch?v=1khK6is-Bfs.

8 In the contemporary United States, laws legalizing abortion would be in this regard paradigmatic.

9 It has been alleged that on account of overcriminalization, each American commits an average of three felonies a day. See Harvey Silverglate, *Three Felonies a Day: How the Feds Target the Innocent* (New York: Encounter Books, 2011).

10 Our thinking here is indebted to Robert M. Cover, "Nomos and Narrative," *Harvard Law Review* 97 (November 1983): 4–68.

11 Paul W. Kahn, *The Cultural Study of Law: Reconstructing Legal Scholarship* (Chicago: University of Chicago Press, 1999); Benjamin L. Berger, *Law's Religion: Religious Difference and the Claims of Constitutionalism* (Toronto: University of Toronto Press, 2015).

12 Robert A. Yelle, "Moses' Veil: Secularization as Christian Myth," in *After Secular Law*, ed. Winnifred Fallers Sullivan, Robert A. Yelle, and Mateo Taussig-Rubbo (Stanford, CA: Stanford University Press, 2011), 23–42.

13 On "jurispathic courts," see Cover, "Nomos and Narrative," 40–54.

14 Philip Schaff, *America, a Sketch of Its Political, Social, and Religious Character*, ed. Perry Miller (Cambridge, MA: Belknap Press, 1961), 74, 76. Also see Robert Baird, *Religion in America; or, An Account of the Origin, Relation to the State, and Present Condition of the Evangelical Churches in the United States. With Notices of the Unevangelical Denominations* (New York: Harper & Brothers, 1856).

15 Alexis de Tocqueville makes a similar argument in his classic work *Democracy in America*, ed. J. P. Mayer (New York: Harper Perennial, 1988), 294–301.

16 Sidney E. Mead, *The Lively Experiment: The Shaping of Christianity in America* (New York: Harper & Row, 1963).

17 Cantwell v. Connecticut, 310 U.S. 296 (1940); Everson v. Board of Education, 330 U.S. 1 (1947).

18 Sarah Barringer Gordon, *The Spirit of the Law: Religious Voices and the Constitution in Modern America* (Cambridge, MA: Belknap Press, 2010).

19 For some of the best early work in this field, see Mark De Wolfe Howe, *The Garden and the Wilderness: Religion and Government in American Constitutional History* (Chicago: University of Chicago Press, 1965); Philip B. Kurland, ed., *Church and State: The Supreme Court and the First Amendment* (Chicago: University of Chicago Press, 1975).

20 In fact, the castigation or even mockery of the court for its inconsistency was a recurring theme of these works, a trope that eventually itself became a subject of derision by later scholars.

21 "Toward a Constitutional Definition of Religion," *Harvard Law Review* 91, no. 5 (March 1978): 1056. For other efforts among legal academics to define "religion" for First Amendment purposes, see Jesse Choper, "Defining Religion in the First Amendment," *University of Illinois Law Review* 1982, no. 3 (January 1, 1982): 579–613; Kent Greenawalt, "Religion as a Concept in Constitutional Law," *California Law Review* 72, no. 5 (1984): 753–816; Eduardo Penalver, "The Concept of Religion," *Yale Law Journal* 107, no. 3 (1997): 791–822.

22 Robert Michaelsen, "The Study of Religion: A Quiet Revolution in American Universities," *Journal of Higher Education* 37, no. 4 (April 1966): 181–86; D. G. Hart, *The University Gets Religion: Religious Studies in American Higher Education* (Baltimore: Johns Hopkins University Press, 2002); Russell T. McCutcheon, "'Just Follow the Money': The Cold War, the Humanistic Study of Religion, and the Fallacy of Insufficient Cynicism," *Culture and Religion* 5, no. 1 (March 1, 2004): 41–69; Sarah Imhoff, "The Creation Story, or How We Learned to Stop Worrying and Love Schempp," *Journal of the American Academy of Religion* 84, no. 2 (June 1, 2016): 466–97.

23 See, for example, Robert A. Orsi, *The Madonna of 115th Street: Faith and Community in Italian Harlem, 1880–1950* (New Haven, CT: Yale University Press, 1985); Carol J. Greenhouse, *Praying for Justice: Faith, Order, and Community in an American Town* (Ithaca, NY: Cornell University Press, 1986); David D. Hall, ed., *Lived Religion in America: Toward a History of Practice* (Princeton, NJ: Princeton University Press, 1997); Karen McCarthy Brown, *Mama Lola: A Vodou Priestess in Brooklyn*, rev. and expanded ed. (Berkeley: University of California Press, 2001).

24 Winnifred Fallers Sullivan, *The Impossibility of Religious Freedom* (Princeton, NJ: Princeton University Press, 2005), 1, 155; Winnifred Fallers Sullivan, *Prison Religion: Faith-Based Reform and the Constitution* (Princeton, NJ: Princeton University Press, 2009); Winnifred Fallers Sullivan, *A Ministry of Presence: Chaplaincy, Spiritual Care, and the Law* (Chicago: University of Chicago Press, 2014).

25 For representative works, see Eric Michael Mazur, *The Americanization of Religious Minorities: Confronting the Constitutional Order* (Baltimore: Johns Hop-

kins University Press, 1999); Philip Hamburger, *Separation of Church and State* (Cambridge, MA: Harvard University Press, 2002); Sarah Barringer Gordon, *The Mormon Question: Polygamy and Constitutional Conflict in Nineteenth-Century America* (Chapel Hill: University of North Carolina Press, 2002); Tracy Fessenden, *Culture and Redemption: Religion, the Secular, and American Literature* (Princeton, NJ: Princeton University Press, 2007); David Sehat, *The Myth of American Religious Freedom* (New York: Oxford University Press, 2011); Finbarr Curtis, *The Production of American Religious Freedom* (New York: New York University Press, 2016); Tisa Wenger, *Religious Freedom: The Contested History of an American Ideal* (Chapel Hill: University of North Carolina Press, 2017).

26 For representative works, see Winnifred Fallers Sullivan, Robert A. Yelle, and Mateo Taussig-Rubbo, eds., *After Secular Law* (Stanford, CA: Stanford University Press, 2011); Winnifred Fallers Sullivan et al., eds., *Politics of Religious Freedom* (Chicago: University of Chicago Press, 2015); Elizabeth Shakman Hurd, *Beyond Religious Freedom: The New Global Politics of Religion* (Princeton, NJ: Princeton University Press, 2015).

27 Jonathan Z. Smith, "God Save This Honourable Court: Religion and Civic Discourse," in *Relating Religion: Essays in the Study of Religion* (Chicago: University of Chicago Press, 2004), 375.

28 See Sehat, *Myth of American Religious Freedom*; Wenger, *Religious Freedom*.

29 Greg Johnson, *Sacred Claims: Repatriation and Living Tradition* (Charlottesville: University of Virginia Press, 2007); Michael D. McNally, "Native American Religious Freedom beyond the First Amendment," in *After Pluralism: Reimagining Religious Engagement*, ed. Courtney Bender and Pamela E. Klassen (New York: Columbia University Press, 2010), 225–51.

PART I

Definition

The chapters of the volume's first section break down the heralded promise of religious freedom into some of its constitutive parts: belief, conscience, exercise, establishment. If, in certain scholarly modes, terms for analysis are stipulated, and analysis proceeds from there, here the impulse to define is turned inside out. For our contributors, definitions are themselves products of discursive practices. To define a term is to uncover the history by which a given term acquired its meaning and significance. We zero in on definition not to fix terms' meanings but rather to track and assess how the meanings that have been affixed have served, knowingly and unknowingly, to advance certain ends.

In the United States, religious freedom is generally associated with the freedom to believe, not the freedom to act on those beliefs. By means of a genealogy that spans nineteenth-century rulings over the regulation of polygamy and twenty-first century corporate exemptions over the Affordable Care Act's birth control mandate, Sarah Imhoff shows that while the jurisprudence has continually centered on religious belief, the precise contours of what belief entails have in no way remained stable. Sliding around as well has been the relationship between belief and practice. Landing on the category of sincerity, Imhoff argues that if the court has had a pervasive tendency, it has been its will to obscure the obvious fact that within any religious group there necessarily exists a diversity of religious beliefs.

A legal concept that has floated in and out of alignment with religious belief is "conscience." Excavating the history of conscientious objection to military service, Ronit Stahl traces the secular drift of the court's reasoning, which has afforded conscience ever greater prominence. Whereas in the nineteenth century an objector needed to establish his membership in a peace church, by the middle of the twentieth century, religion's putative monopoly over acts of conscience had been busted. Nonetheless, to avoid conscription, objectors had to establish that their motivation transcended "personal moral code" and was rooted in more than politics, sociology, or philosophy. Belief in God had been rendered optional, but to qualify for conscientious-objector status petitioners nonetheless had to articulate their ethics in universalizing terms. This life-saving lane that liberal petitioners and jurists had expanded for the purposes of individual protection invited new travelers as the court shifted to the right. In the sphere of women's reproductive health most especially, a tool crafted by individuals to evade war now enables corporations to evade legislatively mandated obligations to their workers.

In writing for the majority in *Hobby Lobby*, for example, Justice Samuel Alito cites the company's statement of purpose, which binds its owners with the obligation to operate "in a manner consistent with Biblical principles." This, the court intimates with a nod to the fact that Hobby Lobby shops are closed on Sundays, entails substantial sacrifice to the tune of the millions of dollars lost annually. The resulting paradox, as Finbarr Curtis observes, is that free religious exercise is anything but "free." Precisely the opposite, actually. To win in court one must present the putative demands of their free-exercise claim as being nothing short of obligatory. What then, Curtis asks, is being "exercised" in free religious exercise? His answer? The religious person's body, resolve, and conviction. Rigid regimentation, discipline, and self-governance: these are the bodily expressions that one is "free" to religiously exercise. Deference to exercise claims, one might say, is the tribute secular slack pays to religious virtue. Whereas liberals have long glorified the principle of tolerance exhibited in such deference, they are suspicious of the excessive sovereignty it grants to religious individuals and groups. Meanwhile, conservatives' celebration of religious freedom as an absolute and inalienable individual right masks the coercive force exerted upon these putatively sovereign selves by family structures, religious institutions, and, perhaps most saliently, capital.

If free exercise jurisprudence favors rigidity, then by contrast, disputes on the establishment side have incentivized various kinds of flexibility. Returning to the early republic, Anna Su tracks the ways that the disestablishment of religion fostered the disaggregation of religious practices from religious behaviors. The result—what would come to be known as the Second Great Awakening—was the saturation of religion into American public and social life. It was not until after World War II, and the school prayer cases, that courts substantively enforced Jefferson's now famous "wall of separation." But the story did not end there. As driven by movement conservatives and, eventually, by conservative jurists as well, religious expressions were welcomed back into the public square—so long as the symbols were used in a vague cultural way that stopped short of endorsing these symbols' religious content. As comes as little surprise, however, these symbols have a curious way of lining up with the religious preferences of the majority culture.

1

Belief

SARAH IMHOFF

Wikipedia redirects the "Freedom of Worship" page and the "Freedom to Worship" page to the "Freedom of Religion" page, where the first sentence glosses freedom of religion as "freedom of belief." So, at least as I write this, a person curious about something called freedom of worship would be quickly redirected to a page about something called freedom of belief, which suggests that if you want to understand something about worship in the context of law and rights, you had better start with reading about belief. Why trust Wikipedia, that online compendium of crowdsourced knowledge about which scholars warn their students, to tell us anything? Precisely because Wikipedia draws on lay understandings, it provides an ethnographic window into how American culture sees itself.

The state also engages in freedom-talk and religion-talk. New applicants for American citizenship read that the Bill of Rights guarantees "freedom of religion."[1] Unlike "freedom of assembly" or "freedom of speech," which the new citizen civics test also lists, there is no apparent verb for "religion": one is free to *assemble*, one is free to *speak*, but we would not say that one is free to *religion*. So what is the right verb? What freedoms, precisely, does a person have if she has freedom of religion?

Two common contenders are "to believe" and "to practice." Americans have imagined religion—not just freedom of religion, but also religion more generally, as a matter of belief and a matter of practice. Under US law, for example, Christians can believe in the divinity of Jesus Christ, Jews can believe in a law-giving God, and Rastafarians can believe in the return of Haile Selassie. Then everyone can act accordingly: Catholics can take communion, Jews can fast on Yom Kippur, and Rastafarians can address a God who was incarnated as an emperor of Ethiopia in their prayers. Or so the story goes.

But unlike this understanding of religion as a combination of belief and practice might at first suggest, it does not give the two equal roles: in this picture, religion is fundamentally a matter of belief and faith. The law protects (to some extent) what a person does with her body because of belief or faith, but the real essence of religion is what goes on in her head and her heart. Religious practice is an outgrowth, a second-order occurrence stemming from religious belief. The mind and the heart are primary; the body is secondary. Americans often talk about a "belief system" as a way to describe a religion, or "believers" to denote members of a religious community. They talk about "interfaith" events to describe gatherings of multiple religious groups. Courts talk about "faith or creed," "faith traditions," and a "person of another faith" when they mean religion and religious affiliation.[2] Even scholar Wilfred Cantwell Smith, in his groundbreaking historicization of the concept of religion in the West, *The Meaning and the End of Religion*, called religion "faith."[3]

The concept of belief, then, is crucial to understanding religion in the United States. From the vernacular, such as Wikipedia and "interfaith" community events, to formal appearances of law, such as Supreme Court rulings, belief most frequently appears as the true center of religion. Thinking about belief gets to the heart of fundamental cultural assumptions about what religion is. This chapter shows that through shifting histories of American law, the idea that belief is central has remained a constant, though what exactly "belief" entails and the scope of its protection has continually shifted.

To explore this idea of belief, this chapter will first gesture toward a genealogy of belief and then look briefly at three separate cases—the 1879 *Reynolds v. United States*, the 1914 *Order of St. Benedict v. Steinhauser*, and the 2014 *Burwell v. Hobby Lobby*—to show some of the different ways the Supreme Court has posited the scope and meaning of religious belief. These three cases are not intended to be a history, or even to mark the most important legal moments for the idea of religious belief, but rather to be three examples of the diverse ways that Americans, as actors within the legal system, have worked to configure religious belief. As each case shows, the law never creates religion in a vacuum; it is always in conversation with other cultural and legal movements. Whether these larger political issues involve the inclusion of territory, the ascendency of contracts, the social role of corporations, or other things, legal understandings and court documents construct religion in dialogue with these elements. Put more forcefully, even when the courts discuss religion as if it is a transhistorical phenomenon, it isn't: religion is a product of its time, place, culture, politics, and other contextual factors.

One place we can see this contextual nature of religion is in American assumptions about what religion is: because of the historical, social, and legal power of Protestants, many contemporary American assumptions are indebted to Protestant Christianity. Scholars from a variety of disciplines have noted that one feature of this indebtedness is the idea that belief is—or at least should be—central to religion.[4] Donald Lopez Jr. explains that Christian theologians, philosophers, and even scholars of religion have long figured belief as the foundational aspect of religion. "The accumulated weight of this discourse has resulted in the generally unquestioned assumption that adherents of a given religion, any religion, understand that adherence in terms of belief."[5] Americans have also tended to assume the same, both in the past and in the present. They also see religions across the globe in these same terms. These constructions of religion do not stop with cognitive or imaginative constructions; rather, courts, legislatures, town councils, and even many religious communities themselves use this assumption when they make practical decisions about religion. As Talal Asad argues, "In all these legal functions, liberal democracy (whether at home or abroad in its colonies) not only works through secularity, it requires that *belief* be taken as the essence of religiosity."[6] Religious people and communities can express their beliefs through practices like worship and rituals, but these embodied acts stem from belief. And as Elizabeth Shakman Hurd argues, American projects dedicated to promoting religious freedom abroad likewise assume that what they are protecting is the freedom to believe.[7] Protestant notions of belief as the essence of religion permeate American culture, from philosophers to courts and government.

What, then, is belief? It has something to do with interiority, it is usually something other than what we would call knowledge, it seems personal, and it often has some sort of relationship to conscience. There is belief *in*, and there is belief *that*. There might be belief in a God or belief that there is an afterlife. But the idea of religious belief and how it can be known are not constants. Belief's relationship to practice is similarly unsteady: different people in different historical and cultural moments assume quite different configurations of the belief-practice relationship. Observant Jews who do not believe in God may keep religious commandments. Their communities do not consider them hypocritical, and some suggest that keeping commandments can cultivate belief in God. Even Protestant children may do things, such as say the Lord's Prayer at night before they understand its meaning, not because they already believe but because their parents understand that practicing religion can help create belief. Here, then, I will not define it, because it does not have a stable definition or a fixed relationship to related concepts, such as practice and religious freedom.

American jurisprudence has had a long and complex engagement with the idea of belief, and whenever the law encounters the idea of religious belief, it always does so through specific cultural and historical contingencies. While scholars of religion often theorize what role belief can and does play in the study of religion, courts only decide the specific case before them, with its specific and historically located facts. By looking at these cases and courts' interpretations, the religious studies scholar can glimpse the constructed nature of the concept of religious belief through the courts' rulings about religion. These three cases display judicial ideas about the role of belief from three different historical moments and with reference to three different religious groups. Together they highlight the contingency and malleability of the category of religious belief.

Reynolds v. United States, a well-known 1879 Supreme Court case, became a public occasion for considering the relationship of belief and practice and for staking out legal claims about what precisely the First Amendment protected. In fact, this was the first time that the Supreme Court explicitly interpreted the free exercise clause. Briefly, here are the facts of the case: George Reynolds, a member of the Church of Jesus Christ of Latter-Day Saints (LDS) and secretary to Brigham Young, married a second woman while remaining married to his first wife. Reynolds never denied that he had married more than one woman, and he maintained that because his religion required men to enter into polygamous marriages if they could, he should be found not guilty. A Utah territorial district court found him guilty of bigamy, and the territorial supreme court upheld the ruling.

Even though it was a case about actions and practice, both sides of the case presented a case in which belief was the foundation of religion. Reynolds claimed that the court should acquit him because "he had contracted such second marriage pursuant to, and in conformity with, what he believed at the time to be a religious duty."[8] In this, Reynolds represented belief as primary: he was, he claimed, only doing the thing which his religious belief demanded. True freedom of religion required the protection of any action that stemmed from what he believed to be his religious duties.

The court, however, did not see it that way. In his opinion, Chief Justice Morrison Waite posited that when we talk about "religious freedom," belief *is* real religion. Religious belief, but not the actions that follow from that belief, is what is protected. "A party's religious belief cannot be accepted as a justification for his committing an overt act, made criminal by the law of the land." Given this, the overarching question for the court became whether or not the law prohibiting polygamy violated the free exercise clause: "Congress cannot pass a law for the government of the Territories which shall prohibit the free exercise of religion. The First Amendment to the Constitution expressly forbids such legislation." Because Utah was a territory and not a state, it was under federal jurisdiction. He then shifted seamlessly to "religious freedom," a move which seemed to equate it with free exercise: "Religious freedom is guaranteed everywhere throughout the United States, so far as congressional interference is concerned. The question to be determined is, whether the law now under consideration comes within this prohibition." Waite understood this case to be about the free exercise clause and implied that free exercise was freedom of religion, but in the end, much like the Wikipedia articles, he managed to circle around to belief.

The court noted that it was hard to define religion . . . but then it went ahead and found a definition anyway. "The word 'religion' is not defined in the Constitution," and so, it reasoned, "we must go elsewhere, therefore, to ascertain its meaning, and nowhere more appropriately, we think, than to the history of the times in the midst of which the provision was adopted. The precise point of the inquiry is what is the religious freedom which has been guaranteed." Here the court made a move we still see today: it appealed to the founders' intentions as a source of authority for its own interpretation. The opinion quoted Jefferson, who had declared that courts could not interfere in "the field of opinion" or "the profession or propagation of principles" and that "it is time enough for the rightful purposes of civil government for its officers to interfere when principles break out into overt acts against peace and good order."[9] Here in Jefferson's words, the court found what it called "the true distinction between what properly belongs to the church and what to the State": "church" is about opinion and principles; "State" is about keeping order. In other words, "church" operates in the realm of beliefs, and "State" operates in the realm of actions.

In the end, the court ruled against George Reynolds: "So here, as a law of the organization of society under the exclusive dominion of the United States, it is provided that plural marriages shall not be allowed. Can a man excuse his practices to the contrary because of his religious belief? To permit this would be to make the professed doctrines of religious belief superior to the law of the land, and, in effect, to permit every citizen to become a law unto himself." The First Amendment protected a man's right to believe that God had recommended plural marriage. But freedom of conscience—that is, an interior personal state—was no justification for lawbreaking. Plural marriage was illegal, no matter what a person believed about God's prescriptions. Here we also see the workings of what scholars Janet Jakobsen and Ann Pellegrini call "stealth Protestantism"[10]: concerns about public order often justified limits on religious freedom in the nineteenth century in ways that advanced Protestant moral precepts, even when they denied that they were privileging Protestant Christianity.

Although *Reynolds* looks typical in its focus on belief, it is also distinctive from many later cases in the extent to which the court made explicit proclamations about what was theologically true and not true. According to the legal ruling, the belief that God intended the practice of polygamy was "a delusion." When it made this pronouncement, the court made decisions about what was and was not a proper belief; it made judgments about what was theologically true and therefore appropriate to believe or not believe. The court instructed the jury to "consider what are to be the consequences to the innocent victims of this delusion [the doctrine of polygamy]."[11] Here, Reynolds was entitled to his religious belief about marriage—the court did not convict him of blasphemy or heresy, for example—but that was where the protection stopped. And even though the court could not convict him of blasphemy or heresy, it nevertheless made judgments about the falsity of his beliefs.

The court reasoned similarly in *Davis v. Beason*, an 1890 polygamy case from Idaho. When Samuel Davis registered to vote, he signed a form affirming that he was neither a polygamist nor part of an organization that promoted polygamy. (It was clearly a statute targeting Mormons in the territory.) Though he was a member of the LDS Church, he signed anyway and was subsequently convicted of election fraud. Davis claimed that requiring the oath violated the free exercise clause of the First Amendment. The court ruled against him. Writing for the court, Justice Stephen Field declared:

> The term "religion" has reference to one's views of his relations to his Creator, and to the obligations they impose of reverence for his being and character, and of obedience to his will. It is often confounded with the *cultus* or form of worship of a particular sect, but is distinguishable from the latter.[12]

Field's distinctions here are worth drawing out. Religion, for Field, was belief in God and the "reverence and character" that should follow from it. Worship and other religious practices were "cultus," which was separable and distinguishable from belief. It was historically contingent and farther from the heart of what required legal protection. No legislation guaranteed "freedom of cultus," after all. Although this distinction did not appear in *Reynolds*, it is very much of the same milieu: it suggests that good religion is belief and a closely related set of personal moral norms that look surprisingly Protestant in practice. In both *Reynolds* and *Davis*, the court suggested that belief could be separated from practice, though scholars of religion, and even later justices, would be less confident about the separability of belief from practice.

The wider political context can help us understand this legal construction of religion: these two cases took place at a time when the Western territories constituted a prominent political issue. How could these frontier regions, lawless in many Americans' imaginations, come to be part of the United States? The LDS Church and its practices became one object of these anxieties. The *Reynolds* opinion read:

As this contest goes on, they multiply, and there are pure-minded women and there are innocent children—innocent in a sense even beyond the degree of the innocence of childhood itself. These are to be the sufferers; and as jurors fail to do their duty, and as these cases come up in the Territory of Utah, just so do these victims multiply and spread themselves over the land.[13]

When the court used the rhetoric of protecting women and children, it was in part impugning the specific practice of polygamy. But it was also imagining the domestication of the Wild West so that it could fit American cultural norms. With this, it becomes clear that legal rulings about religion and religious freedom are not ahistorical concepts, even if some jurists write as if they are.

The *Reynolds* and *Davis* decisions suggested that belief *is* religion, at least for the purposes of thinking about what demands legal protection. Almost forty years later, in a less well-known case, the Supreme Court framed it differently. According to the 1914 decision in *Order of St. Benedict v. Steinhauser*, belief was an essential part of religion, but so too were some of the actions that followed from it, such as associating and entering into contracts. At issue were the book royalties of a recently deceased member of a monastic order. In part, *Order of St. Benedict* is little known because it is not a First Amendment case. It was not really even a religion case—the courts did not take their task to be interpreting either religion clause—but the way the justices wrote about religion in their decision is telling. The casualness of their discussion provides a view into how the court saw religion.

Augustin Wirth had taken the solemn vows of the Benedictine order at St. Vincent's Abbey in Pennsylvania in 1852 and joined the monastery of St. Benedict in Kansas during the following decade. Throughout his career, the priest authored quite a few copyrighted books on religious subjects, many of which sold well. The Benedictine abbot gave Wirth special permission to keep control over how the royalties from these books were used, rather than relinquishing them totally and immediately to the religious community. After Wirth's death, the administrator of his estate, Albert Steinhauser, kept the royalties rather than transferring them to the order. The order sued.

The court decided that the copyright rightly belonged to the order. In the course of doing so, it suggested that religion, and more specifically religious belonging, depended on personal belief and choice. The court ruled that Wirth's time living away from the abbey did not signal the end of his religious membership in the brotherhood; the abbot could grant a member use of that member's income from the books he wrote without canceling the agreement that "gains and acquisitions of the members"[14] belong to the order; and the contract giving the religious order ownership of the copyrights to his books was valid. After his death, the proceeds from his books should go to the order, the court explained, because Wirth's vows to be a part of the order were revocable and he did not revoke them during his life.

The decision explained that the order's vow of poverty was not void on the grounds of "being against public policy" because the vows allowed the member to act in accordance with his belief. That is, he took the vow because of his religious belief, and in the years that followed he continued to follow the rules of the vow because of his religious belief. By contrast, if it were the case that "the vows in connection with the [Rule of St. Benedict] bind the member in complete servitude to the order for life, or until the head of the church absolves him from his obligations," the vow of poverty would have been "opposed to individual liberty" as well as the right to own property. Structured in this way, the court said, such a vow would have been against public policy and therefore void.[15] Vows that were irrevocable or excusable only by authority of the order would have signaled bad religion—or not even real religion—in the eyes of the court. Bad religion was "binding" and "opposed to liberty"; perhaps a vow that was "against public policy" shouldn't even qualify as religion because it was an invalid contract. Good religion would provide the space to act in accordance with one's beliefs, even if those beliefs changed.

Like *Reynolds*, though perhaps less explicitly, the justices' own ideas about true and false beliefs played a role in what they saw as legal. In 1914, mass immigration had changed, and was continuing to change, the face of religion in the United States. Many of the millions of immigrants were Catholics and Jews, which challenged many Americans' vision of a Protestant America. But in marked distinction to the popular anti-Catholic mood of its era, in *Order of St. Benedict*, the court documents approved of the religious beliefs they saw at play in the case. Writing for the circuit court, Justice J. Willard wrote: "That the purposes of the order are not contrary to public policy cannot for a moment be doubted." All could agree that the purpose of the Order of St. Benedict was perfectly legal under the standards of public policy. He might have made this argument in many ways, but the reasoning he provided was striking: "To doubt upon that point would be to doubt the doctrines of the Christian religion and the teachings of the moralists of all ages." The ruling also noted that the state had chartered the Benedictine order as a society of "religious men living in community" and by doing so had already granted it state recognition.[16]

As long as Wirth believed in the tenets of his monastic order, he belonged. Had he stopped believing, he could have left freely. Entering into a contract, then—and the ongoing decision to remain in that contract—was a reflection of Wirth's religious belief. And vows of poverty, however odd they might seem to some, were not against public policy. The decision quoted from an earlier ruling about the Oneida community, a Christian communalist society that preached the possibility of human perfection on earth. The ruling described the Oneida community as "fashioned according to the pentecostal ideal, that all who believed should be together and have all things in common."[17] Both *Order of St. Benedict* and the Oneida ruling suggested that the foundation of religion was belief and that religious belief entailed associating and entering into contracts according to the principles of that belief.

More recently, in the 2014 *Burwell v. Hobby Lobby* case, the owners of two for-profit companies wanted to be exempt from providing the required health insurance coverage for methods of birth control that they saw as infringing on their religion. The Supreme Court ruled 5 to 4 in favor of the companies. Despite their differences of opinion, all of the justices seemed to concur about two things: first, that religion has an identifiable core and essence, and second, that the core and essence of religion is belief. Only if we see "sincere religious belief," they suggest, do we see religion.[18]

In his concurrence, Justice Anthony Kennedy framed religious freedom in terms of belief:

> In our constitutional tradition, freedom means that all persons have the
> right to believe or strive to believe in a divine creator and a divine law. For

those who choose this course, free exercise is essential in preserving their own dignity and in striving for a self-definition shaped by their religious precepts. Free exercise in this sense implicates more than just freedom of belief . . . It means, too, the right to express those beliefs and to establish one's religious (or nonreligious) self-definition in the political, civic, and economic life of our larger community.[19]

For Kennedy, freedom begins with freedom to believe. More than that, it means the freedom to believe "in a divine creator and a divine law." If you choose the "course" of belief, then free exercise follows. Free exercise, for Kennedy, is crucial because it allows the believing person to live a life of consistency and dignity shaped by her beliefs. The free exercise of religion here is the "freedom of belief" plus the "right to express [one's] beliefs." Throughout Kennedy's concurrence, the "believing" aspect of religion is primary and foundational. The practice is secondary and depends on belief. Belief is a prerequisite for religious exercise.

Religion, in this view, is not a practice but rather beliefs that one puts into practice. Writing for the court, Justice Samuel Alito offered a fundamentally similar picture of religion. He explained: "Because the contraceptive mandate forces [the plaintiffs] to pay an enormous sum of money—as much as $475 million per year in the case of Hobby Lobby—if they insist on providing insurance coverage in accordance with their religious beliefs, the mandate clearly imposes a substantial burden on those beliefs."[20] But this is not true. No amount of payment burdens *beliefs*. We might say it burdens the people or places a burden on their religious practice. But it neither challenges nor burdens belief. And surely Alito doesn't mean this. He means that it burdens religious people. If, in *Citizens United v. FEC*, corporations have become people, in *Hobby Lobby*, it seems that beliefs have become religion.[21]

Justice Ginsburg, in her dissent, showed how "religion" and "belief" functioned synonymously for her: "The distinction between a community made up of believers in the same religion and one embracing persons of diverse beliefs, clear as it is, constantly escapes the court's attention."[22] Religion and belief seem interchangeable here, and this sentence highlights the problem with conflating the two. Any thoughtful observer of American religion—or anyone who has ever belonged to a religious community, for that matter—knows that every religious community "made up of believers in the same religion" is still a community of people with "diverse beliefs."[23] While her point about the recognition of employers' potential religious difference from their employees stands, Ginsburg's conception of religion still assumes the primacy of belief.

But how can a court discern a person's belief? Or her sincerity? Especially since the courts have come to understand religious belief as personal—that is, a person need not belong to a widespread religious group nor subscribe to the tenets of a religious group in order to gain protection—this has become an increasingly visible question. In reality, it is not so far from other things courts and juries routinely decide, such as motives and premeditation. As Faisal Devji explains, "The term sincerity came into the English language with the rise of Protestantism, in order to name the internal agreement of statement and belief it required. Ascertaining sincerity, however, was tricky."[24] It still is.

And yet sincerity was crucial in this case. Because the court sought to protect not only beliefs but also practices stemming from those beliefs, it needed to see the sincerity of the owners of Hobby Lobby. Sincerity is the court's way of trying to unite the two parts of religion: it seeks to match beliefs with practices. In *Hobby Lobby*, then, belief's relationship to practice became much more intimate—far more intimate than it was in, say, *Reynolds* or even *Order of St. Benedict*.

What are the implications of these belief-heavy conceptions of religion? We might simply note that the court has a Protestant-influenced conception of what religion is and then move along. But this is not merely a philosophical preference for one idea over another. The effect of this conception is to render some kinds of religion more visible than others. This legal picture of religion offers no guidance about what to make of religious arrangements in which practice is primary and belief is secondary. For instance, Saba Mahmood and Talal Asad have offered anthropological accounts of religion wherein Muslims and Christians carry out bodily religious rituals not *because* they already have some internal state of unwavering belief or faith but *in order to* believe or cultivate faith.[25] These religious lives and expressions are nearly unintelligible as religion, or seem backward if we begin with an account that takes sincere religious belief to be the foundation and starting point of religion.

The belief model of religion also raises questions about religious practices that are not motivated by—or even supported by—"sincere religious belief." When would these count as protected religious exercise? What if it's not my sincere religious belief that this bread becomes Jesus's body, but I want to take communion anyway because I value the ritual aspect or because my grandmother believes and that matters deeply to me? What if I'm six years old and I don't really know what I believe? What if I take off work because it is Yom Kippur and I fast all day but I don't believe in God? What if I'm not sure? What if my beliefs waver? These questions would have posed little problem to the court under a *Reynolds*-type discourse, but they are not easily addressed by a legal language that privileges sincerity and belief as the foundations of religion.

Belief and beliefs, as we have seen here, are not fixed concepts, especially when considering their relationship to practices, religious freedom, or religion as such. And yet paying attention to these various configurations of belief and its related concepts provides a crucial view of American religion and law.

NOTES

1 "What is one right or freedom from the First Amendment?" it asks. "Religion" is one correct answer. "What are two rights of everyone living in the United States?" "Freedom of religion" is one correct answer. *Learn about the United States: Quick Civic Lessons for the Naturalization Test* (Washington, DC: US Citizenship and Immigration Services, 2017), 2, 12.

2 In just the last decade, examples of this language include *Holt v. Hobbs*, *Hobby Lobby*, and *Town of Greece v. Galloway*, among others.

3 Wilfred Cantwell Smith, *The Meaning and End of Religion* (Minneapolis: Fortress, 1963).

4 For just one conversation about the role and definition of belief in religious studies scholarship, see Wilfred Cantwell Smith, *Belief and History* (Charlottesville: University of Virginia Press, 1977); Donald Wiebe, "The Role of 'Belief' in the Study of Religion," *Numen* 26, no. 2 (1979): 234–49; Wilfred Cantwell Smith, "Belief: A Reply to a Response," *Numen* 27, no. 2 (1980): 247–55; Craig Martin, "On 'Belief': A Story of Protectionism," in *Theory and Method in the Study of Religion: Twenty Five Years On*, ed. Aaron W. Hughes (Boston: Brill, 2013), 103–6.

5 Donald Lopez Jr., "Belief," in *Critical Terms for Religious Studies*, ed. Mark C. Taylor (Chicago: University of Chicago Press, 1998), 21.

6 Talal Asad, "Thinking about Religion, Belief, and Politics," in *Cambridge Companion to Religious Studies*, ed. Robert Orsi (Cambridge: Cambridge University Press, 2012), 40.

7 Elizabeth Shakman Hurd, "Believing in Religious Freedom," *Immanent Frame* (blog), March 1, 2012, https://tif.ssrc.org.

8 Reynolds v. United States, 98 U.S. 145 (1879).

9 Ibid.

10 Janet Jakobsen and Ann Pellegrini, *Love the Sin: Sexual Regulations and the Limits of Religious Tolerance* (New York: New York University Press, 2003).

11 Ibid.

12 Davis v. Beason, 133 U.S. 333 (1890).

13 *Reynolds v. United States.*

14 Order of St. Benedict of N.J. v. Steinhauser, 234 U.S. 640 (1914).

15 Ibid.

16 Ibid.

17 Ibid.

18 Thank you to the *Immanent Frame* for allowing me to reprint here parts of my analysis of *Hobby Lobby*: Sarah Imhoff, "The Supreme Court's Faith in Belief," *Immanent Frame* (blog), December 16, 2014, https://tif.ssrc.org.

19 Burwell v. Hobby Lobby Stores, Inc., 573 U.S. _____ (2014).

20 Ibid.

21 Citizens United v. Federal Election Commission, 558 U.S. 310 (2010).

22 Ibid.

23 Ibid.

24 Faisal Devji, "Age of Sincerity," Aeon, April 17, 2017, https://aeon.co.

25 Saba Mahmood, *Politics of Piety: The Islamic Revival and the Feminist Subject* (Princeton, NJ: Princeton University Press, 2004); Talal Asad, *Genealogies of Religion: Discipline and Reasons of Power in Christianity and Islam* (Baltimore: Johns Hopkins University Press, 1993).

2

Conscience

RONIT Y. STAHL

Daniel Andrew Seeger conscientiously opposed war and, in 1957, sought an exemption from the draft as a conscientious objector. There was just one problem. By law, conscientious objectors had to affirm their belief in a Supreme Being, and Seeger didn't believe in God. When he submitted the paperwork to his local draft board, Seeger finessed his claim. As he put it, he was simply seeking the same accommodations granted to his clearly religious peers—the Quaker or Mennonite or Catholic or Jewish men—who resisted military service because of their twin beliefs in God and against war. He did not lack faith but understood the world through a "belief in and devotion to goodness and virtue for their own sakes." Looking to philosophers such as Plato, Aristotle, and Spinoza, he enunciated his sincerely held "religious faith in a purely ethical creed."[1] Neither Congress nor Selective Service director Lewis Hershey was inclined to agree that his view warranted classification as a conscientious objector. Thwarted by his local draft board, Seeger refused to enter the armed forces. His choice garnered him a series of court appearances—a conviction by the district court, a reversal by the appellate court, and finally a date with the US Supreme Court, which was presided over by Chief Justice Earl Warren. Heard in November 1964 and decided in March 1965, *United States v. Seeger* centered on how much latitude draft boards ought to grant to definitions of a Supreme Being. In other words, the Supreme Court wondered, to what degree did conscience require belief in an entity that resembled a religious God?

Almost fifty years after the Warren Court heard oral arguments in *Seeger*, the Roberts Court listened to attorneys debating another plea for an exemption on the basis of conscience, albeit in the realm of health insurance rather than military service. By the late twentieth and early twenty-first centuries, conscience had become a legal and political tool through which to register dissent more broadly—often in support of conservative social, rather than liberal antiwar, views. In *Burwell v. Hobby Lobby* (2014), the Green and Hahn families objected to providing health insurance coverage for four specific contraceptives they considered abortifacients—mechanisms to end rather than prevent pregnancy.[2] As devout Christians, they sincerely believed that life begins at conception and that facilitating access to these contraceptives violated their consciences by making them complicit in their use. There was no doubt that the Greens and the Hahns expressed religious objection to these forms of contraception, so why did arguments about providing comprehensive health care invoke the language of conscience?

Seeger and *Hobby Lobby* differ in significant ways, but together they expose how conscience represents "a special puzzle" in the American legal system, a puzzle distinct from yet tied to religion.[3] Conscience claims rely on an alchemy of religion and morality, fused, in differing amounts, to garner protection from participating, directly or indirectly, in systems to which one is opposed. In *Seeger*, an individual sought personal relief from direct military service on moral grounds. His case highlighted the fuzzy boundary between religious and nonreligious claims. It asked that his view, grounded in moral philosophy but attenuated from religious doctrine, acquire the same protection as overtly religious antiwar positions. In *Hobby Lobby*, business owners requested reprieve from complying with the Affordable Care Act's contraceptive mandate.[4] This case questioned whether religiously motivated corporate opposition to indirect involvement, or complicity, in employees' potential use of contraception was protected. In other words, whereas *Seeger* centered on whether an individual could morally resist providing his body to the military for not completely religious reasons, *Hobby Lobby* hinged on whether a corporation could refuse to cover contraceptives in its insurance that its owners' religion classified as immoral. Religion thus played distinct roles in each case. In *Seeger*, the question focused on whether an attenuated religious claim could succeed. In *Hobby Lobby*, the question revolved around whether a religious claim of complicity, or indirect involvement, merited legal protection.

In both cases, the petitioners asserted their right to follow their consciences and receive exemptions from duties required of other Americans. Neither case stemmed from infringement on beliefs—the government had not instructed anyone to stop thinking or holding certain truths. Nor did either case arise from interference with the exercise of particular religious practices. No one was forced to work on the Sabbath, remove a religious head covering, or eat a religiously proscribed food. Rather, Daniel Seeger and the Green and Hahn families sought to act upon, or exercise, their ethical convictions. The language of conscience blended religious and moral rationales that intertwined personal, professional, and political claims.

What exactly conscience means or entails has long been the province of moral philosophers grounded in either theological or secular traditions.[5] In the United States, whether religion and conscience fully overlap or simply share some common features may not necessarily matter in social or political contexts. Yet in legal contexts, the boundaries between religion and conscience matter a lot because the Constitution affords significant protection to religion. If conscience is religious, then invoking it may excuse participation from otherwise mandatory responsibilities. However, if conscience insulates religious conscience claims from regulation without according the same protections to nonreligious conscience claims, then conscience may become a tool of favoring religion over not-religion, or some religions over others. Historically, American jurisprudence has not offered a consistent definition of or metric for assessing conscience.

Legal understandings of conscience are amorphous and have shifted over time along two key axes: what it means or encompasses and who can claim it. After a brief examination of the discussion of "conscientious scruples" during debates over the Bill of Rights, this chapter analyzes two efforts to legislate and litigate conscience in the United States: mid-twentieth-century conscientious objection to war and late twentieth- and early twenty-first-century conscientious refusal to provide health care.[6] Paying particular attention to the contexts in which conscience is evoked, by whom, and how it is connected to or disconnected from religion helps highlight the distinct uses of conscience as a religious idea, legal instrument, and political tool. Comparing these instances reveals the challenge of plucking a concept from one arena (war) and applying it to another (medicine). Despite assumed similarities conveyed by the use of the same term, substantively, conscience-related discourse has been used to achieve distinct ends in these two realms. In fact, opening conscientious objection to war to include nonreligious rationales gave conscientious refusal in medicine a cloak of inclusiveness despite pronounced links to particular religious doctrines. In this sense, the law—as crafted by legislators and interpreted by judges—has layered and intermingled ideas about religion and conscience rather than clarifying them.

*　*　*

Questions about the relationship between law and conscience are as old as the republic. In 1789, as the First Continental Congress debated the text of what became the Bill of Rights, early legislators worried about violating individual conscience without defining what, exactly, conscience encompassed. "No religion shall be established by law, nor shall the equal rights of conscience be infringed," stated an early version of the First Amendment, thereby restricting the government from establishing religion while explicitly protecting individual conscience.[7] A flurry of conversation followed. As James Madison (VA) explained, this meant that Congress could not force anyone to observe religious laws or "compel men to worship God in any manner contrary to their conscience."[8] When challenged about the necessity of an amendment focused on religion, Daniel Carroll (MD) answered indirectly, remarking that conscience presented a particularly intricate issue in a nation beset with religious differences.[9] Recognizing this difficulty, Benjamin Huntington (CT) sought an amendment that "would be made in such a way as to secure the rights of conscience, and a free exercise of the rights of religion, but not to patronize those who professed no religion at all."[10] On August 17, 1789, Huntington agreed to limit the government from infringing "the equal rights of conscience."[11] Huntington's contrast between "the rights of conscience" and "a free exercise of the rights of religion" suggests that "conscience" may have referred to beliefs rather than rituals or, perhaps, to values that did not necessarily correlate with formal doctrine. To the extent that early politicians considered conscientious *objection*, they did so in debates over militias and the Second Amendment. Citizens with "conscientious scruples" against bearing arms would not be forced to do so.[12] Conscience escaped mention in the final versions of both the First and Second Amendments, but concern with conscience has occupied legislators, judges, and the American public ever since.

For almost 150 years, the United States allowed religious pacifists to recuse themselves from military service. To avoid bearing arms, objectors could pay fines or hire substitute soldiers. When the United States entered World War I and turned to mass conscription through the creation of a draft, Uncle Sam allowed men (women were not drafted) to conscientiously object to war. The Selective Service Act of 1917 recognized *religious* conscientious objection to war, which allowed members of peace churches, such as Quakers and Mennonites, to avoid combatant duties, provided government officials assessed their convictions as sincere and long-standing. Objectors performed noncombatant military service (e.g., Medical Corps, Quartermaster Corps) or, if they refused any participation, were imprisoned. Americans who did not belong to a peace church faced immense obstacles in attempting to prove that their conscientious objection to war was genuine. That a mere handful succeeded signals the clear limits the federal government placed on claims of conscience in World War I: the state recognized the individual objector only when he belonged to a known pacifist religious group.[13]

By World War II, the federal government no longer required membership in a peace church to acquire conscientious objector status, but it demanded noncombatant work or alternative service in mental hospitals or Civilian Public Service camps.[14] While the state expanded its understanding of conscience by detaching it from pacifist churches, it maintained an understanding of conscience as a subsidiary of religion. Thus the Selective Service Act of 1940 provided exemptions for "any person . . . who, by reason of religious training and belief, is conscientiously opposed to participation in war in any form."[15]

Two cases that bookend World War II highlight how the acceptance of conscientious objectors shifted during this time. In 1929, in *United States v. Schwimmer*, the Supreme Court denied naturalization to a pacifist woman seeking citizenship because she refused to vow to take up arms to defend the country (never mind that the country was not at war and women had not been drafted). Seventeen years later, in *Girouard v. United States*, the Supreme Court reversed itself. Because the Selective Service Act "recognized that one may adequately discharge his obligations as a citizen by rendering noncombatant as well as combatant services," the court decided a Seventh-day Adventist man who would not carry a rifle but promised to pursue a noncombatant role could become an American citizen.[16] By 1946, naturalized citizens, like native-born citizens, could conscientiously object to war on the basis of their "religious scruples."

Although many Americans joined religious institutions after the war, others rejected religion. As American intervention in Southeast Asia accelerated and opposition to the Vietnam War mounted, more draft-age men sought exemptions from military service. Those with clear and convincing religious commitments to pacifism generally found support from local draft boards. But others, like Daniel Seeger, opposed war without grounding their views in theology or direct connection to God. These men constituted a category problem, for conscientious objection, as a matter of law, had been grounded in religious opposition to war. But men like Seeger denied a direct link between religion and conscience.

In a unanimous decision, the Warren Court accepted Seeger's position as sincere and validated his status as a state-sanctioned conscientious objector. The justices also offered the Selective Service what it deemed an "objective" test for prospective objectors: "Does the claimed belief occupy the same place in the life of the objector as an orthodox belief in God holds in the life of one clearly qualified for exemption?" The logic was that of analogy. So long as these objectors' moral convictions mirrored the convictions of religious objectors, they could validly object to participation in the American military. When the Selective Service Act passed in 1948, Justice William Douglas reasoned in a concurring opinion, "We were a nation of Buddhists, Confucianists, and Taoists, as well as Christians." He then "attribute[d] tolerance and sophistication to the Congress, commensurate with the religious complexion of our communities."[17] Accounting for the diversity of the American religious landscape led the court to broaden its definition of religion in order to equalize the opportunity for a wider array of Americans to claim conscience to object to military service.

As Daniel Seeger successfully argued, participation in organized religious communities did not generate conscience. Rather, as a secular individual, he too had a conscience. And, as he argued, he had the right to exercise his conscience by accessing conscientious objector status, even without any professed connection to God. Following the lead of contemporary theologians, the Supreme Court accepted Seeger's expansive view of conscience, but it clung to religion as a necessary condition for conscientious objection.[18] As the *Seeger* decision underscored, no litigant "comes to us an avowedly irreligious person or as an atheist." That, the accompanying footnote pointed out, would produce "quite different problems."[19]

Into that void leapt Elliot Ashton Welsh II. Faced with a 1964 Selective Service form that read, "I am by reason of my religious training and belief, conscientiously opposed to participation in war in any form," Welsh crossed out "my religious training." His local draft board, the appeals board, and, eventually, a Department of Justice officer refused to sanction his revised statement as a defensible interpretation of the law. In 1966, Welsh was convicted and sentenced to three years in prison. This case presented the court with a far more vexing case than *Seeger* because Welsh equivocated about any link between his beliefs and religion. Over the course of his dispute with state officials, he held strongly to a fundamental principle that "war, from the practical standpoint, is futile and self-defeating and that from the more important moral standpoint it is unethical."[20] When challenged about whether he understood this perspective as *religious*, Welsh acknowledged that it did not conform to a conventional use of the adjective and thus did not claim it as such. But, the court observed, in his "long and thoughtful letter" to the appeals board, Welsh stated that his antiwar articles of faith were "certainly religious in the ethical sense of the word."[21] Thus the court's conundrum: Were ethics equivalent to religion? Were ethics like religion but not entirely the same? Or, perhaps, did ethics sufficiently differ from religion so as to make them set apart and distinct?

In the five years following *Seeger*, the Warren Court had become the Burger Court, and in the process it lost its unanimity on the nature of religious objection to the draft. Nevertheless, a plurality of the justices agreed that Welsh deserved conscientious objector status. "[T]he central consideration in determining whether the registrant's beliefs are religious is whether these beliefs play the role of a religion and function as a religion in the registrant's life," the court wrote—and Welsh met this standard.[22] Writing for four members of the court's majority, Justice Hugo Black explained this conclusion by pointing out that the statute "exempts from military service all those whose consciences, spurred by deeply held moral, ethical, or religious beliefs, would give them no rest or peace if they allowed themselves to become a part of an instrument of war."[23] According to this rubric, morals, ethics, and religion stood equal, all justifying—in comparable if not identical ways—state classification as a conscientious objector. Morals, ethics, and religion, in the court's equation, did not fall under the "essentially political, sociological, or philosophical" views or "merely personal moral code" that the draft law excluded.

But this perspective acquired only four votes. Justice John Harlan arrived at the same result—that Welsh was entitled to conscientious objector status—through altogether different logic. According to Harlan, morals and ethics, however sincerely held or fervently believed, neither fell under the same category as religion nor could be camouflaged as religion. The position held in *Seeger*, Harlan wrote, was "a remarkable feat of judicial surgery," and Black's opinion in *Welsh* was nothing less than "a lobotomy." These moves reflected "an Alice-in-Wonderland world where words have no meaning" and denied the obvious fact that Congress had elevated religious objections over nonreligious objections.[24] However, denying conscientious objector status to those opposed to war for nontheistic reasoning, he wrote, "runs afoul of the religious clauses of the First Amendment."[25] For Harlan, *Welsh* presented an establishment clause issue: the question was not how far to stretch the definition of religion but rather whether the state treated religion and secular beliefs equally and consistently.[26] To act nonpreferentially, neither Congress nor the Selective Service could use a religion test to enable conscientious objection.[27] Adhering to the stance that "legislation must, at the very least, be neutral" and allowing for a long history of state-granted exemptions from conscription, Harlan accepted that the "prevailing opinion's conscientious objector test . . . cures the defect of under-inclusion," thus enabling all Americans to access conscientious objector status regardless of creed.[28]

In a dissent, Justice Byron White diagnosed Welsh's antiwar beliefs as constituting "a personal moral code" that, like Justice Harlan contended, was not religion. The nonreligious underpinnings of Welsh's objection propelled White's dissent in the opposite direction from Harlan: if *Welsh* prompted any First Amendment concerns, the case tended toward free exercise clause matters and not the establishment clause. The exclusion of Welsh (and other nontheistic objectors) from draft immunity was constitutionally meaningless because "nothing in the First Amendment prohibits drafting Welsh and other nonreligious objectors to war." In a bit of curlicue logic, White concluded that Welsh had no standing to challenge the draft law on religious grounds because the statute did not recognize the nonbeliever as a participant in a draft-exempt group and thus triggered no First Amendment problem.[29] If Welsh's not-quite-religious beliefs did not constitute allowable conscientious objection, they did help illuminate why religious objection could receive special treatment. As White argued, Congress's constitutional mandate to "raise and support armies" existed pursuant to the constitutional directive to permit free exercise of religion. As a result, religious amnesty became necessary lest conscription force believers, contra their free exercise rights, to participate in combat. Protecting the faithful from mandatory service represented a compelling government interest; enabling the nonreligious to avoid compulsory service, in contrast, did not. From the dissent's perspective, there was nothing ambiguous about Welsh's worldview: it was not religious and deserved no deference. That others found the lines between religiously and nonreligiously motivated antiwar sentiment increasingly blurry mattered little.

As split as the court was, the *Welsh* decision redefined "conscience" within American law. "Conscience" meant claims rooted in "morals, ethics, or religion" that were neither "personal moral code" nor "essentially political, sociological, or philosophical." While this opened conscientious objector status to nonreligious people, it did not end debates over the boundaries of conscience claims. In the heat of Vietnam War protests, several Americans presented the Supreme Court with a new question about the rights of conscience: Could those who objected to *specific* wars, rather than war in general, receive state-sanctioned status as conscientious objectors? Both Guy Gillette, a humanist who refused to comply with his draft notice, and Louis Negre, a Catholic who sought an honorable discharge from the service, viewed Vietnam as an abhorrent overreach of state power. Their aversion to soldiering was not universal but particular, aimed only at US campaigns in Southeast Asia. Like Welsh and Seeger, the men looked to the courts for assistance in living their moral convictions as selective conscientious objectors.

Neither received the relief he sought. Written by Justice Thurgood Marshall, the 8–1 opinion in *Gillette* argued that Congress could limit exemptions to total opposition to war. Draft law, the court declared, clearly indicated "that conscientious scruples relating to war and military service must amount to conscientious opposition to participating personally in any war and all war."[30] Whether or not conscientious objection to particular wars emerged from a religious belief, the Selective Service standard of opposition to all war still applied to every draft-age American male. Indeed, in the interest of equity and fairness to all, it was imperative to maintain a system in which "the relevant individual belief is simply objection to all war, not adherence to any extraneous theological viewpoint," lest the "more articulate, better educated, or better counseled" prevail where the less sophisticated, poorly educated, or poorly advised might fail.[31] The very malleability of objection to particular wars voided its legal plausibility as a matter of public policy. According to the court's majority, nothing less than the integrity of the draft and the democratic impulse at the heart of mass conscription was at stake in *Gillette*. Americans could not expect exemptions simply because they opposed—however conscientiously—a particular war. Antiwar protesters seethed at this decision, which limited conscientious objection, but its impact diminished in 1973 when President Richard Nixon ended the draft. The rise of the all-volunteer military effectively ended legal debates about the right to conscientiously object to war, but the language of conscience was bubbling up in other realms.

* * *

Reproductive health care became the next battleground for conscience, a contest in which both proponents and opponents of abortion and contraception asserted positions grounded in morals, ethics, and religion. For "doctors of conscience" in the 1960s, providing illegal abortions to women who needed them represented an act of conscience, a legal and professional risk worth taking to ethically serve their patients. Opponents of abortion—especially Catholics, whose church doctrine made its prohibitions morally binding on all providers and institutions—also appealed to conscience.[32] In the fall of 1972, a district court in Montana enabled Gloria Taylor to get a tubal ligation (sterilization) after a caesarean section at St. Vincent's, a Catholic hospital that housed Billings's only maternity unit. Taylor had turned to the courts because the *Ethical and Religious Directives for Catholic Hospitals*, which governed St. Vincent's, prohibited sterilizations. Then, in January 1973, the Supreme

Court delivered its 7–2 decision in *Roe v. Wade*, which struck down abortion bans nationwide.[33] Together, these court decisions prompted new legislation regulating conscience rights.

The Church Amendment, which became law in June 1973, was the first health care conscience clause. It insulated hospitals, doctors, and nurses who objected to abortion or sterilization because of "religious beliefs or moral convictions" from being required to perform, assist, or make its facilities available for those procedures. Specifically, it stated that neither courts nor any "public authority" could compel recipients of federal funds to participate in these procedures. Passed with broad bipartisan support, the amendment also made federal funding contingent on employment nondiscrimination toward both willing and refusing providers of abortions and sterilizations. The Church Amendment incorporated the *Seeger* and *Welsh* decisions into its formulation by accepting "religious beliefs or moral convictions" as grounds for conscience claims. As Senator James L. Buckley (C-NY) said during Senate hearings, the legislation emulated "the right of conscience which is protected in our draft laws."[34] If this new statute built on case law in acknowledging that conscience could arise from religious or moral views, it simultaneously ignored the Selective Service System's infrastructure of accommodation. In other words, unlike conscientious objectors to war, those who refused to partake in abortions or sterilizations did not have to register or compensate society for their refusal.

Although the Church Amendment started out somewhat narrowly tailored—focused on direct providers of two specific medical procedures—it became the starting point for a whole new terrain of conscience legislation. States quickly followed with conscience clauses of their own. Subsequent federal and state conscience clauses increased the scope of who was protected while limiting protections to refusal instead of both refusing and willing providers. For example, subsequent statutes exempted researchers and trainees (including medical students and residents) from participation in work "contrary to religious beliefs or moral convictions." In the 1990s and 2000s, legislation extended the scope of these conscience protections even further. Insurance companies could refuse to cover abortions or referrals for abortions. No "institutional or individual health care entity," ranging from clinicians to hospitals and insurers, could receive federal funding without guaranteeing it would not discriminate against those who refuse to perform, refer to, or cover abortion services. Congress likewise required the accreditation of ob-gyn residencies that did not teach doctors how to perform abortions, despite professional association requirements to the contrary. In the waning days of his administration, George W. Bush issued the Provider Conscience Regulation, which allowed any health care providers to refuse treatment or referral for any services to which they objected on religious or moral grounds. Barack Obama rescinded the executive order, but recent state legislation has created conscience protections that shield health care providers from treating LGBT patients and businesses from serving LGBT people.[35] Through executive orders, administrative rules, and the creation of the Division of Conscience and Religious Freedom in the Department of Health and Human Services, the Trump administration has expanded one-sided conscience rights for medical professionals refusing to provide care.[36]

When the Supreme Court heard oral arguments in *Hobby Lobby* in March 2014, the range of individuals and groups who had acquired the right to conscientiously object to health care services had grown tremendously. What had started as an accommodation for doctors, nurses, and hospitals directly involved in abortions or sterilizations had mushroomed into exemptions for people and entities indirectly connected to patient care. Moreover, while the Supreme Court had insisted that conscientious objection to war be categorical, these newer conscience clauses could be quite selective. In Louisiana, for example, broad language appears to insulate all health care professions from civil or criminal liability, discrimination, or prejudice "for declining to participate in any health care service that violates his conscience." What appears to be all-encompassing, however, is not so vast. For the purposes of immunizing health care workers from malpractice lawsuits or employment repercussions, the statute defines "health care" to mean only "abortion, dispensation of abortifacient drugs, human embryonic stem cell research, human embryo cloning, euthanasia, or physician-assisted suicide." As a result, any religious or moral principles can undergird a Louisiana health care worker's right to refuse to do six things.[37]

Hobby Lobby likewise presented the court with a case of selective conscientious objection to the Affordable Care Act (ACA). The business owners did not protest providing health insurance but rather facilitating access to four specific forms of birth control. *Hobby Lobby* differed from the draft law cases in significant ways. First, the Green and Hahn families pursued a conscience claim not for themselves but on behalf of a closely held for-profit corporation. Second, the objection invoked a blend of religious and moral rationales not as distinct justifications deserving of equal treatment but as additive rationales designed to strengthen their claim. Thus, the families asserted it was "immoral and sinful for [them] to intentionally participate in, pay for, facilitate, or otherwise support these drugs." Why did building a case based on both religion and morals matter? Because, third, according to the families, following the law implicated or would make them "morally complicit in 'the death of [an] embryo'" (or what they considered to be an abortion).[38] The objection was not to a government mandate to use birth control akin to a government mandate to serve as a combatant soldier in war. Rather, as Justice Samuel Alito's majority opinion framed it, the case raised "a difficult and important question of religion and moral philosophy, namely, the circumstances under which it is immoral for a person to perform an act that is innocent in itself but that has the effect of enabling or facilitating the commission of an immoral act by another."[39]

Hobby Lobby centered on a distinct form of conscientious objection, what some legal scholars have classified as "complicity-based conscience claims." The Affordable Care Act did not require Hobby Lobby's owners to personally violate their beliefs by forcing them to use contraception. Instead, the owners sought an exemption from providing health insurance that enabled *other people*—their employees—to acquire contraception that the owners disavowed as immoral.[40] By declaring the ACA to be a moral problem as well as a religious problem, Alito was able to vindicate the claim. In her dissent Justice Ruth Bader Ginsburg worried that the logic undergirding *Hobby Lobby* would enable any number of religious employers to resist particular elements of health care—say, Jehovah's Witnesses being forced to supply health insurance that covered blood transfusions—but the majority flicked that away. *Hobby Lobby* involved more than a mere religious matter, reasoned the majority; it pivoted on what the business owners considered both a moral and religious imperative.

* * *

Over the past century, conscience has become more deeply embedded in legal conflicts over claims to religious free exercise. During the
mid-twentieth century, the courts expanded the right to conscientiously
object to military service by untethering conscience from organized religion and then religion altogether. The process incrementally opened the
umbrella of combatant military service exemptions from members of
peace churches to individual believers and then from religiously rooted
objection to any form of religious, moral, or ethical objection. By 1971,
conscientious objection to war no longer relied upon religious reasoning
but still required opposition to all wars.

Starting in 1973, legislators transferred conscience rights from military conscription to health care. In so doing, they carried over the
idea that conscientious objection could arise from either religious or
moral worldviews, thus seeming to offer anyone the possibility of invoking conscientious refusal in medicine. The first conscience clause
was limited to two procedures—abortion and sterilization—and to direct participants (doctors and nurses) and institutions (hospitals). But
here, too, the scope of conscience rights swelled. From the beginning,
legislation transformed conscience claims from a right claimed by an
individual to a right that could be claimed by an institution. Later this
came to encompass larger entities such as insurance companies, health-
maintenance organizations, closely held for-profit corporations, and,
most recently, any employer. Similarly, individuals claiming exemptions
snowballed from direct providers to indirect or tangentially involved
workers such as pharmacists, EMTs, and schedulers. The rationale for
demanding conscience-based exemptions grew from direct participation to the specter of complicity—a Catholic doctrine now embraced
by other religious groups. And, over the past forty-five years, objectors
began applying the rhetoric of conscience to additional elements of
health care and, beyond medicine, to "culture war" issues such as gay
marriage and adoption.[41] Conscience now provides a language for making rights claims that transform moral and religious objections to other
people's life choices into practices deserving personal legal protection.

This admixture of religion and morality is potent and often obscures
or ignores the costs of conscience. In contrast to military conscientious
objection, which was vetted and required noncombatant or alternative service, health care conscience legislation has created rights of ab-

solute refusal. What is cost-free and consequence-free to the objector can be costly, consequential, and discriminatory for others. Releasing the individual, institutional, and corporate objector from obligations in medicine passes the burden to the patient seeking treatment, the doctor seeking to treat patients according to medical standards of care, and the employee seeking the best personal form of contraception.[42] In both health care and gay marriage, religious objectors have adopted the language of conscience, with its valence of overlapping religious and moral claims.[43] Espousing this rhetoric but eschewing the regulatory system that oversaw conscientious objection to war has created an unbalanced framework in which some religious ideas receive automatic deference while others are ignored.

"Taking conscience seriously," in contrast, requires considering the conscience of everyone involved and affected. Courts, scholars, and public discourse tend to view contests over conscience as religious versus secular conflicts. Yet they often pit religious and moral convictions against religious and moral convictions.[44] Just as religious and moral arguments support and oppose fighting war, so too do religious and moral arguments support and oppose a range of choices in health care, including contraception, in-vitro fertilization, abortion, LGBT care, organ donation, and end-of-life decisions.

Nevertheless, the very elasticity granted to conscience by mid-twentieth-century courts has accelerated its use in other domains, for more attenuated concerns, and against other people. Because conscientious objection does not depend on religious doctrine, it appears accessible to everyone; after all, anyone from a devout churchgoer to a dogmatic atheist can cite his or her conscience as a basis for refusing to bear weapons in war, provide contraception, or bake a cake for a gay wedding. But, as deployed in health care, used in public discourse, and accepted by courts, conscience tends to protect and exempt the identifiably pious social conservative more than others. Conscience has therefore shifted from serving as a shield protecting the individual from state conscription to a sword attempting to block others from accessing services, from comprehensive health care to wedding vendors.

But conscience is not inherently preferential of certain types of religious and moral arguments. Neither law nor religion conclusively defines what conscience is, while history reveals only when it has been recognized and how it has been used or, in some circumstances, constrained. If conscience emerges from the individual, then it may reinforce or contradict prevailing religious doctrine or current social mores. Attention to who uses the language of conscience, in what circumstances, and to achieve what goals—as well as how the public, politicians, and judges defer to or curb those claims—illuminates how individuals and groups sit in relation to the state and with one another. Conscience initially offered a limited number of Americans a tool with which to resist state conscription to bear arms. Over the twentieth century, the Supreme Court granted all Americans, regardless of religious commitments, the possibility of asserting conscientious objection to all war, thus making it a more inclusive right. As conscience claims migrated from the military to other realms of American society, they shifted from an inclusive implement that empowered individuals against the state to an exclusive instrument that privileged particular religious views. Democratizing access to legal rights of conscience thus had the unintended consequence of turning a state-granted olive branch into a legal and political weapon that individuals, institutions, and corporations could deploy against their fellow Americans.

NOTES

1   United States v. Seeger, 380 U.S. 163, 167 (1965).
2   Science and medicine do not support this view. IUDs and emergency contraception prevent the implantation of a fertilized egg, and from a scientific perspective, implantation marks the start of pregnancy. However, some religious groups identify the beginning of pregnancy as fertilization, and scientific validity is not a requirement for litigation. Annie Sneed, "Fact or Fiction?: Emergency Contraceptives Cause Abortions," *Scientific American*, July 3, 2014, www.scientificamerican.com/; Gregory M. Lipper, "Zubik v. Burwell, Part 3: Birth Control Is Not Abortion," *Bill of Health* (blog), March 19, 2016, http://blogs.harvard.edu.
3   Kent Greenawalt, "Granting Exemptions from Legal Duties: When Are They Warranted and What Is the Place of Religion?" (McElroy Lecture), *University of Detroit Mercy Law Review* 93 (Winter 2016): 93.
4   *Hobby Lobby* rested on the application of the Religious Freedom Restoration Act, which made it a statutory, rather than a constitutional, case.
5   For a sharp and concise distillation of many of these debates over conscience, see Elizabeth Sepper, "Taking Conscience Seriously," *Virginia Law Review* 98 (2012): 1526–31. As a matter of theology, Catholicism offers an elaborate history of defining and discussing "conscience," but these discussions occur in other faith traditions as well.

6 I focus on these two contexts because the legislators who created conscience rights for health care providers and institutions assumed they were simply borrowing from the military, as I will discuss later. Conscientious objection in medicine can also apply to patients refusing treatment or interventions for religious reasons, such as Jehovah's Witnesses declining blood transfusions or Christian Scientists spurning vaccinations. However, these are different in two ways: First, adults can always refuse to consent to treatment for any reason. Second, the one exception, upheld by the Supreme Court in *Jacobson v. Massachusetts* (1905), is compulsory vaccination, in which public health needs outweigh civil liberties. The public interest is notably absent from arguments supporting religious refusal to provide health care.

7 1 Annals of Cong. 757 (1789) (Joseph Gales ed., 1834).

8 1 Annals of Cong. 758 (1789).

9 1 Annals of Cong. 757 (1789).

10 1 Annals of Cong. 758 (1789).

11 1 Annals of Cong. 783 (1789).

12 On debates about the Second Amendment, see Nathan Kozuskanich, "Originalism, History, and the Second Amendment: What Did Bearing Arms Really Mean to the Founders?," *Journal of Constitutional Law* 10, no. 3 (2008): 413–46.

13 John Chambers, "Conscientious Objectors and the American State from Colonial Times to the Present," in *The New Conscientious Objection: From Sacred to Secular Resistance*, ed. Charles Moskos and John Chambers (New York: Oxford University Press, 1993), 23–46; Christopher Capozzola, *Uncle Sam Wants You: World War I and the Making of the Modern American Citizen* (New York: Oxford University Press, 2008), 55–82.

14 Chambers, "Conscientious Objectors." Of the approximately 34.5 million men who registered for the draft in World War II, about seventy-two thousand sought conscientious objector status. More than one-third failed the military physical (excusing them from service), slightly more than one-third accepted noncombatant roles, one-sixth chose Civilian Public Service camps, and about six thousand men went to jail for refusing any service.

15 Selective Training and Service Act of 1940, P.L. 76–783, 54 Stat. 885 (1940).

16 Girouard v. United States, 328 U.S. 61, 67 (1946).

17 *Seeger*, 380 U.S. at 185, 192–3.

18 Theologians cited include Paul Tillich (Lutheran), John A. T. Robinson (Anglican), the Ecumenical Council (Catholic), and David Saville Muzzey (Ethical Culture).

19 *Seeger*, 380 U.S. at 194.

20 Quoted in Welsh v. United States, 398 U.S. 333, 339 (1970).

21 *Welsh*, 398 U.S. at 343.

22 *Welsh*, 398 U.S. at 340.

23 *Welsh*, 398 U.S. at 345.

24 *Welsh*, 398 U.S. at 352, 355. In a footnote, Harlan argues that the very elasticity of Black's definition of "religion" avoided an establishment clause problem.

25 *Welsh*, 398 U.S. at 346.

26 Whether the state treated religious and nonreligious views equally was a central question of religion-state jurisprudence at midcentury.

27 A multitude of religion-state cases in the 1960s pushed the court to adopt positions that required legislative neutrality or nonpreferentialism between religion and secular positions. See, for example, Torcaso v. Watkins, 367 U.S. 488 (1961) (no test oaths for public office); Engel v. Vitale, 370 U.S. 421 (1962) (no school prayer, however generic); Sherbert v. Verner, 374 U.S. 398 (1963) (denying unemployment benefits to someone fired for religious beliefs requires a compelling government interest); Abington Township v. Schempp, 374 U.S. 203 (1963) (no school-sponsored Bible readings); and Epperson v. Arkansas, 393 U.S. 97 (1968) (no prohibitions on teaching evolution).

28 *Welsh*, 398 U.S. at 362, 366–67.

29 *Welsh*, 398 U.S. at 370.

30 Gillette v. U.S., 401 U.S. 437, 444 (1971).

31 *Gillette*, 401 U.S. at 455, 458. The rhetoric of fairness echoes the 1967 Selective Service report, *In Pursuit of Equity: Who Serves When Not All Serve?* (Washington, DC: Government Printing Office, 1967). The data on enlisted men during Vietnam clearly demonstrate, however, that the "more articulate, better educated, or better counseled" avoided the military or escaped deployment in Vietnam. See Christian Appy, *Working Class War: American Combat Soldiers and Vietnam* (Chapel Hill: University of North Carolina, 1993).

32 There is a vast literature on abortion in twentieth-century America. See, for example, Carol Joffe, *Doctors of Conscience: The Struggle to Provide Abortion before and after* Roe v. Wade (Boston: Beacon, 1995); Cynthia Gorney, *Articles of Faith: A Frontline History of the Abortion Wars* (New York: Touchstone, 1998); Daniel K. Williams, *Defenders of the Unborn: The Pro-Life Movement before* Roe v. Wade (New York: Oxford University Press, 2016).

33 Taylor v. St. Vincent's Hospital, 369 F. Supp. 948 (D. Mont. 1973); Roe v. Wade, 410 U.S. 113 (1973).

34 Church Amendment to the Health Programs Extension Act of 1973, P.L. 93-45, § 401(b), (c), 87 Stat. 91 (1973); James Buckley, *Congressional Record* (March 27, 1973), S9601.

35 Sara Dubow, "A Constitutional Right Rendered Utterly Meaningless": Religious Exemptions and Reproductive Politics, 1973–2014," *Journal of Policy History* 27, no. 1 (2014): 1–35; Kimberly A. Parr, "Beyond Politics: A Social and Cultural History of Federal Healthcare Conscience Protections," *American Journal of Law & Medicine* 35, no. 4 (2009): 620–46.

36 Juliet Eilperin, "Trump Moves to Allow Broad Exemption from ACA Birth-Control Coverage," *Washington Post*, May 31, 2017; Religious Exemptions and Accommodations for Coverage of Certain Preventive Services Under the Affordable Care Act, Federal Register, Interim Final Rule, October 6, 2017, https://federalregister.gov; Moral Exemptions and Accommodations for Coverage of Certain

Preventive Services under the Affordable Care Act. Federal Register, Interim Final Rule, October 6, 2017, https://federalregister.gov; Alison Kodjak, "Trump Admin Will Protect Health Workers Who Refuse Services on Religious Grounds," National Public Radio, January 18, 2018, www.npr.org.

37 LA Rev Stat § 40:1061.20 (2016).

38 Burwell v. Hobby Lobby, 573 U.S. __ (2014), 13; Brief for Respondents, No. 13–354, at 5, 11.

39 *Hobby Lobby*, Brief for Respondents, at 5.

40 Douglas NeJaime and Reva B. Siegel, "Conscience Wars: Complicity-Based Conscience Claims in Religion and Politics," *Yale Law Journal* 124 (2015): 2516–91.

41 Micah Schwartzman, Chad Flanders, and Zoe Robinson, eds., *The Rise of Corporate Religious Liberty* (New York: Oxford University Press, 2016).

42 One exception is in end-of-life care as most state laws require providers and institutions to transfer a patient if they will not comply with the patient's advanced directives (e.g., declining a ventilator or requesting aggressive treatment). This does not include physician-assisted suicide.

43 For recent examples, see Masterpiece Cakeshop, Ltd. v. Colorado Civil Rights Commission, 584 U.S. __ (2018); NIFLA v. Becerra, 585 U.S. __ (2018).

44 Elizabeth Sepper, "Taking Conscience Seriously," *Virginia Law Review* 98, no. 7 (November 2012): 1501–75. In his book *Exemptions: Necessary, Justified, or Misguided?* (Cambridge, MA: Harvard University Press, 2016), Kent Greenawalt dismisses the need to balance the patient and the provider as well as the provider and the institution, not seeing those conflicts as especially significant because, he writes, "a sense of religious or moral obligation not to perform is broader than a sense that one must perform" (111). Yet other evidence contradicts his claim, especially in a time when the ability to perform certain procedures has been restricted and stigmatized. See Lori R. Freedman, *Willing and Unable: Doctors' Constraints in Abortion Care* (Nashville: Vanderbilt University Press, 2010); Lisa Harris, "Recognizing Conscience in Abortion Provision," *New England Journal of Medicine* 367, no. 11 (2012): 981–83; Mara Buchbinder et al., "Reframing Conscientious Care: Providing Abortion Care When Law and Conscience Collide," *Hastings Center Report* 46, no. 2 (2016): 22–30.

3

Exercise

FINBARR CURTIS

I'm sure you'll understand my point of view
We know each other mentally
You gotta know that you're bringin' out
The animal in me
—Olivia Newton-John

While the word "exercise" does not appear in Olivia Newton-John's 1981 hit "Physical," the music video's images of her in her iconic 1980s aerobics gear made it a prophetic anthem for working out. Any association with exercise in the gym is an invention of the video, which depicts Newton-John coaxing several hapless men into an exercise routine before miraculously transforming them into muscle-bound exemplars of physical fitness. The song's injunction to "get physical" is clearly about sex, at least "clearly" in the sense that innuendo can be clear. Newton-John expresses her impatient desire to transform affection into physical activity, announcing that "There's nothing left to talk about / Unless it's horizontally."

Questions about the ability to transform sentiment into action are familiar features of debates over the free exercise of religion. There is a great deal at stake in deciding whether religious freedom resides in a believer's mind or is manifested in the exercise of a religious body. It is unclear exactly what one does when one exercises religion. Discussions about the First Amendment often take "free exercise" as synonymous with "personal religious freedom" without clarifying what aspects of religion are to be exercised. Possible usages of the word "exercise" receive less scholarly attention than the contested meanings of "establishment." If anything, what is taken to be problematic about the free exercise of religion is what defines the words "free" and "religion."

This chapter will consider what kind of activity is protected by free exercise and will suggest that religious freedom claims are most persuasive in the courts when they prescribe habits of bodily regulation and discipline. Rather than removing institutional constraints on individual behavior, free exercise claims tend to strengthen private forms of authority like families, churches, and corporations that seek freedom from government regulation so that they can more effectively govern persons.

Get Physical

The Latin *exercere* has the sense of "to train," "to practice," or "to keep oneself busy." As a verb, *exercere* anticipates the sort of physical exercise that people do at the gym. Rituals of exercise are performed with the conviction that sustained, repeated activity is necessary to cultivate and maintain something, to keep it in shape. Staying in shape is not easy. It requires strenuous exertion in the service of diligent adherence to an exercise routine. For many people, this discipline is voluntary but can still feel like a duty or obligation. A commitment to exercise is a common goal of New Year's resolutions, but keeping this promise can be easier said than done. Exercise regimes are hard to sustain. They can sometimes mark a distance between actual behavior and idealized behavioral norms.

Voluntary exercise in the gym is a project of bodily self-governance. To exercise is to follow rules that discipline bodies to conform to socially normative ideals of fitness. The freedom to follow rules might be a good way of thinking about religious exercise. While "freedom" often connotes the ability to do what one wants without regard for external constraints, free exercise is not usually invoked to protect acts of uninhibited personal expression. Free exercise of religion tends to be invoked by people seeking to undertake strenuous activity in the service of regulation, restraint, discipline, and self-control. This sense of restriction hearkens back to early usages of the Latin *religio*. As Carlin A. Barton and Daniel Boyarin explain, "*Religio* was most often . . . used by Romans to describe *not* an institution or set of institutions but rather a range of emotions arising from heightened attention: hesitation, caution, anxiety, fear—feelings of being bound, restricted, inhibited, stopped short."[1] The binding obligations of *religio* required care, caution, and scrupulous attention to observing social boundaries. This boundary-observing sensibility was tied to the intuitive feelings that compel people to follow rules as well as to the anxiety and shame that come with breaking them.

To think about exercise in the context of law in the United States, it might be helpful to revisit these rule-bound and anxiety-inducing qualities of religious practice. Examining strenuous efforts of self-governance can complicate the idea that the primary work of free exercise is to protect authentic selves expressing inner convictions.[2] Of course, associations of religious freedom with interiority and sincerity are common features of the rhetoric of religious freedom. In his influential letter on religious toleration, for example, John Locke explained: "[T]rue and saving religion consists in an inward conviction of mind; without it, nothing has value in the eyes of God."[3] Americans like Thomas Jefferson and James Madison, arguably the two most influential figures in shaping the First Amendment, were influenced by Locke's insistence that true religion was a matter of inward conviction. In Jefferson's famous letter to a Connecticut Baptist congregation, he defined religion as "a matter which lies solely between Man & his God, that he owes account to none other for his faith or his worship, that the legitimate powers of government reach actions only, & not opinions."[4] Jefferson's insistence that religious freedom is protected because the reach of government concerns only "actions" did not address activity that many would classify as religious. In practice, legal controversies have arisen in response to disputes about rules that govern visible behavior.

Know Each Other Mentally

Later English usages of "exercise," and those possibly most germane to the First Amendment, have to do with the assertion of rights. One sense of "exercise" that might describe how American law has used the term is the exercise of some right, power, or authority over one's choice of religion. This has often meant that citizens have the right to believe what they want, to associate with others who share those beliefs, and sometimes to act on those beliefs.[5] Decisions like *Reynolds v. United States* (1879), however, specified that free exercise protected religious opinions but not the right to act on those opinions. In this case predating the rejection of polygamy by the Church of Jesus Christ of

Latter-Day Saints, a Mormon resident of the Utah territory argued that it was his religious obligation to enter into multiple marriages. The court responded that while he was free to believe in polygamy, he was not free to practice it. As the *Reynolds* decision explained, "Laws are made for the government of actions, and while they cannot interfere with mere religious belief and opinions, they may with practices."[6] A bright line was drawn between mind and body, beliefs and actions. Minds are free to believe whatever they wish, but bodies are not necessarily free to follow after. In the twentieth and twenty-first centuries, the jurisprudence expanded beyond *Reynolds* to consider practices in addition to beliefs, but confusion remains over the extent to which the state is expected to accommodate activity that violates otherwise religiously neutral laws.

It is not clear that the restriction of "exercise" to belief reflects the older use of the term. The Maryland Toleration Act of 1649 specifies that no one will be "compelled to the beliefe [*sic*] or exercise of any other Religion against his or her consent." Exercise, this language suggests, is some activity supplemental to belief, and the ability to perform rituals or sacraments is a component of religious freedom. Exercising religion was distinct from having ideas in one's head. Writing two decades later, the English Quaker William Penn made a clear distinction between liberty of mind and liberty of exercise in the form of visible worship. As he stated, "By *Liberty of Conscience*, we understand not only a meer [*sic*] *Liberty of the Mind*, in believing or disbelieving this or that Principle or Doctrine, *but the Exercise of ourselves in a visible Way of Worship, upon our believing it to be indispensably required at our hands, that if we neglect it for Fear or Favour of any Moral Man, we Sin, and incur divine wrath*."[7] For Penn, exercise was tied both to visibility and to binding obligation. The point here was descriptive but also normative. For Penn, mere belief without action would lead to moral dissolution and divine censure. His assertion that exercise includes a "visible Way of Worship" raises a question about whether religious rituals are in the same category as moral behavior consistent with religious teachings. In some ways ritual and moral action appear to be distinct social phenomena, but one thing these forms of exercise have in common is that they both involve bodies that follow rules.

In an attempt to reconstruct what the framers of the Constitution meant by restricting Congress from passing any law "prohibiting the free exercise" of religion, legal scholar Michael McConnell has argued that "exercise" does indeed mean something different from "belief." As McConnell asserts, the phrase "free exercise" was used in the place usually held by "liberty of conscience," and this substitution signaled a robust view of religious freedom that not only tolerated but encouraged religion.[8] In McConnell's view, the framers sought to encourage religious exercise because they thought it was a good thing when churches played a prominent role in shaping civic discourse and governing personal behavior.[9] Therefore, a Lockean call for civil toleration of inward convictions was not the primary motivation for those making free exercise arguments.

Not everyone agrees with McConnell's analysis. Phillip Hammond, David Machacek, and Eric Mazur insist that free exercise and liberty of conscience are interchangeable concepts and that protecting conscience is the primary aim of the First Amendment. As they argue, "The freedom of conscience . . . is the source from which the freedoms of religion, speech, the press, and association are derived. Indeed, without the freedom of conscience—the freedom of the individual to decide for him- or herself questions of morality, truth, and beauty—the First Amendment protections would amount to little more than pleasant words."[10] This interpretation focuses on the individual's right to make decisions. Decisions could be the basis for action, but the freedom of conscience is tasked with protecting the mental space that allows for independent judgment.

Regardless of who is right about the framer's intent, the suggestion that there might be a difference between conscience and exercise raises the question of whether there is a difference between having a right and exercising a right. Is religion something that someone has or something that someone does? Does free exercise protect an interior freedom that is satisfied by being left alone, or does it require activity involving assertion and effort? What I am getting at is not so much the familiar distinction between belief and ritual (although it is related to this) but a tension between passivity and activity, between protection and assertion. This tension is especially evident when citizens are not satisfied with protecting their own worship or moral behavior but insist on asserting that their rules should govern the social order. In cases like opposition to abortion or same-sex marriage, citizens have asserted that their moral precepts should be encoded in civil law while still claiming that their beliefs are distinctly religious convictions that require protection from the state.

There's Nothing Left to Talk About

It makes intuitive sense to think of religious freedom in terms of protection rather than assertion, because free exercise is often invoked as the right to not do something, to be exempt from some law that other citizens are compelled to follow. Not everyone has agreed that such exemptions should exist. As some scholars and courts have contended, free exercise is not inhibited so long as laws do not target specific religions. This was the logic of the *Reynolds* decision as well as the much maligned majority opinion in *Employment Division v. Smith*.[11] In the *Smith* case, two members of the Native American Church were denied unemployment benefits because they were fired for ingesting peyote. Although they argued that peyote was part of a religious ritual, the court ruled that they had no right to an exemption from drug laws because these were neutral regulations that applied to everyone.

Liberals, especially those that see religious diversity as a social good, have conflicted feelings about exemptions. On the one hand, they tend to sympathize with religious minorities and believe those minorities should have the right to act in ways that are not subject to the imposition of majoritarian social norms. To this end, they support decisions that protect the free exercise of public school students who do not wish to pray or salute the flag.[12] According to Sarah Barringer Gordon, groups like Jews, Mormons, Jehovah's Witnesses, and others were able to use the free exercise of religion to fight for their place within American civic life. As Gordon explains, "The embrace of religious diversity as a positive value in constitutional jurisprudence, and in the broader society, blended a new and dynamic legal innovation with a religious movement toward ecumenicism."[13] On the other hand, the ability to opt out of laws that govern public policy can raise liberal concerns about the erosion of the public good in favor of a retreat to private freedom.[14] According to legal theorist Robin West, citing religious convictions in order to opt out of civic duties amounts to an "exit right" that allows citizens to avoid broader discussions of public goods in favor of loyalty to specific concerns of subcommunities. As she explains, "[A]n exit right, virtually regardless of its textual foundation, is justified by the purported importance—moral, political, or otherwise—of the nongovernmental sovereign to which allegiance of the subcommunity that will be covered by the exit right is owed."[15] It is possible that the association of religious exercise with privacy intensifies the nongovernmental quality of subcommunities that seek to shape the conscience and conduct of their members.[16] When subcommunities are classified as religious, the logic of the separation of church and state places claims based on conscience in a zone outside of political contestation.[17] To act in a nongovernmental zone, however, is not to free oneself from institutional regulation. Rather, framed as an affirmation of communal values, the free exercise of religion protects the rights of citizens to choose which institutional authorities will govern them.

Thinking about exercise in terms of self-governance requires thinking about the institutional conditions necessary to make such governance possible. To have an athletic ability does not guarantee that one will be a successful athlete (the same could be said for other forms of discipline, like music). One needs to practice. Practice requires time, dedication, and resources. These resources, in turn, depend on prior institutional arrangements that enable people to practice in order to transform aptitude into ability. Free exercise, especially as tested under the law, addresses the work put into producing the forms of social authority necessary to maintain institutional spaces that allow one to practice religion. To ascertain how churches and corporations practice religion, courts have to decide who is authorized to speak for these institutions. This requires practical decisions about legitimate structures of organizational governance as well as the distribution of institutional resources. There is a great deal at stake in deciding who can use religious freedom to govern and who is to be governed by religious freedom.

Recent decisions like *Hosanna-Tabor Evangelical Lutheran Church and School v. EEOC* (2012) and *Burwell v. Hobby Lobby Stores, Inc.* (2014) presume that exercise includes institutional power over individual actions.[18] These cases do not empower individual forms of belief or practice as much as they protect institutional authority over religious persons. In *Hosanna-Tabor*, the court decided that a church had the legal power to fire a teacher who could have filed a disability claim if she was not employed by a religious organization. By protecting a church's right to discipline its employees, the court protected a private institution from public oversight even in a case that did not involve what would be obviously classified as religious worship. *Hobby Lobby* enabled a corporation to opt out of providing for its employees forms of contraception coverage mandated by the Affordable Care Act. In both cases, the Roberts court decided, the religious institutional rules trumped the legal protections generally afforded to private citizens. Free exercise allowed religious organizations to be left alone to govern people in autonomous zones protected from democratic institutions. As Mary Ann Case points out, the right to be left alone is distributed unequally in favor of political advocates of sexual regulation: "[T]he proposal to live-and-let-live is radically asymmetrical, with religious opponents of sexual rights demanding both legal protection for their own space and the legal right to invade the space of others."[19] As is the case with many abstract freedoms, in practice, free exercise depends on the distribution of social and institutional power.

Animal in Me?

One may be tempted to see religious accommodation as a ruse to avoid regulations, but in practice this characterization gets things backward. Rather than the freedom to do less than what the law requires, free exercise empowers nongovernmental institutions to insist on more personal regulation. It is possible that free exercise exemptions are most persuasive when citizens enter into voluntary agreements to police their behavior in ways that are more strenuous than would be required by the state, and this in turn is enforced by consensual submission to some authoritative body that enforces these rules. Free exercise, then, is the ability to follow or enforce one set of rules when they come into conflict with another set of rules.

An example of what happens when people attempt to use religious freedom to improvise rather than follow institutional rules can be found in Winnifred Fallers Sullivan's analysis of the failed free exercise claim adjudicated in *Warner v. Boca Raton* (2001). In this case, people had decorated cemetery plots in ways that reflected personal expressions of religious sentiment but violated city ordinances prohibiting vertical markers on graves. These personal religious preferences were judged to be sincere, but because they were insufficiently institutionalized and amounted to what the city called a form of "cemetery anarchy," they were deemed to be inadequate grounds for an exemption. As Sullivan notes, "Religiously motivated activity, as the City understood it, would be authoritatively prescribed and defined from above, not improvised from below."[20] Free exercise was the freedom to follow sectarian rules; it was not the freedom to ignore or make up one's own rules.

Part of the reason why political conservatives often prize the free exercise of religion over all else is that it gives private institutions the power to regulate behavior.[21] Of course, Christian majorities have had a practical interest in favoring exercise over establishment. A group of people who want to pray in public will insist it is their voluntary right to do so rather than an establishment clause violation of the separation of church and state. Almost uniformly, this logic is applied when they are confident that the religious practices to be exercised will be ones they like. But another reason for the intuitive connection between religious freedom and conservatism is the affirmation of choices to follow what seem to be more restrictive forms of self-governance. Successful free exercise claims have been made by people who are more rigorous Sabbatarians, who cover their heads in public, who insist on more restrictive forms of sexual regulation, or who are sect members who cannot attend public school lest it impose a worldly influence that would contradict an "entire mode of life" that is "regulated in great detail."[22] These exercises are socially conservative in the technical sense that they conserve (maintain) social boundaries and institutional authority. I am not proposing that the preference for recognizing the exercise rights of socially conservative practices is a fixed rule, but there might be an intuitive association of religion with binding obligations and boundary policing.

One illustration of this intuitive connection between religion and restraint can be found in the dissenting quality of free exercise arguments for greater sexual freedom. For example, Janet R. Jakobsen and Ann Pellegrini propose that free exercise should promote improvisational and experimental expressions of bodily freedom on the grounds that religious freedom for everyone would affirm personal choices about bodily pleasure. Frustrated with the equation of religious freedom and sexual restriction, Jakobsen and Pellegrini advocate instead for a "Free Exercise of Sex." They lament the use of religious reasons for sexual regulation by the same

Christian conservatives who refuse to consider religious reasons for economic regulation, arguing, "Conservatives rarely offer any explanation as to why sexual freedom is the height of immorality and selfishness, while other types of freedom—political and economic freedom, for example, or freedom of speech and thought—are not only expressions of high moral principles, but are, in fact, the central values of the American nation."[23] If people valued sex the way they valued speech or money, they would be more likely to see institutions that regulated sex as threats to personal freedom. Instead, conservative arguments for religious freedom see bodily pleasure as selfish and immoral while financial indulgence is perfectly fine. Whatever the normative value of Jakobsen and Pellegrini's call for reshaping the relationship between free exercise and sex, however, it is clear that they are thinking against the grain. In the discourse of religious freedom, sexual restraint goes hand-in-hand with economic hedonism.

If there is an internal coherence to conservative advocacy for free markets and sexual restrictions, it is that both economic and religious freedom expand the power of private institutions. Conservatives claim that their efforts to outlaw abortion or endorse abstinence-only education are motivated by their desire to protect the sanctity of families, the unit, in their judgment, best suited to governing private behavior. Similarly, a marketplace liberated from state regulation makes strenuous demands on the labor of citizens in order to benefit nongovernmental corporations. Economic freedom is accompanied by suspicion of "freeloaders," people who benefit from state entitlements at the expense of those who have to work for a living. According to Jerry Falwell, religious freedom was a resource to combat government policies that eroded sexual and economic discipline. In his view, modern Americans "have been reared by the family and by the public school in a society that is greatly devoid of discipline and character-building. These same young people have been reared under the influence of a government that has taught them socialism and welfarism. They have been taught to believe that the world owes them a living whether they work or not."[24] For Falwell, families and markets free from government regulation provide the discipline that can serve as the antidote to modern practices of bodily self-indulgence. Bodies ungoverned by work pose a social threat similar to the danger posed by bodies ungoverned by sexual rules. Both require rigorous religious and economic exercise to get them into shape.

It is fitting, then, that recent cases have blurred the lines between corporations, churches, and families. As with Hobby Lobby's right to protect itself from the sexual freedom of others, the case of *Masterpiece Cakeshop v. Colorado Civil Rights Commission* involved a baker who cited religious freedom as the grounds for refusing to bake a cake for a same-sex wedding. The baker's defense team argued that by forcing him to bake a cake for a same-sex wedding, the state of Colorado was "ordering him to sketch, sculpt, and hand-paint cakes that celebrate a view of marriage in violation of his religious convictions."[25] The baker held that same-sex unions violated the rules of marriage, and it was a matter of religious conviction not only to follow his own rules but also to refuse to be complicit in the rule breaking of others. Deciding in the baker's favor, the court held that the Colorado Civil Rights Commission had demonstrated "hostility to religion" in their deliberations.[26] In its rulings on complicity cases like *Masterpiece Cakeshop* and *Hobby Lobby*, the court accepts several principles as axiomatic: a corporation is an extension of the religious will of the owner, criticism of religious intolerance is itself a violation of freedom of religion, and conservative regulations of sex are religious while expressions of sexual freedom are irreligious. As Sullivan notes, it is so obvious to the court that religion restricts sex that the point does not even need to be argued: "There is an easy assumption by the Court [in *Masterpiece Cakeshop*] and in the *Hobby Lobby* opinions that conservative views about sex are religious while liberal ones are secular. No explanation need be given."[27]

The substitution of exercise for sex in the music video for Olivia Newton-John's "Physical" illustrates what might be a familiar theme of First Amendment jurisprudence. It makes sense to think about free exercise not as freedom from norms but as the ability of institutions to more effectively and authoritatively regulate human bodies in the absence of state forms of bodily regulation. For this reason, "religious freedom" has become the buzzword of attempts to mobilize against the threats posed by sexual freedom and its concomitant regime of "political correctness."[28] When religious freedom advocates lose public battles over sexual regulation, they seek to protect their rights to at least live in nongovernmental subcommunities. Conservative usages of free exercise seek to empower private institutions to avoid paying for birth control or having to bake a wedding cake for a couple whose bodily discipline seems to threaten their own forms of familial, church, and corporate governance. Instead of seeing free exercise claims as tied to the promotion of diversity and pluralism, it might be possible that free exercise claims are also attempts to protect relatively homogenous social spaces against the threats posed by a religiously, ethnically, racially, and sexually diverse world.

NOTES

1 Carlin A. Barton and Daniel Boyarin, *Imagine No Religion: How Modern Abstractions Hide Ancient Realities* (New York: Fordham University Press, 2016), 19. While Barton and Boyarin emphasize that religion was not an institution in this particular passage, much of the book chronicles the eventual institutionalization of *religio* in the writing of Cicero and Tertullian. This relationship between binding obligation and institutional governance resonates with contemporary usages of "the free exercise of religion."

2 A number of postcolonial critics have argued that the nexus of religious freedom, sincerity, authenticity, and interiority derives from Protestant assumptions that have shaped the development of the modern category of religion. For genealogical approaches that consider religious freedom beyond the US context, see Talal Asad, *Genealogies of Religion: Discipline and Reasons of Power in Christianity and Islam* (Baltimore: Johns Hopkins University Press, 1993); Webb Keane, *Christian Moderns: Freedom and Fetish in the Missionary Encounter* (Berkeley: University of California Press, 2007).

3 John Locke, "A Letter Concerning Toleration," in *Locke on Toleration*, ed. Richard Vernon (New York: Cambridge University Press, 2010), 8. It should be noted that the inward conviction of which Locke speaks was displayed through a "life of goodness and piety," so his ideas about religious toleration were not solely concerned with disputes about truth claims.

4 Thomas Jefferson, "To messers Nehemiah Dodge, Ephraim Robbins, & Stephen S. Nelson, a committee of the Danbury Baptist association in the state of Connecticut," January 1, 1802, Library of Congress, www.loc.gov.

5 For more on the centrality of belief to legal conceptions of religious freedom, see Sarah Imhoff's chapter in this volume.

6 Reynolds v. United States, 98 U.S. 145, 166 (1879).

7 William Penn, *The Great Case of Liberty of Conscience Once More Briefly Debated and Defended* (Ann Arbor, MI: ProQuest, 2011 [1670]), 11.

8 Michael W. McConnell, "The Origins and Historical Understanding of Free Exercise of Religion," *Harvard Law Review* 103, no. 7 (May 1990): 1443–44.

9 For a similar view that the purpose of free exercise was to create conditions under which Christianity would flourish, see Steven D. Smith, *The Rise and Decline of American Religious Freedom* (Cambridge, MA: Harvard University Press, 2014).

10 Phillip E. Hammond, David W. Machacek, and Eric Michael Mazur, *Religion on Trial: How Supreme Court Trends Threaten Freedom of Conscience in America* (New York: AltaMira, 2004), 39.

11 Employment Division v. Smith, 494 U.S. 872 (1990).

12 Engel v. Vitale, 370 U.S. 421 (1962); Abington School District v. Schempp, 374 U.S. 203 (1963); West Virginia State Board of Education v. Barnette, 319 U.S. 624 (1943).

13 Sarah Barringer Gordon, *The Spirit of the Law: Religious Voices and the Constitution in Modern America* (Cambridge, MA: Belknap Press, 2010), 17.

14 In some ways, this would hearken back to the classic liberal concern that minority groups are protected from what John Stuart Mill called the "tyranny of the majority," in which a majority of citizens could use democratic institutions to violate the rights of a few. As Patricia J. Williams points out, however, this tyranny might be just as vexing as the public sphere emptied out in favor of private institutions. As she explains, "The tyranny of the majority has survived in liberal political theory as a justification for all manner of legislative restraint, particularly economic restraint. But what Mill did not anticipate was that the persuasive power of the forum itself would subvert the polis, as well as the law, to the extent that there is today precious little 'public' left, just the tyranny of what we called the private." See Patricia J. Williams, *The Alchemy of Race and Rights* (Cambridge, MA: Harvard University Press, 1991), 43.

15 Robin West, "Freedom of the Church and Our Endangered Civil Rights: Exiting the Social Contract," in *The Rise of Corporate Religious Liberty*, ed. Micah Schwartzman, Chad Flanders, and Zoë Robinson (New York: Oxford University Press, 2016), 405. While it is unclear whether there is any intrinsic difference between a subcommunity and a community, the "sub" here emphasizes the limits of communal obligations. Membership in a subcommunity implies something distinct from inclusion in a broader community or public.

16 In addition to creating spaces for subcommunities, exit rights also create the possibility that relative consensus about moral precepts within local communities might create alternative legal zones. If enough people in a given area cited religious freedom as a reason to opt out of laws that protected sexual or religious minorities, then those minority groups would enjoy little practical protection from discrimination. As Douglas NeJaime and Reva Siegel explain, "Ultimately, in more conservative, religious, and rural parts of the country, complicity-based refusals have the capacity to construct separate, localized legal orders in which same-sex couples face an unpredictable marketplace and labor market and continue to encounter stigma and rejection"; see "Conscience Wars: Complicity-Based Conscience Claims in Religion and Politics," *Yale Law Journal* 124 (2014): 2574.

17 This is not to say that consciences are not produced within political and economic institutions, but only that they are imagined as apolitical. For more on the production of conscience, see Isaac Weiner, "The Corporately Produced Conscience:

Emergency Contraception and the Politics of Workplace Accommodations," *Journal of the American Academy of Religion* 85, no. 1 (March 2017): 31–63.

18 Hosanna-Tabor Evangelical Lutheran Church and School v. EEOC, 132 S. Ct. 694 (2012); Burwell v. Hobby Lobby Stores, Inc., 134 S. Ct. 2751 (2014). It is significant that the religious freedom claim of the owners of Hobby Lobby resonated because, unlike other corporations, it was closely held and tied to a family. This illustrates the court's deference to private forms of institutional regulation.

19 Mary Ann Case, "Why 'Live and Let Live' Is Not a Viable Solution to the Difficult Problems of Religious Accommodation in the Age of Sexual Civil Rights," *Southern California Law Review* 88 (2015): 476.

20 Winnifred Fallers Sullivan, *The Impossibility of Religious Freedom* (Princeton, NJ: Princeton University Press, 2005), 35.

21 "Conservative" is not the most precise label, as contemporary conservatism can include everyone from evangelical activists to libertarian free marketeers with little interest in religious regulation. What I am attempting to get at in this usage is not so much an absolute principle as a tendency for self-identified conservatives to support expansive religious freedom claims made by churches and corporations.

22 Sherbert v. Verner, 374 U.S. 398 (1963); EEOC v. Abercrombie & Fitch Stores, 135 S. Ct. 2028 (2015); Burwell v. Hobby Lobby Stores, Inc., 134 S. Ct. 2751 (2014); Wisconsin v. Yoder, 406 U.S. 205, 210 (1972).

23 Janet R. Jakobsen and Ann Pellegrini, *Love the Sin: Sexual Regulation and the Limits of Tolerance* (Boston: Beacon, 2004), 129.

24 Jerry Falwell, *Listen, America!* (New York: Bantam, 1980), 15–16.

25 Oral Argument at 4, Masterpiece Cakeshop v. Colorado Civil Rights Commission, 137 S. Ct. 2290 (2017).

26 Masterpiece Cakeshop v. Colorado Civil Rights Commission, 584 U.S. _____ (2018).

27 Winnifred Fallers Sullivan, "Is Masterpiece Cakeshop a Church?," *Immanent Frame* (blog), June 8, 2018, https://tif.ssrc.org/.

28 By "political correctness," I do not mean any analytically coherent category. Rather, I refer to popular usages of the term that identify a pervasive assault on expressive freedom caused by civic expectations that white Christians consider and respond to the diverse sensibilities of people other than themselves.

4

Establishment

ANNA SU

"In the words of Jefferson, the clause against establishment of religion by law was intended to erect a wall of separation between church and state."[1] With that one sentence, Justice Hugo Black, writing for the majority of the Supreme Court in the 1947 case of *Everson v. Board of Education of the Township of Ewing*, laid down the foundation for a separationist rhetoric that would form the bedrock of popular and academic discourse about the purposes of nonestablishment. It was the first case to expound on the history of the establishment clause, and the first to hold the clause applicable to the states.

Everson involved the question of whether a New Jersey program subsidizing the transportation of students to schools, including religious schools, was constitutionally valid. The Supreme Court found no violation, but not without elevating the metaphor of "wall of separation" as the predominant frame of popular and legal discussion for the role of religion in American public life. How did this conclusion come about? Justice Black vividly recounted the history of religious persecution in seventeenth-century Europe, in particular singling out the compelled payment of tithes and taxes to government-sponsored churches, as the primary evil that the First Amendment sought to address, noting:

> A large proportion of the early settlers of this country came here from Europe to escape the bondage of laws which compelled them to support and attend government-favored churches. The centuries immediately before and contemporaneous with the colonization of America had been filled with turmoil, civil strife and persecutions generated in large part by established sects determined to maintain their absolute political and religious supremacy.[2]

From *Everson* onward, nonestablishment meant that there can be no government aid to religion. There was one problem, however. No evidence lends authority to Justice Black's sweeping interpretation of the establishment clause. To be sure, conflict involving religion and politics has been a constant fixture of American history since the founding era, but as the case illustrates, the Supreme Court's interpretation of the establishment clause proved to be crucial in shaping the future of nonestablishment. These decisions set the parameters, however shifting, within which Americans continue to give life to the words of the First Amendment of the US Constitution, particularly, "Congress shall make no law respecting an establishment of religion." Court opinions thus cast a long shadow on how citizens debate and discuss religion.

In this chapter, I look at the transformation of how the Supreme Court understood nonestablishment and explore the consequences of such understandings. If nonestablishment started out as the means by which an individual's liberty of conscience would be protected—that is, there has to be separation of church and state in order to protect a person's individual conscience—it has since become a guarantor of political equality. That transformation brought about a greater visibility of religion in the public square, for example, the recitation of prayer before municipal legislative sessions, the funding of religious schools, and the creation of religious monuments throughout the country, much to the consternation of many. More importantly, the transformation comes with a hidden cost. Religion might be on full display in America all right, but only after shedding itself of any claim to divine transcendence or objective truth. A religiously themed war memorial is now simply a patriotic monument. A Ten Commandments monument is only a historical message. A prayer is just like any other kind of speech. Perhaps this is a price that those who support the greater visibility of religion in the public square are willing to pay.

At the very least, recalling this strange career of nonestablishment, and as a corollary, what Americans really mean when they invoke the metaphor of a "wall of separation," invites us to be more skeptical of purported wins or losses on either side of the ongoing culture wars.

Beginnings of Separation

Law professor Gerard Bradley once wrote, "Separation of church and state is right up there with Mom, apple pie and baseball in American iconography."[3] But the hold and ubiquity of the phrase in the national imaginary is a bit of a puzzle. It is nowhere to be found in the Constitution. It is also probably not what the Founders intended. For most of the eighteenth and nineteenth centuries, religion was widely considered to be necessary to create publicly minded citizens and thus crucial to a healthy republic. Contrary to the popular myth, the establishment clause had a limited ambition at the outset. It simply meant to prevent the newly formed federal government from establishing a national religion and from interfering with existing religious establishments of the states at that time.[4] Note that Massachusetts, for instance, had an official state religion—Congregationalism—as late as 1833. From a narrow historical perspective, the best plausible interpretation, then, was that the clause was designed to protect the existing status quo. This converged with a narrow view of what establishment meant during the founding period. According to legal scholar Michael McConnell, the states could not control religious doctrine, could not use physical church property to conduct public business, and could not compel church attendance.[5] Beyond these examples, it was unclear what separation or disestablishment actually meant at that time. At best, it protected dissenters' liberty of conscience. After all, Christianity was deemed to be part of the common law in many states. Moreover, even after the last state church was disestablished in Massachusetts, religion remained a staple in public life. Though citizens were no longer taxed for the support of particular churches, churches were nonetheless politically paramount. Traveling across the United States for nine months in 1831, Alexis de Tocqueville observed that despite the removal of religion from government in America, it remains the "foremost of their political institutions."[6]

Throughout the nineteenth century, courts slowly fleshed out the contours of disestablishment by explicitly disconnecting religious practices from their religious origins. Sunday closing laws, for example, were justified as a legitimate state measure to ensure a day of rest.[7] In an Ohio state supreme court decision upholding a similar statute, the opinion read: "The statute upon which the defendant relies, prohibiting common labor on the Sabbath, could not stand for a moment as a law of this state if its sole foundation was the Christian duty of keeping that day holy and its sole motive to enforce the observance of that duty."[8] Other state courts made similar rulings that Sunday closing laws were valid civil regulations notwithstanding their religious origins. The government, courts reiterated, has no power over anything spiritual, and any preference of one religion over the other would violate the Constitution. In a seminal decision involving a schism within a Presbyterian church in Louisville, Kentucky, the Supreme Court gave birth to the "hands-off" approach, that is, the rule forbidding courts from evaluating the substance of religious claims advanced by believers and groups. In that same case, the court stated that "the law knows no heresy and is committed to the support of no dogma, the establishment of no sect."[9]

Curiously enough, these cases sat comfortably alongside prevalent practices—which would later fall prey to constitutional scrutiny—such as Bible reading in public schools, Thanksgiving proclamations, state funding of missionary schools, and congressional and military chaplaincies.[10] Historians and legal scholars alike attribute this seeming disjunction to the widespread anti-Catholic animus that emerged in the wake of the massive European, mostly Irish, immigration of the mid-1800s. Among other sites of contestation, American Catholics complained that the mandatory Bible reading in public schools—from the Protestant King James Bible, of course—violated their liberty of conscience and was in no meaningful sense nonsectarian.[11] Court doctrines that prohibited the state from meddling with religion or granting preference to one religion over another became a double-edged sword that Catholics sought to use against the Protestant majority. These efforts made few legal inroads and were met, not infrequently, with violent resistance. Consequently, Catholics established their own parochial schools. In response, Protestants charged that Catholic opposition to Bible reading made them unsuited for republican government because of their allegiance to a foreign authority—the pope. The controversy over public funding of Catholic schools eventually led to the 1875 proposal of the Blaine Amendment which would have mandated free public schools and prohibited the use of public monies for sectarian—read *Catholic*—schools. While the amendment failed to secure the necessary votes in the Senate, it spurred several states to adopt their own versions, many of which are still in effect today.

The meaning of nonestablishment thus changed. Calls against a union of church and state were, in effect, directed against the new immigrants. As legal historian Kurt Lash has argued, it was during the period between the founding and Reconstruction that the meaning of the establishment clause shifted from its initial, simple federalist ambition of protecting the states' prerogatives to a more expansive purpose of protecting individual freedom. Even as legislatures enacted religiously motivated laws, under the emerging nonestablishment regime, these laws were justified by secular rationales. As far as the Protestant majority was concerned, the odd juxtaposition worked in the meantime. Christianity was no longer the law of the land, but through government sanction, it remained the religion of the people.[12] Many laws, which in design and effect were solicitous of the prevailing religious sentiment, were enforced as religiously neutral measures for public order. In a sense, the Christian majority could have their cake and eat it too.

Minority religionists did not fare nearly as well. Thus, for instance, polygamy, insofar as it formed a key tenet of the Mormon religion, was deemed to be one of the "twin relics of barbarism"[13] alongside slavery. As such, Mormons were relentlessly persecuted by Protestant Americans throughout the late nineteenth century. In *Davis v. Beason*, a decision clearly aimed at Mormons, the Supreme Court upheld the constitutionality of a law that criminalized bigamy and polygamy on the grounds that these deviant arrangements were "inimical to the peace, good order, and morals of a society."[14] In a related case decided in the same year, the court also disincorporated the Mormon Church.[15] Within a few months, the church capitulated to the federal government and officially discontinued the practice of plural marriage.

The Supreme Court Weighs In

For its selective history, the *Everson* decision was met with intense criticism by lawyers and historians. As the dissenting opinion by Justice Wiley Blount Rutledge stated, "No provision of the Constitution is more closely tied or given content by its generating history than the religious clause of the First Amendment."[16] Rutledge's complaint was directed against the outcome, not necessarily Black's narrative. Despite the strong separationist rhetoric of the decision, the court actually allowed the state of New Jersey to subsidize transportation costs of students attending parochial schools. Like Black, Rutledge believed that the object of the clause was to create a complete and permanent separation of the spheres of religious activity and civil authority, which categorically meant the prohibition of public support or aid for religion, even if based on secular criteria.[17] As part of the aftermath, a group of scholars and clergy formed an organization called Protestants and Other Americans United for the Separation of Church and State, which dedicated itself to eliminating all government aid to parochial schools.

The separationist line inaugurated by *Everson* continued in the 1960s with the court's decisions in *Engel v. Vitale* and *Abington School District v. Schempp*, each of which concerned school-sponsored prayers. In *Engel*, the more controversial decision of the two, Justice Black struck down the "Regents' prayer" as inconsistent with the establishment clause, noting, "No doubt that New York's program of daily classroom invocation of God's blessings . . . is a religious activity, even absent evidence of any coercion."[18] If in *Everson* the primary justification for the separation of church and state given by the Supreme Court was to avoid religious persecution, then *Engel* posited that the mixture of religion and government tended to corrupt both.[19] *Engel* was and remains one of the most controversial decisions in the court's history, prompting hundreds of proposals in Congress to overturn the decision by statute.[20] At first, large swaths of school districts across the United States simply ignored the decision, but the number of Bible readings in schools dropped dramatically. In *Schempp*, plaintiffs challenged a Pennsylvania public school ritual that involved the brief recitation of Bible verses without any commentary. The court likewise invalidated the practice. Together, these two cases shifted the understanding of nonestablishment from its original rationale of avoidance of religious persecution to one of state neutrality, where "neutrality" meant the elimination of religious practices from public spaces. Indeed, in *Schempp,* the mere fact that the religious exercise was happening within a public school building was sufficient to make it a violation of the First Amendment.

The wall of separation began to crack in the 1970s, however. In *Lemon v. Kurtzman*, another case involving state funding to parochial schools, the court pronounced a tripartite test to assess the constitutionality of laws restricting religion: (1) the law must have a secular purpose, (2) its primary effect must neither advance nor inhibit religion, and (3) it must not create excessive government entanglement with religion.[21] Oddly enough, even as the secular-purpose requirement appeared to serve separationist ends, the court took pains to state the "line of separation, far from being a wall, is a blurred, indistinct, and variable barrier."[22] Chief Justice Warren Burger further confounded matters when he wrote, "religion must be a private matter for the individual."[23] It was clear, however, that, unlike in its earlier cases, the court now understood separation to be important because it was concerned about aggravating political division along religious lines—hence the mandate to avoid government entanglement with religion. Breaking from its previous rulings, the decision stated that "political division along religious lines was one of the principal evils against which the First Amendment was intended to protect."[24]

This was a significant shift. As legal scholar Noah Feldman has suggested, elevating the political divisiveness rationale in *Lemon* brought the court a step closer to the view that the establishment clause was meant to guarantee the equality of religious minorities, and a step away from the view that the establishment clause was intended to protect the liberty of religious dissenters.[25] If that was indeed the case, the court would set the clause on a different trajectory from where it began. Among other effects, it would allow religion to have a far more pronounced presence in American public life than it did, leading one observer to proclaim the relative irrelevance of the establishment clause.[26]

If the goal was to avoid political divisiveness owing to religious differences, then the key step was to remove religion as a relevant quality in assessing a person's status in the political community. That was precisely what Justice Sandra Day O'Connor did in formulating the so-called endorsement test in a concurring opinion in *Lynch v. Donnelly*,[27] one of the early cases involving public displays of religious symbols, which would be adopted as the rule in *County of Allegheny v. ACLU*.[28] *Allegheny* concerned a crèche placed on the staircase of a county courthouse and, separately, a collection of Chanukah menorahs, a Christmas tree, and a sign saluting liberty. Were either of these displays tantamount to government endorsement of religion and therefore a violation of the Constitution?

Given its prominent location, the sole crèche was held to be a violation; the menorah collection, by contrast, was not. According to Justice O'Connor's formulation, a display would be considered a violation of the establishment clause if it sent a message of exclusion to a reasonable observer by conveying favor or preference for a particular religion or religious belief. The idea was to avoid any religious display that might convey the impression that citizens who do not share similar beliefs are somehow, in the eyes of the state, outsiders.[29] The same reasoning was behind the court striking down a Ten Commandments monument standing alone in front of a Kentucky courthouse as similarly unconstitutional,[30] whereas another monument, strategically placed amongst seventeen other monuments and historical markers commemorating Texas history, was deemed valid.[31]

The endorsement test extended to areas beyond public religious displays, although strictly speaking, the governing test is the so-called neutrality test. The idea is that when it comes to questions of money and state subsidies, religion and nonreligion should be subject to the same treatment. In any case, underlying both tests is the value of equality. In subsequent years, the neutrality test was used to assess the constitutionality of student-led prayers in Texas football games,[32] the use of public school facilities by a religious organization,[33] the use of a state university's student activities fund to support the speech of a religious student organization,[34] the indirect provision of federal funds to local state schools, including religious schools,[35] and of an Ohio school-voucher program that allowed vouchers to be used for attendance at private religious schools.[36] Notable in the latter case was that both the majority opinion by Chief Justice William Rehnquist and the dissent by Justice John Paul Stevens voiced concerns about whether equal access to public funds would convey the impression that the state was endorsing a particular religion.[37]

The success of the endorsement test or even the neutrality test as the predominant test used by courts to evaluate constitutionality did not emerge from nowhere. The key value underpinning the principle of nonendorsement—or, stated affirmatively, the principle of neutrality—is equality. Because of the prominence of racial inequality as the single most important challenge to the American constitutional order, it is not surprising that the legal understanding of equality that originated from cases involving race migrated to other areas of constitutional law, including the religion clauses. But that migration transformed the original understanding of the clauses and generated some unintended consequences.

The Question of Religion in the Public Square

If the foregoing discussion about constitutional and legal tests sounds confusing, that is because it is. The Supreme Court's case law on the establishment clause is widely and quite notoriously described as "arbitrary, incoherent, and inconsistent."[38] For the purposes of our discussion, however, it suffices to note that the elevation of political equality as the overarching purpose of nonestablishment made for an attractive, prevailing framework. Hence, in theory, the law should not distinguish between religious and nonreligious entities insofar as access to government services is concerned. In practice, that means the principle of neutrality allows for the greater visibility of religion in the public square because there is no reason to exclude them, given a neutral set of criteria. If one can donate a secular historical monument to be built on a state park, why not a Ten Commandments monument? In a period of heightened religious diversity, this development, which pays homage to the Christian roots of American culture,[39] has become a flashpoint of the ongoing culture wars. One could even argue that this is a reactionary attempt by conservative Christians who feel, rightly or wrongly, that their traditions are no longer welcome in their own country. Otherwise, why insist on a Ten Commandments monument in a place where there was previously none?

Still, it pays to ask the question: Precisely what kind of religion has risen to public prominence? In *Salazar v. Buono*,[40] the religious form under scrutiny was a Latin cross in the Mojave Desert, mounted on a rock as a memorial to deceased soldiers. After lengthy litigation, the Supreme Court held that the cross could stay, but it nonetheless sent the case back to the lower courts for final resolution. The opinion acknowledged the cross as a Christian symbol but noted, in light of the cross's intended commemorative function, that removal would be tantamount to disrespecting fallen veterans and thus seen as a sign of hostility on all matters of religion.[41] That the late Justice Antonin Scalia could make a straight-faced claim that "the cross is the most common symbol of the resting place of the dead"[42] shows the lasting power of conflating religious sentiment with patriotic symbols.

More recently, an appellate court upheld another religious public monument on the grounds that the so-called Montana Jesus does not convey to a reasonable and informed observer that the government, rather than a private party, endorses Christianity or any other religion. Tellingly the court relied on four criteria: (1) the statute was placed on a mountain rather than in a government building, (2) the plaque itself identified it as privately owned and maintained, (3) the mountain's role as a summer and winter destination for recreational activities such as hiking and skiing suggested a secular context, and (4) the flippant interactions of locals and tourists, such as adorning the statue in ski gear or high-fiving it as they pass by, suggest secular perceptions. This combination established the statue as constitutionally permissible.[43] Given the ideological inclinations of the sitting justices, the complainant, Freedom from Religion Foundation Inc., a Wisconsin nonprofit group, decided not to appeal to the Supreme Court.

State neutrality does not necessarily require the eradication of all public religious symbols. But in the process of making religion visible and constitutional, the religious elements of these symbols have all been pushed into the background in favor of a superficial secular cast. I would argue that religion qua religion is not the thing being justified in these cases; rather, religion's manifestations, such as prayer, practice, and symbol, are defended in terms other than its divine or transcendent character, perhaps as a matter of tradition, culture, or patriotism. As the abovementioned decisions illustrate, these symbols have been somewhat drained of their religious meaning and significance. In *Van Orden v. Perry*,[44] for instance, the case that upheld the constitutionality of a Ten Commandments monument displayed on the grounds of the Texas state capitol, Justice Stephen Breyer's concurrence paid respect to the constitutive role of religion in US founding history while at the same time emphasizing the secular "broader moral and historical message reflective of a cultural heritage."[45] Similarly, another Ten Commandments case involved the question of whether a private group, the Fraternal Order of Eagles, could insist that a municipality permit it to erect a permanent monument in a city park. Interestingly, the court decided the dispute under the free speech clause of the First Amendment.[46] Justice Scalia, concurring with the majority, asserted that the circumstances under question were indistinguishable from the circumstances in *Van Orden*, adding that the monument "was donated by the Eagles as part of its national effort to combat juvenile delinquency."[47] Municipal prayers have gone the same direction as these monuments. In 2014, the Supreme Court upheld the practice of opening town hall meetings with a prayer—even a sectarian prayer—on the ground that this tradition has been practiced by Congress and dozens of state legislatures since the founding period.[48] Even as the court acknowledged that the practice of opening prayers serves the spiritual needs of the lawmakers, it emphasized that this was a practice borne out of tradition. Today, seasonal holiday displays such as nativity scenes, which are often erected in places where Christmas is celebrated by a large number of the local population, have become part of an odd amalgamations of symbols; that is, they normally have to stand beside secular Christmas objects such as candy canes and Santa Claus in order to pass constitutional muster.

The dilution and reduction of religion to simply one phenomenon or human activity among many is easily evident vis-à-vis public displays of religious symbols and practice, but a similar drift governs access to public money. For example, in *Rosenberger v. Rector and Visitors of the University of Virginia*, a case involving the question of whether a public university could deny funds to a student publication produced from a religious viewpoint, the court removed any legal hurdles against state funding of religious speech and activities by invoking the neutrality test. It reconceived the funding for the Christian student magazine *Wide Awake* as equal provision of resources for all kinds of student viewpoints, including religious ones. No longer is religious speech seen as part of religious practice but rather as speech that happens to be spoken by religious groups.[49] In other words, it holds religious speech as not more important but simply as one mode of speech among many. This is the core idea behind *Rosenberger* and the line of cases on which it relied. So long as the government employs religion-neutral criteria, the identity of the recipient does not matter. For instance, the court did not find any problem with the use of state tax credits to fund student scholarships in private schools, many of which are religious schools.[50] This formulation of equal access made it easier for religious groups to obtain funding they would have been surely denied under the old, stricter, separationist regime.

In subsequent cases involving funding to public schools, a rule has thus emerged. If the incidental aid to religious institutions is reached through a neutral program open to both religious and nonreligious beneficiaries, it cannot be inferred that the state is unconstitutionally endorsing a religious practice or belief.[51] Indeed, more recently, the Supreme Court held that the state of Missouri could not deny public funds to a church that sought to use state funds to resurface its playground with rubber simply because it is a religious organization.[52] As Justice Breyer wrote in that case, the scenario was easy enough to imagine: "If government could not deny general services like police and fire protection to religious places, there was no reason for the state to cut off the church from participating in a general welfare program designed to secure or to improve the health and safety of children."[53]

Such developments have led some to lament that this arrangement has paved the way for breaching the wall of separation.[54] Or perhaps its real fate remains to be seen. It is striking, however, that state neutrality, which originally sprang from concerns animating the endorsement test and aimed to protect the sensibilities of religious minorities, has become the avenue by which the Christian religious majority has come to reassert its place in the American public square. Currently, there is greater congruence between the law and the religious preferences of the majority, however debated. But in achieving this, religious organizations and actors have flattened their religious identities and deemphasized the religious character of their messages, at least in the context of legal nonestablishment. Perhaps one explanation is that truly religious claims, that is, claims that foreground the spiritual or divine basis of the speech or activity, have simply migrated to claims of accommodation under the free exercise clause, although that is a subject to be examined another day. I suspect that analysis would come to a similar conclusion.[55] Whether this was the kind of bargain required in order to avoid the phenomenon of, in the words of theologian Richard John Neuhaus, a naked public square, it remains an important question that must be confronted by religious believers.

* * *

To state that the separation of church and state no longer exists under American law would be a gross exaggeration. What is true, however, is that the current understanding of separation and nonestablishment, now viewed through the prism of equality, has allowed for a greater integration between religion and government. Rhetoric and symbols matter. This is especially true for courts that translate the basic values animating the establishment clause into technical legal doctrine. Separation of church and state, to the extent that it actually worked to separate *some* religion from politics in a legally meaningful way, worked for a period of time because it required parties to provide justifications, and those justifications were often premised on the essentially religious nature of the activity. The current approach by the Supreme Court requires no more than fair treatment, that is, religious entities cannot be denied access to public spaces and public monies because they are religious. Religious symbols can stay if they are amidst other, secular symbols.

This is a remarkable transformation in how we understand separation in the past fifty years, thanks in large part to the Supreme Court. It sheds some insight on the ongoing question of whether religion should be considered special at all as a matter of law.[56] Constitutionally speaking, if religion is special enough to merit accommodation under the free exercise clause, it also labors under a special disability mandated by the establishment clause. But that constitutional balance teeters on the edge of obsolescence today. Majoritarian religious actors, in recent years, while they have been vindicated by courts and awarded with increased public visibility of their heritage and tradition, may be Pyrrhic victors. That Christianity has come to be legally articulated in terms devoid of any transcendence ought for no one be a cause for celebration.

NOTES

1 Everson v. Board of Education, 330 U.S. 1 (1947).
2 *Everson*, 330 U.S. at 10.
3 Gerard Bradley, "Church Autonomy in the Constitutional Order: The End of Church and State," *Louisiana Law Review* 49 (1988): 1057.
4 Akhil Reed Amar, *America's Constitution: A Biography* (New York: Random House, 2005); Kurt Lash, "The Second Adoption of the Establishment Clause: The Rise of the Nonestablishment Principle," *Arizona State Law Journal* 27 (1995): 1085.
5 Michael McConnell, "Establishment and Disestablishment at the Founding, Part I: Establishment of Religion," *William and Mary Law Review* 44 (2003): 2105, 2131–80.

6 Alexis de Tocqueville, *Democracy in America*, ed. Isaac Kramnick (New York: Penguin, 2003), 280.

7 Lash, "Second Adoption," 1105–11.

8 Bloom v. Richards, 20 Ohio St. 387 (1853).

9 Watson v. Jones, 80 U.S. 679, 729 (1872).

10 See generally Steven Green, *The Second Disestablishment: Church and State in Nineteenth-Century America* (New York: Oxford University Press, 2010).

11 Noah Feldman, "Nonsectarianism Reconsidered," *Journal of Law and Politics* 18 (2002): 65.

12 David Sehat, *The Myth of American Religious Freedom* (New York: Oxford University Press, 2010).

13 Sarah Barringer Gordon, *The Mormon Question: Polygamy and Constitutional Conflict in Nineteenth-Century America* (Chapel Hill: University of North Carolina Press, 2002).

14 Davis v. Beason, 133 U.S. 333 (1890).

15 Late Corp. of the Church of Jesus Christ of Latter-Day Saints v. U.S., 136 U.S. 1 (1890).

16 *Everson*, 330 U.S. at 33.

17 *Everson*, 330 U.S. at 58–59 (Rutledge J. dissenting).

18 Engel v. Vitale, 370 U.S. 421, 424 (1962).

19 *Engel*, 370 U.S. at 431–32.

20 Thomas C. Berg, "The Story of the School Prayer Decisions: Civil Religion under Assault," in *First Amendment Stories*, ed. Richard Garnett and Andrew Koppelman (New York: Foundation, 2011), 193.

21 Lemon v. Kurtzman, 403 U.S. 602, 613 (1971).

22 *Lemon*, 403 U.S. at 614

23 *Lemon*, 403 U.S. at 625.

24 *Lemon*, 403 U.S. at 624.

25 Noah Feldman, "From Liberty to Equality: The Transformation of the Establishment Clause," *California Law Review* 90 (2002): 673, 693.

26 Richard C. Schragger, "The Relative Irrelevance of the Establishment Clause," *Texas Law Review* 89 (2011): 583.

27 Lynch v. Donnelly, 465 U.S. 668 (1984).

28 County of Allegheny v. ACLU, 492 U.S. 573 (1989).

29 *Allegheny*, 492 U.S. at 579–80.

30 McCreary County v. ACLU of Kentucky, 545 U.S. 844 (2005).

31 Van Orden v. Perry, 545 U.S. 677 (2005).

32 Santa Fe Independent School District v. Doe, 530 U.S. 290 (2000).

33 Lamb's Chapel v. Center Moriches Union Free School District, 508 U.S. 384 (1993).

34 Rosenberger v. Rector and Visitors of the University of Virginia, 515 U.S. 819 (1995).

35 Mitchell v. Helms, 530 U.S. 793 (2000).

36 Zelman v. Simmons Harris, 536 U.S. 639 (2002).

37 Ibid.

38 Alan Brownstein, *Introduction to the First Amendment: The Establishment of Religion Clause* (New York: Prometheus, 2008), 15. See also Marc DeGirolami, "The Bloating of the Constitution: Equality and the US Establishment Clause," in *The Social Equality of Religion of Belief: A New View of Religion's Place in Society*, ed. Alan Carling (Hampshire, England: Palgrave Macmillan, 2016), 226–38.

39 See Mark Tushnet, "Religion and the Roberts Court: The Limits of Religious Pluralism in Constitutional Law," in *The Rise of Corporate Religious Liberty*, ed. Micah Schwartzman, Chad Flanders, and Zoe Robinson (New York: Oxford University Press, 2016), 465–77 (arguing that Christianity is the default religion in all cases).

40 Salazar v. Buono, 130 S. Ct. 1803 (2010).

41 *Salazar*, 130 S. Ct. at 1823.

42 Transcript of Oral Argument at 38, *Salazar*, 130 S. Ct. at 1803.

43 Freedom from Religion Foundation v. Weber (9th Cir. 2015), No. 13–35770.

44 *Van Orden*, 545 U.S.

45 *Van Orden*, 545 U.S. at 703.

46 Pleasant Grove City v. Summum, 555 U.S. 460 (2009).

47 *Pleasant Grove*, 555 U.S. (Scalia J. concurring).

48 Town of Greece v. Galloway, 134 S. Ct. 1811 (2014), 1824 ("The prayers delivered in the town of Greece do not fall outside the tradition this Court has recognized").

49 Paul Kahn, "The Jurisprudence of Religion in a Secular Age: From Ornamentalism to Hobby Lobby," *Law and Ethics of Human Rights* 10, no. 1 (2016): 19.

50 Arizona Christian School Tuition Org. v. Winn, 131 S. Ct. 1436 (2011) (resolved on the ground that the parties did not have the proper standing to challenge).

51 Mitchell v. Helms, 530 U.S. 793 (2000); Zelman v. Simmons-Harris, 536 U.S. 639 (2002).

52 Trinity Lutheran v. Comer, 137 S. Ct. 2012 (2017).

53 Ibid.

54 Christian Joppke, "Beyond the Wall of Separation: Religion and the American State in Comparative Perspective," *International Journal of Constitutional Law* 14, no. 4 (October 2016): 984–1008.

55 Kahn, "Jurisprudence of Religion," 29.

56 See Micah Schwartzman, "What If Religion Is Not Special?," *University of Chicago Law Review* 9, no. 4 (2012): 1351–1427.

PART II

Contestation

The legal definitions examined in the previous section were never hammered out for theory's sake. Rather, those who crafted the determinative judicial decisions were forced into such judgments by motivated citizens and tactically minded organizations. Without exception, those that filed the lawsuits that yielded consequential precedents *wanted* things. On the free exercise side, they wanted permission to do things that were prohibited or exemption from doing things that were civically obligated. On the establishment side, they wanted to disrupt long-standing public practices. As is true of all jurisprudence, these were stories of contestation: contestation over ideas and principles, bodily and communal sovereignty, public funding and resources. In this section our contributors examine separation, sovereignty, and protection as sites and weapons of contestation. In so doing, they reveal one of this volume's dominant themes: how, over the course of US history, the boundaries of what counts as public matters—and thus which matters are open to public contestation—have continually shifted.

Schools have been an especially fraught and productive site for contestation—between liberals and conservatives and between Protestants and Catholics. The rise of public education in the latter part of the nineteenth century led to a push to deny public funding to schools run by religious sects. Albeit often "unmarked" as religious, this Protestant preference for religious disestablishment dovetailed with the assertion of another kind of hegemony. In examining disputes over Catholic schools in Indian territory, Kathleen Holscher shows how the termination of Catholic-funded mission schools also belonged to an imperialist project. While the doctrine of separation was "saving" public education from the Roman Catholic Church, it simultaneously supplied an organizing principle for the management of Native populations. The extension of state control into the field of public education also signaled the triumph of settler sovereignty over Indigenous sovereignty.

From the days of first encounter, settler colonialism in the Americas displayed a Christian spirit. As derived from the Book of Genesis, the doctrine of discovery entitled Europeans first, and American colonialists second, to the heathen lands of the new world. A textbook political theology, this divine dispensation licensed any exception. The sovereign, one might say with a nod to Carl Schmitt, is the one who decides which treaty to break and when. Connecting the dots between this originary license and the recent assault on the water protectors of Standing Rock Indian Reservation, Tisa Wenger explores the role the analytic of religion has played in this process of persistent dispossession. While Native Americans have occasionally used the categories of religion and spirituality to their advantage, more often than not, the designation of Native practices as "religion" has undermined Indigenous claims to sovereignty. Strategically placed in opposition to the Native's "pagan theocracy" and "priestcraft," white settler sovereignty takes on the appearance of rationality and inevitability. Indeed, as Wenger argues, even when First Amendment claims brought by Native Americans pay material dividends, the "secular contract" undergirding such victories concedes sovereignty to the Christian settlers.

The legal construction of the religious other has long played a role in determinations of precisely who gets to become an American. Using President Trump's "Muslim ban" as the irresistible point of departure, Rosemary Corbett shows how barriers to Muslim naturalization on explicitly religious grounds are by no means a twenty-first-century innovation. Tried and true as well are the moral panics that are affixed to religious others, particularly to Muslims. Today's "terrorist" lives on a family tree with the polygamists of yesteryear. Constructed in this way across lines of religious difference, each cursed designation conjures an essentially unassimilable body, a body warranting exclusion at the very least and application of lethal force when deemed necessary. From the Barbary pirates to ISIS, the trumped-up nativist imperative to protect the homeland from such alien threats has furnished the administrators of American state violence with a highly elastic political weapon.

5

Separation

KATHLEEN HOLSCHER

In August 1904, the Jesuit priests and brothers and Franciscan sisters at St. Francis Mission School on the Rosebud Reservation received welcome news. Several years earlier, Congress had ended financial support for Catholic "contract schools" like St. Francis, and lately the Catholic educators had scrambled to fund what was the nation's largest Roman Catholic Indian boarding school.[1] Now the Commissioner of Indian Affairs, acting under the direction of President Roosevelt, extended a new contract for the sprawling complex.[2] In return for meeting a laundry list of curricular requirements, including "to instruct pupils as to the duties and privileges of American citizenship," the teachers at St. Francis would once again have access to publicly administered funds: $108 annually for each of their 250 Lakota charges.[3] This time, though, the money to operate Catholic Indian schools would not come from congressional appropriations. Instead it would come exclusively from "treaty and trust funds"—funds held and administered by the government on behalf of the Sicangu Oyate (Rosebud Sioux) and other tribes as their due in exchange for past cessions of land and property.[4] In the case of St. Francis School, Commissioner Francis E. Leupp was clear that he dispensed this money at the bidding of the tribe itself. A petition signed by 212 tribal members ratified the payments.[5]

Three years later, this three-way arrangement between the Sicangu Oyate, the federal government, and the Catholic Church was subjected to Supreme Court review. In *Quick Bear v. Leupp* (1908) three Lakota men from the Rosebud Reservation—Rueben Quick Bear, Ralph Eagle Feather, and Charles Tackett—filed suit, objecting to the government's new form of payments to the Church. The complaint stopped short of calling the arrangement unconstitutional, but it did appeal to "the 'wall of separation between Church and State' [which] undoubtedly makes it inconsistent and undesirable for the Government to participate . . . in the maintenance of a sectarian institution."[6] In its decision, the court confirmed the legality of tribal-fund payments under the First Amendment's establishment clause. Unlike congressional appropriations, Chief Justice Melville Fuller explained, treaty money was *not* public money. Rather, it was the tribe's money to spend as it saw fit:

> The two subjects . . . are essentially different in character. One is the gratuitous appropriation of public moneys for the purpose of Indian education; but the "treaty fund" is not public money in this sense. It is the Indians' money, or, at least, is dealt with by the government as if it belonged to them, as morally it does.[7]

In its conclusion, the court reflected on the religious freedom of the tribe. To prohibit the Sicangu Oyate "from receiving religious education at their own cost if they desire it . . . would be . . . to prohibit the free exercise of religion amongst the Indians."[8]

Quick Bear was among the earliest establishment clause cases decided by the US Supreme Court.[9] Limited in scope to the federal government's execution of trustee and treaty responsibilities, however, *Quick Bear* left no mark on establishment clause jurisprudence. Likewise, it has left barely a trace on histories of church and state.[10] For historians, the case is esoteric in its attention to treaty and trustee matters, but it is also ordinary. In an era with dozens of state-level legislative and judicial efforts to keep public money from the coffers of the Catholic Church, the *Quick Bear* suit generically sought to stop the Church from providing public schooling. These episodes are well-worn terrain. Abundant scholarship on US anti-Catholicism has analyzed the varieties of discomfort nineteenth-century Protestants harbored toward Catholics and their Church.[11] Nativism, anticlericalism, and phobia of Catholicism's hyper-ritualized and "antibiblical" character mingled in the Protestant imagination with concerns about the Church's compatibility (or lack thereof) with the US political system. Well into the twentieth century, recurrent cries about Catholicism's threat to freedom and democracy echoed throughout US legal and political discourse. Nowhere did this rhetoric show more strongly than in initiatives to remove public money from Catholic schools.[12] As Phillip Hamburger has argued, not only did anti-Catholicism propel such initiatives, but this antagonism was also consequently responsible for church-state separation's rise as a guiding principle in US law and politics between the mid-nineteenth and the mid-twentieth centuries.[13] In this register, the *Quick Bear* plaintiffs' appeal to a "wall of separation" to obstruct Catholic work rings all too familiar. So too does the involvement of Protestant-aligned groups, including the Indian Rights Association (which the defense called the "real plaintiff" in the case) and the nativist American Protective Association, in the litigation.[14]

Here I consider the fight over public money and Catholic Indian schools that culminated in *Quick Bear* differently. In what follows I chart the rise of church-state separation as an organizing principle in Indian affairs between 1885 and 1905 and the shifting shape of schooling for Indigenous children that accompanied the principle's ascent, not only as a consequence of "anti-Catholic feeling" but also as an extension of the federal government's project of Indigenous lands colonization, in the form that project took at the close of the nineteenth century.[15] Anti-Catholicism was but one dimension of this enterprise. As such I argue that separation discourse, as taken up by settlers involved in Indian affairs, tells us more about the state than its Protestant nature. Importantly, that discourse reveals the historical work that went into constructing the sovereignty of that state over and against Indigenous sovereignty and the role religion (and discussion about religion) played in that work. Following the failure of the proposed Blaine Amendment to the US Constitution in 1876, which had sought to bar public funds from schools "under the control of any religious sect," most separationists in the United States turned their attention to state law.[16] At the federal level, church-state separation was salient at century's end only in the adjacent worlds of Indian affairs and imperial projects overseas.[17] In the 1890s, armed with separation appeals, a small but influential group of reformers convinced Congress to do for Indian schools what Congressman James G. Blaine had tried to do for all US schools two decades earlier. By 1897 Congress had terminated the federal government's contract system with the Catholic Church. Going forward, religious organizations would no longer receive public funds to assist the state in its responsibility of educating Indigenous children.[18] Congress distributed funds for the last contracts two years later. The treaty-and-trust funds arrangement that thrilled the

Catholic teachers at St. Francis School, and incited the plaintiffs in *Quick Bear*, emerged from the rubble of this defunct school contracts system.

Calls for church-state separation during the school contracts fight, and in its aftermath, had a valence unique to their context: support of the federal government's work educating Indigenous children. During the 1880s and '90s, the United States was consolidating its authority over tribes that, a few decades earlier, it had treated (and treated *with*)—albeit in already-qualified and asymmetrical ways—as external polities. Amid this large-scale shift, the principle of church-state separation offered its advocates more than cover for anti-Catholic feeling; it was an essential tool in the expansion of federal imperial power. Separation brought the guarantee that schools would perform exclusively as appendages of the state, as sites where the "duty" of the federal government would become real, in unmediated fashion, in the lives of Indians, whom it had come to know as its wards. Cast in the light of US imperial ambition, the Catholic Church, with its different-but-overlapping interests in Indian education, was an ambiguous specter. For reformers who worried about it, the Church not only threatened to derail state efforts at Indian assimilation but also lingered awkwardly between the "guardian" federal government and its accumulating responsibilities. The entire project of Indigenous lands colonization turned on the ability of the state to demonstrate its power to govern in absolute, unlimited fashion. Within Indian affairs, church-state separation did more than reinforce the Protestant character of the state; it clarified the model of state sovereignty upon which US imperialism relied.

* * *

The language of separation does not appear in the US Constitution. Although Thomas Jefferson famously introduced the metaphor of a "wall of separation between Church and State" to lay out the implications of the establishment clause, as he saw them, in an 1802 letter to the Danbury Baptists, separation as constitutional doctrine is a product of the twentieth century and of the US Supreme Court.[19] The court contemplated Jefferson's wall in broad terms as early as *Reynolds v. United States* (1879), but it was not until *Everson v. Board of Education* (1947) that it settled on separation as its measure for determining the scope of the establishment clause.[20] Writing for the majority in *Everson*, Justice

Hugo Black revived Jefferson's model when he concluded, "The clause against establishment of religion by law was intended to erect 'a wall of separation between church and State.'" At Black's hand, the "wall of separation" became a constitutional standard, newly binding on both federal law and state law.[21]

Long before Black hitched separation to the establishment clause, however, the principle carried legal and political weight in the United States. As early as the mid-nineteenth century, advocates celebrated church-state separation and looked for ways to translate it into both federal and state law. These efforts were on display in 1875 with the proposed constitutional amendment, the Blaine Amendment, which would have required that

> no money raised by taxation . . . for the support of public schools . . . , nor any public lands devoted thereto, shall ever be under the control of any religious sect; nor shall any money so raised or lands so devoted be divided between religious sects or denominations.[22]

The Blaine Amendment fell four votes short of the two-thirds majority it needed to pass the Senate. In the decades surrounding its failure, however, a majority of state legislatures did what the federal government had declined to do and approved a slew of "little Blaine Amendments," which prohibited the use of public funds for religious schools at the state level.[23]

From the Blaine Amendment through the *Everson* era, public debate over church-state separation focused almost exclusively on education and was driven by advocates who highlighted the need to separate "sectarian" religion from publicly funded schools. Across this period, "sectarian" referred reliably to "Catholic." Separation was something that, for Americans who considered it through most of the nation's history, primarily made sense in relation to concerns about the Catholic Church, its clergy and religious, its amassing laity, and the threats (real or imagined) these groups presented to the United States.[24] It was also a principle that worked—alongside its counterpart, religious freedom—to assist Protestantism's passage into what Tracy Fessenden has named "an unmarked category" comprising the American secular. In other words, it was by means of separation rhetoric that the norms and styles of Protestantism moved from being discretely "religious" into being the un-signified "how things are." Well into the twentieth century, for example, separation discourse effected the elimination of Catholic lessons from public schools while indirectly preserving devotional reading of the Protestant King James Bible and other "nonsectarian" forms of prayer as legitimate practices, something other than troublesome "religion."[25]

This history of the separation principle as it developed amid fear of Catholicism is both familiar and important, but the work church-state separation has done amid US imperial initiatives requires another sort of analysis. Recognizing colonization as foundational to the US enterprise in turn means reconsidering separation. In *An Indigenous Peoples' History of the United States*, Roxanne Dunbar-Ortiz centers colonization and its accompanying violence as analytics for the study of US history: "Everything in US history is about the land—who oversaw and cultivated it, fished its waters, maintained its wildlife; who invaded and stole it; how it became a commodity . . . broken into pieces to be bought and sold on the market."[26] Dunbar-Ortiz is one of a group of Indigenous and non-Indigenous scholars who have called attention to the historical processes via which the United States government, accompanied by "all kinds of agencies, voluntary militias and . . . settlers themselves," has acted to terminate Indigenous nations for the purpose of making their territory free and available for the US to claim and settle.[27] Dunbar-Ortiz explains what termination entails—and does not entail—in the context of the colonization project: "The objective of US colonialist authorities was to terminate [Indians'] existence *as peoples* [my emphasis]—not as random individuals."[28] At the *Quick Bear* moment, not only federal Indian policy but also the appeals to church-state separation that shaped it conformed closely to this termination-of-peoples logic.

Over the course of the nineteenth century, Congress and the Supreme Court acted in tandem to terminate Indigenous sovereignty by recategorizing Indians as legal dependents. However qualified, earlier consideration of tribes as foreign polities with the authority to enter into nation-to-nation treaties had, by the 1870s, given way to the exercise of federal plenary power. According to this colonialist logic, tribes were reclassified as domestic entities. No longer "territorially and treaty-based peoples, they came to be understood as internal beneficiaries of 'gifted' land."[29] Congress completed this shift with its 1871 Indian Appropriations Act, which declared that no Indian tribe henceforth would be recognized "as an independent nation, tribe, or power with whom the United States may contract by treaty."[30] Relying on language introduced by the Supreme Court forty years earlier in *Cherokee Nation v. Georgia* (1831), the act also affirmed the legal status of Indians as wards of the US.[31] The federal government's most ambitious exercise of authority over tribes came the next decade, with the General Allotment Act of 1887. The Dawes Act, as it came to be known, "ushered in the . . . assimilation era of federal Indian policy" by allotting parcels of tribal lands as private holdings to individual tribal members and their families. It made allotment-holders subject to US civil and criminal law and extended US citizenship to those who conformed to the terms of the arrangement.[32] The act served the complementary ends of releasing "surplus" (i.e., non-allotted) tribal land for white settlement and assimilating Indigenous individuals. In both of its ends, the Dawes Act dealt a long-term blow to the integrity of tribes as distinct, land-based, self-governing peoples.[33]

Allotment and education reform—in particular, reforms intended to bring schools for Indians under exclusive control of the state—were tightly joined in the minds of Indian policy architects during the Dawes Act period. Reformers talked about them together as necessary for the "complete absorption [of the Indian] into the body politic."[34] In the months after the Dawes Act, the Friends of the Indians conference in Lake Mohonk, New York, turned its attention to education. The 1888 conference kicked off with a paper by Congregationalist minister Lyman Abbott. "The Indian problem is three problems—land, law, and education," Abbott told those gathered. "The country has entered upon the solution to the land problem. It has resolved to break up the reservation system . . . But nothing has yet been done toward the solution of the education problem."[35] For Abbott, the "education problem"—by which he meant the failure to "convert" Indians into "communities of intelligent, industrious, and self-supporting citizens"—was a product of the government's delay in building a state-run system of Indian education and its reliance instead upon religious contract schools, most of which the Bureau of Catholic Indian Missions managed by 1888.[36]

To solve the problem, Abbott presented his colleagues with a multipart plan—what he called the "outlines of a possible educational system."[37] Reminding his audience that "the education of the wards of the nation is a duty imposed on the nation itself," he called first for the end of federal contracts with religious groups.[38] The nation's wealth, he reasoned, was "produced by the lands where these Indians once roamed in savage freedom." It properly fell then to the nation to "provide the means necessary to enable those same Indians to adjust themselves to the conditions of civilized life." That responsibility, Abbott stressed, *must not be handed to other actors*: "The United States Government must undertake to provide education, not to supplement provision made by others; not to aid it with appropriations . . . ; not to try tentative experiments here and there, dependent upon the idiosyncrasy of individual agents."[39] Abbott's fervent emphasis on state obligation echoed in other parts of his plan as well. He insisted, for example, that the government itself, via its own state-run schools, ultimately "[assume] the entire charge of all primary education."[40] Abbott also recommended that the schooling of Indian children be made compulsory, regardless of parents' wishes. For Abbott, the state's duty was clear, and its execution was paramount. Proper execution justified the negation of parental authority, and it demanded too the marginalization of meddling "idiosyncratic" religious agencies.

The Friends of the Indians vigorously debated Abbott's proposals in 1888 and the years following. There were disagreements among them, and those who allied themselves with Abbott to end school contracts justified their position not only in terms of the nation's special responsibility for Indians but also in terms of separation of church and state. In 1890 J. M. King, secretary for the National League for the Protection of American Institutions, beseeched Lake Mohonk attendees to "let the nation do its work of education, and trust to the churches . . . for Christianization." The end of contract schools, King told them, is "first, in the best interests of the Indians; and, second, in the best interests of the American principle of the entire separation of Church and State."[41] In his 1891 annual report, T. J. Morgan, the Commissioner of Indian Affairs, similarly invoked the state's obligation to its wards alongside church-state separation to explain his own position against contract schools:

> It is contrary to the letter and the spirit of the Constitution of the United States . . . to take from the public moneys funds for the support of sectarian institutions. I believe that the Government ought to assume, ab-

solutely and completely, the control of Indian education, and that these wards should be trained in the Government institutions with the specific end of fitting them for American citizenship . . . I believe I am giving expression to the American idea of the entire separation of church and state.[42]

The year following, at the urging of advocates fighting the contract system, the Protestant denominations that had historically benefited from school contracts—Methodists, Episcopalians, Presbyterians, and Abbot's own Congregationalists—voluntarily withdrew from contract work. In so doing they expressed their support for ending an arrangement that disproportionately funded Catholic-run schools.[43] Their leadership also invoked separation. The executive committee of the Congregationalist American Missionary Association, for example, explained itself in an appeal to benefactors for funds to replace federal dollars. "We gave up money for the sake of a principle," the committee wrote. "We find ourselves counseled and compelled . . . to surrender twenty-two thousand dollars in obedience to the principle of separation between Church and State."[44]

Efforts to cut off public money for Catholic Indian schools, and the appeals to church-state separation to support them, resembled the simultaneous efforts in the dozens of initiatives to procure state Blaine Amendments. The 1897 Indian Appropriations Act, which conclusively declared "the settled policy of the Government to hereafter make no appropriation whatever for education in any sectarian school," echoed the Blaine Amendment language that was becoming law across the country.[45] Within Indian affairs, however, separation appeals functioned differently than they did in state legislatures. When it came to Indian schooling, church-state separation served not only to marginalize Catholicism but also to affirm the special obligations of the state—and by extension the consolidated power of that state—in relation to the lives of Indians. As early as the 1830s, the Supreme Court had decided that Indians were dependents who fell "under the protection of the United States, *and of no other power* [my emphasis]."[46] A half century later, in the face of both stubbornly "unassimilated" Indigenous communities *and* ambiguities of the Catholic missions enterprise, church-state separation helped to create an education system through which the federal government could perform undivided and unmediated guardianship over its wards.

In the analysis of Eugene Provenzo Jr. and Gary McClosky, the US government and the Catholic Church enacted "opposed colonial models" of Indian education during the 1890s.[47] I contend that the flows of Catholic power in relation to US colonization have always been more complicated than the Provenzo-McClosky model suggests. Public money funded the work of Catholic missionaries within Indigenous communities for decades before the fight of the 1890s, and that money continued to flow (through more circumscribed channels) for decades after.[48] The long ambivalence among federal officials and their allies over support for Catholic Indian schools indicates, among other things, parallel ambivalence about the Church's overall position within (or outside of) the state's colonizing enterprise. There *were*, however, plenty of Americans who at the end of the century speculated about the Catholic Church in Provenzo and McClosky's general terms. For many who cried foul at Catholicism during these years, the Church was, if not its own coherent and oppositional colonial system, at least a lingering thorn in the side of the nation's colonization achievement. Its missions represented—sometimes, if not all the time—disruptions to an otherwise "closed" frontier: an enterprise of land acquisition and settlement that white America fantasized in the 1890s as newly complete.[49]

In *Our Country* (1885), Josiah Strong famously juxtaposed concerns about Catholicism alongside his enthusiastic accounting of the newly secured agricultural and mineral resources in the western United States. In doing so, he relied on the language of Catholic colonization. "When the Jesuits were driven out of Berlin," he wrote, "they declared that they would plant themselves in the western territories of America. And they are there today with empires in their brains . . . They are free to colonize the great West, and are there gathering and plotting to Romanize and control our western empire."[50]

Strong himself stayed clear of the treaty-and-trust payments dispute.[51] Among those who *did* advocate to cut funding for Catholic Indian schools, however, the era's familiar rhetoric of Catholicism as un-American mingled with more specific references to Catholicism as a separate colonial enterprise. "Is it consistent to allow to be taught in the Indian schools, at the expense of the government, doctrines that militate against the interests of the United States?" Addison Foster queried his colleagues at Lake Mohonk. "When it comes to our government acting as trustee, I protest."[52] Marking the quadricentennial anniversary of Columbus's landfall in an 1892 address calling for an end to contract schools, J. M. King emphasized the explorer's Catholic (rather than Spanish) ambitions of empire. "In this Columbian year it becomes us to remember that our civilization is not Latin," King exhorted, "because God did not permit North America to be settled and controlled by that civilization . . . Let us not put a premium by national grants [contracts] on a rejected civilization in the education of a race who were here when Columbus came."[53] If Catholicism regularly appeared as a challenge to the US political project during the nineteenth century, it also at times presented more specifically as a competitor to the state as colonial enterprise.

Concern about the Catholic Church and skepticism about its relationship to US colonial authority underlie the Bureau of Indian Affairs' enactment of a rule that made state-run education for Indian children effectively compulsory. In 1896 Commissioner of Indian Affairs Daniel M. Browning made Lyman Abbott's proposal for mandatory state-led education a near reality when, communicating with an agent at Pine Ridge Agency, he established what became known as the Browning Rule. For the next five years, it was Bureau policy that the government could require Indigenous students on reservations to attend state-run day schools in lieu of their religiously administered counterparts. In September 1902 on the Rosebud Reservation, police officers removed eleven children from St. Francis School in accordance with the rule, because the nearby government-run school was under enrollment capacity.[54] "It is [the] duty [of Bureau agents]," Browning explained, "first to build up and maintain the Government Day Schools . . . and the Indian parents have no right to designate which school their children shall attend."[55] The Bureau of Catholic Indian Missions (BCIM) objected to the rule and eventually won its abrogation. In response to the BCIM's objections, Browning's successor clarified the government's reasoning behind the rule: "Under the law . . . Indian parents and children are known as wards of the Government. It is the duty of the Commissioner . . . to look closely after their welfare."[56] Because Indians were wards, the commissioner acted from the assumption that the state (rather than either parents or the Church) retained exclusive authority to determine where children living on reservations attended school. Albeit short-lived, the Browning Rule confirmed state-run public schools as specialized colonial sites; places that ratified the relationship between the federal government and the Indigenous people—colonizer and colonized—as that between guardian and wards.

* * *

After the Dawes Act, officials and settlers with shared investment in "Indian reform" began a new discussion about the state, its duty to Indigenous children, and "separated" government schools as special sites for the state to execute that duty. During the 1890s, this conversation was a backdrop for the congressional decision to end contract schools, and over the next decade it shaped the fight over treaty-and-trust payments to the Catholic Church. The court's determination in *Quick Bear v. Leupp* that tribal money was "not public money," and that government payment of that money to the Catholic Church did not violate the establishment clause, was in this vein a check (however paradoxical) *against* the accumulating power of the guardian state. It was also a boon for Catholic schools like St. Francis. To say the case produced these two effects is not to overlook the Catholic Church's own part in Indigenous lands colonization. If the Church sometimes conjured the specter of competing empire, its priests and its men and women religious were— and remain—notorious across Indian country for the violence that marked their efforts both to make Indigenous children into Catholics and to assimilate them to a Euro-American standard.[57] Recent scholarship has also cast light beyond Indian lands on the critical support Catholic leaders gave US imperial enterprises in Mexico, Puerto Rico, and the Philippines during this period.[58] As colonialism was foundational to the US enterprise, so was it constituent to the Catholicism that flourished alongside it.

My aim here has not been to untangle the knotted history of Catholicism and US Empire but to propose a new framework for considering both church-state separation as a legal principle and the institution of public schooling that principle has historically protected. At the turn of the century, separation saved public education from Catholicism. In doing so, it simultaneously transformed government schools into sites

where federal guardianship was exercised over (and in) the lives of Indigenous children. Church-state separation has an anti-Catholic history
in the United States, and it also has a history as an extender of federal
imperial power. If at times the anti-Catholic character of separation was
synonymous with fear of immigrants or anxiety about errant theology,
at other times the anti-Catholicism baked into the separation doctrine
was an expression of enthusiasm for the undivided, unmediated flow
of federal power, channeled into the enterprise of colonizing land and
building empire. Put another way, the history of separation reveals more
about the United States than its Protestantism. Properly rendered, separation exposes the work entailed in asserting US state sovereignty over
and against the sovereignty of nations the United States has colonized,
and the important role religion has played over time in that work.

NOTES

1 Karla Lee Ekquist, "Federal Indian Policy and the St. Francis Mission School on
   Rosebud Reservation, South Dakota: 1886–1908" (PhD diss., Iowa State University, 1999), 96.
2 Francis Paul Prucha, *The Churches and the Indian Schools, 1888–1912* (Lincoln:
   University of Nebraska Press, 1979), 87.
3 Ibid., 209–10.
4 Brief for Appellees, Transcript of Record at 8–9, Reuben Quick Bear v. Leupp, 210
   U.S. 50 n.569 (1908).
5 Prucha, *Churches*, 207–8.
6 The plaintiffs' primary argument was that the payments violated Congress's Indian Appropriation Act of 1897, which ceased appropriations funding to contract
   schools and which the plaintiffs described as necessary under the principle of
   church-state separation (Appellants' Brief, Transcript of Record at 30–31, Reuben
   Quick Bear v. Leupp, 210 U.S. 50 [1908]).
7 Reuben Quick Bear v. Leupp, 210 U.S. 50 (1908).
8 Ibid.
9 The court handed down its first establishment clause decision in Bradfield v. Roberts, 175 U.S. 291 (1899). In *Bradfield* the court upheld an arrangement providing
   federal funds to the Sisters of Charity, an order of Catholic women religious, for
   an extension to their Providence Hospital in Washington, DC. *Quick Bear* followed *Bradfield* as the court's second establishment clause decision.
10 John C. Jeffries Jr. and James E. Ryan, "A Political History of the Establishment
   Clause," *Michigan Law Review* 100 (November 2001): 279, 284.
11 The historiography of US anti-Catholicism stretches across nearly a century,
   from Ray Allen Billington's foundational study of nineteenth-century nativism,
   The Protestant Crusade, 1800–1860: A Study of the Origins of American Nativism

(Chicago: Quadrangle, 1938), to Mark S. Massa's *Anti-Catholicism in America: The Last Acceptable Prejudice* (New York: Crossroad, 2005) and more recent publications; see, for example, Katie Oxx, *The Nativist Movement in America: Religious Conflict in the Nineteenth Century* (New York: Routledge, 2013); Maura Jane Farrelly, *Anti-Catholicism in America, 1620–1860* (Cambridge: Cambridge University Press, 2017). A standout in this historiography is Jenny Franchot's *Roads to Road: The Antebellum Protestant Encounter with Catholicism* (Berkeley: University of California Press, 1994).

12 On the historical relationship between anti-Catholicism and liberal defenses of freedom and democracy, see especially John McGreevy, *Catholicism and American Freedom: A History* (New York: W. W. Norton, 2004).

13 Philip Hamburger, *Separation of Church and State* (Cambridge, MA: Harvard University Press, 2004). For additional treatment of the Blaine Amendment in this regard, see Steven K. Green, *The Bible, the School, and the Constitution: The Clash That Shaped Modern Church-State Doctrine* (New York: Oxford University Press, 2012).

14 *Quick Bear*, 210 U.S.; Prucha, *Churches*, 110, 114. While Hamburger discusses separation's entanglement with anti-Catholic nativism through the end of the nineteenth century, he makes no mention of *Quick Bear* (see Hamburger, *Separation*, 335–59). The American Protective Association made public aid to Catholic Indian schools one of its chief causes through this era (see Prucha, *Churches*, 27–29).

15 Hamburger contends that "because of the strength of anti-Catholic feeling, [nativist Protestants] managed to secure local versions of the Blaine Amendment in the vast majority of states" during their period (*Separation*, 335).

16 Quoted in ibid., 324.

17 In addition to Indian affairs, church-state separation carried weight during this era in the state's management of its imperial claims to Puerto Rico and the Philippines. See, for example, the Supreme Court's decision in Municipality of Ponce v. Roman Catholic Apostolic Church in Porto Rico, 210 U.S. 296 (1908). In *Ponce* the court upheld property rights of the Catholic Church in Puerto Rico, but in doing so reflected on "the difficult problem incident to the transfer of sovereignty from a regime of union of church and state to the American system of complete separation."

18 Protestant denominations voluntarily withdrew from the contracts system in the early 1890s; see Prucha, *Churches*, 24–25.

19 Thomas Jefferson, "To messers Nehemiah Dodge, Ephraim Robbins, & Stephen S. Nelson, a committee of the Danbury Baptist association in the state of Connecticut," January 1, 1802, Library of Congress, www.loc.gov.

20 Reynolds v. United States, 98 U.S. 145 (1879); Everson v. Board of Education, 33 U.S. 1 (1947).

21 In *Everson* the court upheld the use of state funds to bus children to and from Catholic schools. The decision's main jurisprudential legacy, however, came through the court's incorporation of the wall-of-separation model, which re-

stricted instances of future church-state collaboration. The decision also relied on the due process clause of the Fourteenth Amendment to confirm the establishment clause as binding on state education laws in addition to federal law. For many scholars, *Everson* initiates the era of the "modern establishment clause." See, for example, Jeffries and Ryan, "A Political History," 284.

22 Quoted in Stephen K. Green, "The Blaine Amendment Reconsidered," *American Journal of Legal History* 36, no. 1 (January 1992): 38.

23 See Stephen K. Green, *The Second Disestablishment: Church and State in Nineteenth-Century America* (New York: Oxford University Press, 2010), 251–328. State Blaine Amendments exist in thirty-seven state constitutions; most of these were passed in the first decades after the failure of the federal Blaine Amendment. See also Kyle Duncan, "Secularism's Laws: State Blaine Amendments and Religious Persecution, *Fordham Law Review* 72 (December 2003): 493.

24 On the history of church-state separation and concern about Catholicism during the *Everson* era, see Kathleen Holscher, *Religious Lessons: Catholic Sisters and the Captured Schools Crisis in New Mexico* (New York: Oxford University Press, 2012).

25 Tracy Fessenden, *Culture and Redemption: Religion, the Secular, and American Literature* (Princeton, NJ: Princeton University Press, 2011), 6, 60–83. See also Holscher, *Religious Lessons*. This would change in the 1960s with a pair of US Supreme Court decisions, Engel v. Vitale, 370 U.S. 421 (1962) and Abington School District v. Schempp, 374 U.S. 203 (1963), which found mandatory recitation of the Lord's Prayer (*Engel*) and devotional Bible reading (*Schempp*) in public schools to violate the establishment clause.

26 Roxanne Dunbar-Ortiz, *An Indigenous Peoples' History of the United States* (Boston: Beacon, 2014), 1.

27 Ibid., 10.

28 Ibid., 6.

29 Ibid., 5, 11. On contradictions within the US government's recognition of Indigenous sovereignty during the treaty era, see Joanne Barker, "For Whom Sovereignty Matters," in *Sovereignty Matters: Locations of Contestation and Possibility in Indigenous Struggles for Self-Determination*, ed. Joanne Barker (Lincoln: University of Nebraska Press, 2005), 6; Donna L. Akers, "Decolonizing the Master Narrative: Treaties and Other American Myths," *Wicazo Sa Review* 29, no. 1 (Spring 2014): 58–76.

30 25 U.S.C. § 71.

31 Chief Justice John Marshall defined the relationship between tribal nations and the US government as resembling "that of a ward to a guardian" in Cherokee Nation v. Georgia, 30 U.S. 1 (1831). On the role of the Marshall Court in erasing Indigenous sovereignty via its articulations of "domestic dependent nationhood" and the "ward/guardian analogy," see Barker, "For Whom Sovereignty," 6–16.

32 John P. LaVelle, "The General Allotment Act 'Eligibility' Hoax," *Wicazo Sa Review* 14, no. 1 (Spring 1999): 252.

33 Between 1881 and 1934 Indigenous landholdings declined from 156 million to about 50 million acres, primarily due to allotment (Dunbar-Ortiz, *Indigenous Peoples' History*, 11).

34 Prucha, *Churches*, 4.

35 Lyman Abbott, "Education for the Indian," in *Proceedings of the Sixth Annual Meeting of the Lake Mohonk Conference of Friends of the Indians*, ed. Isabel C. Barrows (New York: Lake Mohonk Conference, 1888), 11.

36 Prucha, *Churches*, 4. The Bureau of Catholic Indian Missions won its first school contracts in 1881. By 1888 Catholic schools were receiving the majority of federal contracts for Indian education: thirty-eight contracts compared to twelve received by Protestant denominations (ibid., 12). The federal government, in the person of the commissioner of Indian Affairs, first laid out plans for a "comprehensive system of Indian education to be owned and controlled exclusively by the federal government" in the early 1880s, and parallel state and church systems had emerged by the 1890s, with federal funding supporting both; see Fredric Mitchell, "Church-State Conflict: A Little Known Part of the Continuing Church-State Conflict Found in Early Indian Education," *Journal of American Indian Education* 2, no. 3 (May 1963): 8.

37 Abbott, "Education for the Indian," 11.

38 Ibid., 13.

39 Ibid., 13, 12.

40 Ibid., 13–14.

41 J. M. King, "The Churches: Their Relationship to the General Government in the Education of the Indian Races," in *Proceedings of the Eighth Annual Meeting of the Lake Mohonk Conference of Friends of the Indians*, ed. Isabel C. Barrows (New York: Lake Mohonk Conference, 1890), 57.

42 US Office of Indian Affairs, *Annual Report of the Commissioner of Indian Affairs, for the Year 1891* (Washington, DC: Government Printing Office, 1891), 68–69, http://digital.library.wisc.edu.

43 Prucha, *Churches*, 24–25.

44 American Missionary Association, "Change in the Indian Policy: The American Missionary Association's Appeal to Churches," *American Missionary*, 47, no. 3 (March 1893): 85.

45 Quoted in Prucha, *Churches*, 34–35. The final appropriations were made in 1899.

46 Worcester v. Georgia, 31 U.S. 515 (1832). See also Barker, "For Whom Sovereignty," 12.

47 Eugene F. Provenzo Jr. and Gary N. McClosky, "Catholic and Federal Indian Education in the Late 19th Century: Opposed Colonial Models," *Journal of American Indian Education* 21, no. 1 (November 1981): 10–18.

48 The first evidence of public funds to support Catholic religious working among Indigenous communities is an 1803 peace treaty between the US government and the Kaskaskia nation. The treaty set aside $100 annually for payment of a Catholic priest (Mitchell, "Church-State Conflict," 7). By the 1930s the Bureau of Catholic

Indian Missions was again receiving approximately $180,000 annually in government contracts; see Kevin Abing, "Directors of the Bureau of Catholic Indian Missions: 4. Monsignor William McDermott Hughes, 1921–1935," 1994, Marquette University Special Collections and University Archives, www.marquette.edu.

49 Frederick Jackson Turner offered a famous articulation of this imagined milestone as the starting point for his "frontier thesis" at the 1893 meeting of the American Historical Association: "The Significance of the Frontier in American History," in *Rereading Frederick Jackson Turner: The Significance of the Frontier in American History and Other Essays*, ed. John Mack Faragher (New York: H. Holt, 1994).

50 Josiah Strong, *Our Country: Its Possible Future and Its Present Crisis* (New York: Baker & Taylor, 1885), 58.

51 Prucha, *Churches*, 98.

52 Quoted in *Proceedings of the Eighth Annual Meeting*, 67–68.

53 Quoted in Martha D. Adams, ed., *Proceedings of the Tenth Annual Meeting of the Lake Mohonk Conference of Friends of the Indians* (New York: Lake Mohonk Conference, 1892), 63.

54 Ekquist, "Federal Indian Policy," 189–90.

55 Quoted in Prucha, *Churches*, 58.

56 Quoted in ibid., 60.

57 See, among many examples, Stephanie Woodard, "South Dakota Boarding School Survivors Detail Sexual Abuse," *Indian Country Today*, July 28, 2011, https://newsmaven.io; Vinni Rotondaro, "Boarding Schools: A Black Hole of Native American History," *National Catholic Reporter*, September 1, 2015, www.ncronline.org. The model of state guardianship that excluded Catholic influences when embedded in the discourse of church-state separation elsewhere benefited Catholic educators, extending to them the authority to retain students at school regardless of their parents' wishes. See, for example, Sarah Shillinger, *A Case Study of the American Indian Boarding School Movement: An Oral History of Saint Joseph's Indian Industrial School* (Lewiston, NY: Edwin Mellen, 2008), 81.

58 See especially Anne Martinez, *Catholic Borderlands: Mapping Catholicism onto American Empire, 1905–1935* (Lincoln: University of Nebraska Press, 2014).

6

Sovereignty

TISA WENGER

The enemy immigrated to a land he claimed for his God.
He named himself as the arbiter of deity in any form.
He beat his Indian children.
The law of the gods I claim state:
When entering another country do not claim ownership.
It's important to address the souls there kindly, with respect.
And ask permission.
I am asking you to leave the country of my body, my mind, if
you have anything other than honorable intentions.
—Joy Harjo, "Returning from the Enemy"

The question of sovereignty—who holds the ultimate authority over a place and its people—lay at the heart of the 2016 protests against the construction of the Dakota Access oil pipeline. The #NODAPL protests that year energized a global network of Indigenous activists not only to protect the land, water, and treaty rights of the Standing Rock Sioux Nation but the broader principle of Indigenous self-determination. When the United States approved the pipeline against their objections, it was also asserting absolute sovereignty over a Native American nation and its land. In so doing it rejected the claim that Indigenous nations are *nations* with the right to govern themselves. As in this example, Native assertions of sovereignty are often hotly contested and must constantly be renegotiated, both on the ground and in the halls of power. More aspirational than fully realized, they have rarely been recognized by settler colonial governments like the United States.

The protestors at Standing Rock, much like Harjo in this chapter's epigraph, identified Christianity as a major source for Indigenous dispossession. In a particularly compelling moment of protest theater, more than five hundred interfaith clergy and lay supporters joined Native "water protectors" around a large campfire to sing hymns and burn the fifteenth-century papal bulls that had helped justify European conquest in the Americas. In 1493 when the news of Columbus's voyage first reached Rome, Pope Alexander VI divided the newly discovered lands between Spain and Portugal. He then assigned Christian rulers the right to any lands not already inhabited by Christians and to overthrow whatever "barbarous nations" they might find there. All the European colonial powers—and later the United States—used much the same "doctrine of discovery" to justify their claims to sovereignty within what Native people knew was not a New World.[1]

Christianity's significance for colonialism developed logically from its role in early modern European systems of governance. As the Holy Roman Empire waned, newly assertive monarchs claimed a greater scope of power and jockeyed for new territories. They grounded this authority in new claims to divine anointment and sometimes, as in the case of France's King Louis XIV, by declaring their own divinity. The notion of God as the ultimate sovereign served as a model for these early modern monarchs and as a way to legitimize their power over the lands they claimed, first in defining their own borders and then others around the world. Christianity was far from the sole impetus for European colonial conquests, but it provided a convenient rationale and would help structure colonial governance in the centuries that followed. Early modern theorists of sovereignty such as Montaigne and Hobbes were beginning to theorize religion as a domain distinct from the state, at least in part to justify the independent authority of the state. At the same time, they envisioned this newly authoritative state as a sanctified force for divine and natural order.[2]

The racially stratified conditions of colonialism crystallized the violent contours of state sovereignty in the modern world.[3] The police and military forces marshaled by the state to crush the protests at Standing Rock—along with the private DAPL security guards who released attack dogs and sprayed mace on protestors—illustrate this violent substratum. As public attention waned in the months that followed, the most visible and persistent of the Indigenous protestors found their futures in peril. Hundreds faced prolonged legal battles and potential incarceration under charges ranging from disorderly conduct to "civil disorder," a politicized charge first created in the 1960s to target protestors in the Black Identity and antiwar movements. Members of the American Indian Movement had faced similar charges after their 1973 occupation of Wounded Knee, where their sovereignty demands likewise met with violent suppression. For most Americans, these legal and extralegal forms of state violence normally simmer below the surface of consciousness. Native Americans, like other racialized minorities, have never had the luxury of ignoring them.[4]

The ultimate sovereign power, according to political theorists in the tradition of Carl Schmitt and Georgio Agamben, is the ability to decide the exception to any rule.[5] This power, directed in raw form against the colonized, is apparent in the ease with which the United States has violated its own treaties with Native nations, including the Standing Rock Sioux. More subtly, the charges brought against the #NODAPL protestors reveal the stark inequities that every level of law enforcement in the United States continues to perpetuate. The law as enacted may be color-blind; the law as enforced is decidedly not. As in other settler colonial societies, the sovereign exception most often works in favor of white and Christian settlers and against colonized and racially marginalized populations.[6]

This settler sovereignty continues to rest on Christian foundations. "The Dakota Access Pipeline crisis is a direct result of the United States government using the religious underpinnings of US federal law against our Nations," explained Yakama Nation chairman JoDe Goudy at a major protest in Washington, DC. "This is the precedent that is relied upon for the continuous failed attempts to protect our resources in the federal courts."[7] Goudy and other Native activists have strategically challenged these foundations as a clear violation of the First Amendment's establishment clause, which prohibits state-sponsored religion or special privileges for any religion in the United States. Within the governing structures of settler modernity, then, the law can serve not only to bolster colonial power but also to challenge it.

This chapter begins with the doctrine of discovery and its Christian foundations as the basis for US sovereignty and then tracks the effects of twentieth-century attempts to separate the domains of law and religion. I argue that secular law in the United States conceals the founding role of Christianity while still maintaining the privileged status of the white settlers who are racially identified with it. Even as US law formally granted equal status to all religions, the legal system and the larger culture defined and delineated religion in ways that continue to privilege Christianity and foster expressions of white Christian nationalism. In so doing, secular law helped make settler colonial rule appear natural and inevitable. At the same time, the systems of settler governance marked Indigenous leaders and traditions as problematically religious and so denied their claims. This "secular contract" manages and delineates both race and religion, proclaiming the principles of racial and religious equality while upholding the underlying structures of normative Christianity and white settler sovereignty.[8] By way of conclusion, the chapter returns to recent Native American efforts to reformulate the concept of sovereignty and examines their relevance for questions of sovereignty, law, and religion in the United States.

Johnson v. M'Intosh: Christianity, Sovereignty, and the Doctrine of Discovery

The US Supreme Court first defined the doctrine of discovery as the foundation for US sovereignty in the 1823 case *Johnson and Graham's Lessee v. William M'Intosh*. The court ruled in favor of defendant William M'Intosh, whose Illinois landholdings dated to a 1779 grant from the newly independent commonwealth of Virginia, and invalidated competing claims based on direct purchases from the Illinois and Piankeshaw Indians. Land rights, the court reasoned, could only be issued by the colonial power that had successfully asserted the rights of discovery and possession. Virginia had inherited (or rather won) these rights from the British Crown. Under this doctrine, Indians enjoyed temporary rights of occupation but lacked true sovereignty over their own land.[9]

The majority opinion by Chief Justice John Marshall readily acknowledged that the doctrine of discovery served European interests and that Christianity provided much of its rationale. When the "nations of Europe" first discovered "this immense continent," Marshall wrote, they were "eager to appropriate to themselves so much of it as they could respectively acquire." They developed the shared understanding "that discovery gave title to the government . . . by whose authority, it was made, against all other European governments." The chief justice outlined the papal decrees that had originated this doctrine and then detailed its subsequent development. Europeans were convinced that as Christians they had a divinely ordained right to conquest—and that the gift of Christianity more than compensated for any losses that Indigenous people might suffer. As Marshall defined it, the doctrine of discovery rested on a basic contrast between European Christians, who deemed themselves "civilized," and Indigenous people, who, by virtue of their "heathenism," were not. The various European powers would never stop fighting over their competing colonial claims. But they agreed that as Christians, they rightfully held the right of sovereignty over whatever lands they "discovered," as long as another Christian power hadn't yet done the same.[10]

The Supreme Court concluded in *Johnson v. M'Intosh* that this doctrine could not be abandoned because it had established the foundations for US sovereignty. England had embraced the principles of discovery every bit as enthusiastically as the other European powers, Marshall explained, and the early leaders of the United States had done the same. The justice admitted that Indigenous land rights were indisputable, making the doctrine logically dubious. But in the final analysis he agreed with his sources that Christian civilization was indeed superior and so could support a superior claim to the land. And whether or not the doctrine was logical or just, he could not undermine the sovereignty of the United States. "However this restriction may be opposed to natural right, and to the usages of civilized nations," he wrote, "yet, if it be indispensable to that system under which the country has been settled, and be adapted to the actual condition of the two people, it may, perhaps, be supported by reason, and certainly cannot be rejected by Courts of justice." Marshall did not invent these rationales for settler conquest. Yet in narrating a history of this doctrine he solidified it for the first time as the legal grounds for US sovereignty over the land and so, retrospectively, as the legal grounds for the United States to exist as a nation at all.[11]

The role of Christianity in this decision was unremarkable at the time. American justices and legal scholars through the nineteenth century mostly assumed that the law and indeed the entire social order rested on Christian foundations.[12] Marshall's colleague on the Supreme Court, the eminent legal scholar Joseph Story, explained in his celebratory history of the Puritans that all European conquerors had founded their claim to Indigenous lands first on the "infidelity and barbarism" of the "natives . . . which allowed them to be treated as the enemies of God," and second "on the prospect of converting them to the Christian faith." The Puritans had improved on this logic, Story wrote, by identifying a further "civil right" granted by divine favor to those who "appropriated some parcels of ground, by enclosing and peculiar manurance," or in other words, by fencing and cultivating the land.[13] This claim followed a distinctly English interpretation of the injunction in Genesis 1:28 to "multiply and *replenish* the earth, and *subdue* it." English and then white American settlers invoked this passage to justify their seizure of lands they considered unimproved and uncultivated "wilderness." In reality Native Americans had a variety of agricultural practices—indeed the early colonists had relied on Indigenous crops to survive—but white settlers were less and less willing to recognize them as such. That Indians did not fence and cultivate the land in the English style became proof that it was not, in fact, their land at all. Conveniently enough, most white settlers believed that God had destined it for them.[14]

Johnson v. M'Intosh was the first of three cases known as the Marshall trilogy that provided a durable legal rationale for US sovereignty. The other two involved the balance of power between the Cherokee Nation, the state of Georgia, and the federal government. As one of the so-called Five Civilized Tribes, the Cherokee had ratified a formal constitution and deliberately adopted many markers of "civilization," including English-style houses, farms, and schools. None of this helped them secure title to their land. The 1828 discovery of gold on Cherokee land in Georgia accelerated that state's ongoing efforts to dissolve the Cherokee Nation. New state legislation effectively nullified Cherokee laws and set up a lottery process for the sale of Cherokee lands to white settlers. In *Cherokee Nation v. Georgia* (1831), the Marshall court rejected Cherokee claims to sovereignty and instead carved out a new legal category of "Indian tribes," which the justices named "domestic dependent nations." With the precedent of *Johnson v. M'Intosh* in place, the Supreme Court granted Georgia free rein against the Cherokee.[15]

The next year in *Worcester v. Georgia* (1832), the Supreme Court attempted to place some limits on state power by vesting ultimate sovereignty in the federal government. Georgia had imprisoned Samuel Worcester, a Congregationalist missionary, because he had violated state law while attempting to defend Cherokee land rights. Individual missionaries took a variety of positions on the question of Indian re-moval; Worcester was among its staunchest opponents. The Supreme Court ruled that Georgia had no right to imprison him. While Indian tribes were not considered "sovereign nations," they held "many of the attributes of sovereignty" and so their laws could not simply be nullified by the state. The federal government alone had the right to manage In-dians and to supersede their sovereignty. Despite this ruling, President Jackson famously refused to lift a finger against Georgia for its assaults on the Cherokee. In accordance with his Indian removal policy, they were soon forced to cede their lands and move west. So many Cherokee men, women, and children died on the wintertime march to their new reservation that they called it the Trail of Tears.[16]

The legitimating role of Christianity remained visible throughout the Marshall trilogy. The chief justice did not detail the doctrine of discov-ery in the Cherokee cases, as he had in *Johnson v. M'Intosh*. Instead he simply cited the earlier decision as legal grounds for federal sovereignty. The doctrine's Christian basis remained unstated but still active through the mechanism of the legal precedent. The benevolent claims of Chris-tian missions remained very much in the foreground, as they did in most nineteenth-century pronouncements on Indian affairs. *Worcester v. Georgia* specifically commended the "civilizing" work of the Protes-tant missionaries among the Cherokee. Indeed, it seems to have been the justices' admiration for missionary benevolence—and their disgust at Georgia's refusal to honor it—that led them to place any limits on state sovereignty at all.

Christianity appears as a double enigma in this history, simultane-ously absent and present both in the Cherokee Nation and in the United States. The doctrine of discovery located Indians as inherently, even ra-cially, uncivilized "heathens" who therefore had no legal claim to their own lands. Christianity's absence from the racialized figure of the "hea-then" justified settler seizures of Indigenous lands. Whether or not Na-tive people converted to Christianity, as many Cherokee had, they were still treated as racially heathen. They were perpetual targets of missions, never fully equal in the church or in the larger society. At the same time the court presented the gift of Christianity as compensation to Indig-enous people for their loss of land. Meanwhile, on the Anglo-American side of the equation, Christianity appeared as a defining characteristic of the "civilized" and so enabled the sovereignty claims of the United States. Yet it would gradually disappear from view in a legal discourse that increasingly presented itself in secular terms.

Johnson v. M'Intosh and particularly the place of Christianity in that case have remained mostly underground as the foundations of federal Indian law. Subsequent decisions involving Indigenous land rights and political sovereignty could simply cite this case without elaboration. *Tee-Hit-Ton Indians v. United States* (1955), which denied the Tlingit people of Alaska any financial compensation for the loss of their land, did not mention Christianity but briefly quoted *Johnson v. M'Intosh* to the effect that "discovery gave an exclusive right to extinguish the Indian title of occupancy, either by purchase or by conquest." According to the majority opinion, the Tlingit had remained "in a hunting and fishing stage of civilization, with shelters fitted to their environment," and had used the land in question "for these activities as well as the gathering of wild products of the earth." In other words, the Tlingit could not be considered "civilized" because they were not farmers in the English style. The court considered them merely occupants of the land rather than its owners. The reference to civilizational stages reflected the influence in twentieth-century jurisprudence of the anthropological theory of social evolution, which provided a secular and scientific way to denigrate Indigenous societies, not an overtly Christian one. Yet the ruling relied silently on Christianity in the legal precedent of *Johnson v. M'Intosh*. Christianity appeared even more subtly in the court's concern for agriculture, which, as we've seen, rested on English traditions of biblical interpretation.[17]

Even when overtly Christian arguments dropped out of the court's vocabulary, then, federal Indian law and the logics of US national sovereignty continued to rest on older assertions of Christian superiority—and therefore European civilizational superiority—as a key rationale for colonial conquest. *Johnson v. M'Intosh* and its continuing reverberations in the law reveal how Christianity still remains at the heart of US secular sovereignty. Europeans had asserted the rights of discovery and possession because they deemed themselves, as Christians, civilized and therefore superior to the people whose land they wanted to seize. Several centuries later, the secular law of US settler sovereignty remains rooted in the logics of white and Christian supremacy.

The Secular Contract and Indigenous Religion

Within the realm of federal Indian law and far beyond it, the historical processes of sovereignty, secularism, and settler colonialism are inextricably intertwined. This dynamic is not unique to the United States. I take the term "secular contract" from Australian scholar Holly Randell-Moon, who expands on Charles Mills's notion of a "racial contract" to theorize the operations of Australian state sovereignty. Locating racism at the heart of the European political order, Mills contends that the putatively universal principles of European civil society—the inalienable rights and liberties of citizens—were articulated from the beginning to serve the racist systems of European imperialism. They were never intended to apply to non-Europeans. Randell-Moon links Australia's official state secularism to this racial contract. State secularism obscures the Christian foundations of Australian sovereignty, she argues, and so continues to privilege white settlers who, by virtue of their whiteness, are presumed (barring evidence to the contrary) to be Christians. Australian politicians explain that the long-standing practice of opening sessions of Parliament with the Lord's Prayer is not an unconstitutional "religious" practice but simply honors the nation's Christian and democratic origins. Randell-Moon explains that such practices continue to center the white settler and so obscure the violence of these origins. "Who is the 'we' that established the Australian state," she asks, "and recognizes 'our' Judeo-Christian heritage?" Australian state secularism, then, is "complicit with the ways indigenous sovereignties in (post)colonial states are negated."[18]

In much the same way, the US secular contract grants Christianity unmarked privileges that allow US settler sovereignty to appear natural and inevitable. The form of this contract has changed over time. Throughout the nineteenth century, Christianity held direct authority in shaping federal Indian policy. Well into the twentieth century, government officials openly named Christianity as the heart of true civilization. This conviction undergirded the US government's efforts to eliminate what officials called Indian "heathenism," including Indigenous models of governance. Well-meaning white reformers and missionaries who wanted to rectify past injustices tried to "civilize" Indians by Christianizing them, hoping to incorporate them into the (white and Christian)

American mainstream. The assimilationist policies of this era sought deliberately to destroy Native American tribal identities and to undercut the ability of Native nations to function as self-governing societies. All of this operated as a multipronged assault on Indigenous sovereignty.[19]

In the day-to-day management of Indian reservations, administrative policies and procedures shaped the realities of colonial governance and the continued salience of Christianity on the ground. Christian missionaries, who often operated the only available schools for Native American children, worked closely with government agents on Indian reservations. Policies enacted by the Office of Indian Affairs—located at first within the Department of War and then moved to the Department of the Interior, where it was renamed the Bureau of Indian Affairs (BIA)—actively criminalized Indigenous practices and traditions. In 1883 the superintendent of Indian Affairs created so-called Courts of Indian Offenses, where government-appointed "Indian judges" ruled on minor disputes and civil offenses.[20] BIA agents, not legislators or the US courts, created most of the systems and rules that governed Indians. This process illustrates how the law is *made*, not merely enforced, through the mechanisms of bureaucracy and executive action. These mechanisms have shaped Native American lives in ways that can seem trivial and quotidian but have cumulatively decimated the sovereignty of Native American nations.

The Indian courts were meant to exemplify and instruct Native people in the principles of modern law. BIA agents installed Indian judges as alternative tribal authorities and pressured Native people to adopt "civilized" models of governance. But concepts like "civilization" and "modernity" were defined by European models and rested on imperial hierarchies of race and religion. These terms are not disinterested descriptors, in other words, but instead emerged as part of the ideological apparatus of European empires. The institutions and practices associated with Europeans were termed "civilized," and the word "modern" denoted a place and a people—Europe and Europeans—far more than it did current events and practices around the world. European settlers in colonies such as Australia and the Americas grafted themselves into these privileged categories while designating Indigenous and enslaved populations as perpetually primitive, premodern, or savage. By the late nineteenth century, US government agents, reformers, and missionaries were linking these well-worn Christian and colonial hierarchies with an increasingly influential social Darwinism that ranked the so-called races according to their "progress" toward a "civilization" that non-Europeans could never fully achieve.[21]

The category of "primitive religion"—and the bunching of virtually all religions other than Christianity into that category—operated as part of this imperial ideology. Christian vocabularies of theological judgment worked with anthropological theories of racial "progress" to denigrate Indigenous practices and traditions as false, deceptive, idolatrous, and even dangerous. Thus the "Indian offenses" enumerated for punishment in 1883 included "savage rites," "heathenish customs," and the "influence of the medicine men" who allegedly used "their conjurer's arts to prevent the people from abandoning" them. This model implicitly valorized Christianity and delegitimized Native American practices and practitioners. It was intended to destroy Indigenous models and replace them with the "modern," delineated spheres of religion and law. To modernize meant to destroy Indigenous identities, life-ways, and models of governance, instilling the "civilizing" balm of Christianity in their place.[22]

The federal government focused its ire on Indigenous "theocracies" while actively endorsing Christianity. "Pagan theocracy," it was said, kept Indians mired in savagery; Christianity and the elimination of Native "priestcraft" were the modernizing solutions. In the name of progress, the BIA sponsored Christian missions to Indians even as it pushed Native Americans to "separate church and state" within their own tribal governments. But the term "theocracy" falsely imposes European models of church and state onto very different cultural systems. Native societies did not generally separate a domain of religion from other aspects of life. Their communal practices of agriculture, hunting, healing, warfare, and diplomacy frequently relied on prayers, dances, and other ceremonies. The ritual specialists who managed these practices were not set apart, defined as religious, and expected to remain aloof from tribal governance. Nor were Native societies autocratic. Indeed, they typically assumed so much individual and small group autonomy that US officials often struggled to identify a "chief" with the authority to speak for a tribe.[23]

Yet BIA officials who considered Christianity essential to civilization failed to see the irony in their attacks on Native "theocracy." In 1892, for example, superintendent of Indian schools Daniel Dorchester—the author of a triumphalist history of American Christianity and architect of the system of government-funded Protestant mission schools—condemned the Pueblo Indian system of government as an "absolute theocracy," where "the church is united with and controls the state." He believed that Christianity would "civilize" the Indians and free them from their "paganism." From his perspective, the role of Christian missions on Indian reservations was not at all incompatible with the American legal system. Instead, Christianity grounded US law, formed subjects capable of responsible citizenship, and could enable Indians to live in the modern world.[24]

Far from aiding Native American claims to land and sovereignty, the category of religion under US law often worked against them. For more than a century, interlaced Christian and anthropological hierarchies of religion had supported the criminalization of Indigenous practices and the denigration of leaders as "savage," "heathen," or "pagan." Christianity conveyed modernity, civilization, and the right to possess and rule the land. Its original absence from Indigenous societies marked a seemingly irreversible state of inferiority. Government officials and missionaries alike advocated conversion to Christianity so as to hasten the civilizing process, but even when Native people became Christians—and many of them did—they remained marked with the racial stain of a hereditary heathenism.[25] Despite the promise that Indians could become "civilized," assimilationist policies did not undo that stain. But they did work to undermine or even eliminate the tribal structures and treaty guarantees that had helped sustain key dimensions of tribal sovereignty.

Government assaults on Indigenous sovereignty changed in the 1930s as Christianity lost most of its governing authority in Indian affairs. In 1933 President Franklin Delano Roosevelt named a former critic of the BIA, John Collier, as his commissioner of Indian Affairs. With the stated goal of restoring sovereignty to Native American tribes, Congress passed the Indian Reorganization Act as the major legislative achievement of the "Indian New Deal." This law encouraged tribes to restructure their governments and enact new constitutions based on models distributed by Collier's BIA. One effect of the provisions on religion was to sharpen emerging distinctions between the religious and the secular within Native societies. "We should form a new government with constitutional regulations, and not in connection with the customs or the religion," argued one reform-minded leader at Santa Clara Pueblo in New Mexico. "Religion has nothing to do with running the pueblo." The resulting constitution recategorized the traditional leaders known as "caciques" as religious figures who could no longer exercise governing authority in the pueblo. The effect was to restructure Native systems of governance along the same lines that Dorchester had recommended. Indigenous traditions had to be remolded to fit a Christian mold for what counted as religion. But instead of Dorchester's overtly Christian approach, Collier's administration grounded these changes in the secular logics of bureaucratic management and constitutional law.[26]

This model of colonial governance marginalized or even delegitimized key aspects of Indigenous traditions as religion. Whether by attacking Native "theocracies" or simply insisting that Native religion should be separate from the institutions of government, the BIA continued to marginalize Native leaders and further diminished the ability of Native societies to meaningfully govern themselves. While Christianity held structural privileges and continued to undergird US sovereignty through the doctrine of discovery, then, the US government also defined and delimited Indigenous religion in ways that undermined Indigenous governance. This is the double bind of the secular contract: even as it rendered normative Christianity invisible and privileged, it marked Indigenous traditions as problematically religious. Whether attacked or admired, these newly delineated religions were increasingly distanced from the material questions of land and sovereignty.

The category of religion has sometimes been useful for Indians, to be sure. Starting in the early twentieth century, in some circles at least, a new public recognition and popular celebration of Native American "religion" and "spirituality" inspired a new respect for Native American traditions and a new level of support for Native religious freedom claims. But Native Americans rarely found success under the banner of religious freedom unless the practices in question easily matched the dominant society's existing models for "religion," and where other powerful interests did not get in the way.[27] And, unfortunately, white enthusiasts often held romanticized views of the so-called primitive. Images of Native Americans as naturally spiritual, close to nature, and possessing a "primal" religion ready for white settler consumption and appropriation have not challenged the secular contract but only reformulated older representations of Indians as perpetual primitives. They place Indians permanently in the past, frozen in a prehistoric time, rather than seeing them as active participants in a modernity that, like other people, they seek to shape for themselves. These images may support a degree of sympathy and support for abstract Indians. But they have tended to work against any understanding of Native Americans as real people in the modern world—and against ongoing efforts to articulate nationhood and sovereignty in Indigenous terms.[28]

The 1978 American Indian Religious Freedom Act (AIRFA) initially looked like a triumph for Indigenous interests. In its most optimistic moments, the Native American Rights Fund hoped that the new law would enable Indians around the country to protect an expansive list of "religious beliefs and practices," and so facilitate the larger cause of cultural and political self-determination. Yet from the beginning Native activists had recognized that the law included no means of enforcement and that turning its promise into reality would require constant vigilance. Too often federal and state agencies could skirt its guarantees in practice. While Native American appeals gained traction in certain arenas—religious rights for those in prison, for example, and the right to use peyote in Native American Church ceremonies—efforts to protect the places that Native people hold sacred have almost always failed in the courts.[29]

Even in the post-AIRFA world, the category of religion often worked against rather than for Native American legal claims. In many of the sacred land cases of the 1980s and 1990s, federal courts suggested that accommodating Indigenous claims would unfairly privilege Native American religions and so could violate the establishment clause. In *Badoni v. Higginson* (1980), for example, the Tenth Circuit Court of Appeals ruled against Navajo Indians who complained that a recent expansion of Glen Canyon Dam on Lake Powell had flooded their sacred sites and that raucous tourists were disrupting their ceremonies and otherwise desecrating the area. The court determined that the public utility of the lake outweighed the Indians' right to free exercise and that restricting tourist traffic in the area would give undue privileges to Native American religions on public lands.[30] Citing that case, the South Dakota District Court ruled in *Crow v. Gullet* (1982) that a proposed expansion of National Park Service facilities at Bear Butte in the Black Hills did not infringe on the First Amendment rights of the Lakota and Tsitsistas (Cheyenne) Indian plaintiffs. According to the majority opinion, later affirmed by the Eighth Circuit Court of Appeals, the park service had already done enough, perhaps too much, "to afford special treatment and privileges to American Indian religious practices at the Butte."[31]

In the courts' eyes, the real danger was not to Native American traditions but to the public's interest in using and enjoying these lands. This situation creates a catch-22 for Native appeals. On the one hand, the language of religion and religious freedom can help garner public sympathy for Native campaigns. On the other, the identification of Indigenous landscapes and traditions as religious can impede rather than aid the effort to protect the places they call sacred. Partly for this reason, Native activists have tended to join the language of religious freedom with other legal strategies. Alongside AIRFA and the First Amendment, they have also appealed to laws protecting cultural heritage, historic sites, or endangered species and the natural environment.[32]

By obscuring the Christian foundations of the doctrine of discovery that still undergirds US sovereignty—and by delineating the category of religion according to a Christian mold—the secular contract has helped defeat Native American sovereignty claims. The normally unmarked but sometimes overt forms of Christianity that stand behind so much American public ritual and political speech making serve constantly to reassert a Christian foundation for the nation. These cultural and legal systems continue to make settler sovereignty appear natural and even divinely ordained. Meanwhile, the belated recognition of Native American traditions as religion has often impeded more than it has aided Indigenous land and sovereignty claims. The ongoing definition and redefinition of religion as a bounded cultural domain, carved out against other spheres such as the political, the legal, and the scientific, has worked to reinforce systems of settler sovereignty by naturalizing Christian norms within the secular and marking off Indigenous traditions as problematically religious. Legal formations of religion have thus served to discipline and control colonized and racialized subjects by designating (and disciplining) certain aspects of their traditions under the sign of religion. Traditions defined in this way have been consigned to the rarified realms of the primitive, the private, or the mythical. Celebrated as religion, they are denied the status of law, which gets coded in contrast as modern, public, and presumably universal.[33]

Conclusion: Indigenous Views of Sovereignty, Law, and Religion

The idea of sovereignty as we know it emerged out of European Christendom, facilitated colonial conquests, and still fosters the dispossession of Indigenous people today. It should not be surprising, then, that many Native American activists and intellectuals consider sovereignty to be a profoundly ambivalent and troubled concept. In the words of Taiaiake Alfred (Mohawk): "The inter/counterplay of state sovereignty doctrines—rooted in notions of dominion—with and against indigenous concepts of political relations—rooted in notions of freedom, respect, and autonomy—frames the discourse on indigenous 'sovereignty' at its broadest level."[34] Alfred sees sovereignty as a European concept that is historically tied to European cultural and political forms. If Native people rely too heavily on this concept, he suggests, they may undermine their own goals and preclude the flourishing of their own societies in Indigenous terms.

Yet Native Americans, with other Indigenous peoples around the world, have found the concept of sovereignty essential to the anticolonial struggle. They have repeatedly called on the United States to recognize their sovereignty by honoring its treaties with them. In their 2016 protests, for example, the Standing Rock Sioux Nation insisted on the continued salience of the 1851 Treaty of Fort Laramie, which delineated the boundaries of the Great Sioux Reservation (a much larger area than the small, scattered Sioux reservations that remain today) and recognized the rights of the Sioux Nation within that territory. Through the winding and torturous history of federal Indian law, the Supreme Court has occasionally acknowledged that Native nations hold a preexisting sovereignty that was not bestowed by the United States and so cannot, in principle, be superseded. In *United States v. Winans* (1905), for example, the court ruled that treaties were "grants of rights from" Indians to the United States, rather than the other way around. This decision, among others, clearly recognized the original sovereignty of Native nations and provided a legal foundation for ongoing Native battles for land, cultural autonomy, and political self-determination.

Some Native intellectuals have sought to reframe the concept of sovereignty in Indigenous ways. Joanne Barker (Lenape) explains that while Native Americans have little choice but to work strategically within the existing order, they must at the same time "decolonize their own concepts and projects of self-determination."[35] As Vine Deloria Jr. (Standing Rock Sioux) put it nearly forty years ago, "'Sovereignty' is a useful word to describe the process of growth and awareness that characterizes a group of people working toward and achieving maturity. If it is restricted to a legal-political context, then it becomes a limiting concept which serves to prevent solutions."[36] Deloria, who also penned scathing critiques of Christianity for its role in the conquest and subordination of Native America, died more than a decade before his own Standing Rock Sioux Nation mobilized their protests against the Dakota Access Pipeline.[37] From a "legal-political" perspective, they lost the battle: the pipeline went through. Yet Deloria might have seen the coalition they mobilized as a hopeful sign. A new generation of activists emerged from Standing Rock determined to keep the fires of sovereignty burning. Lakota people in the protests pointed to a prophecy of a great black snake—the pipeline, some believed—that would devastate Lakota lands and would ultimately be slain by the youth. "The black snake is greed and violence and oppression," reflects the Lakota activist Rattler, who at this writing still faces federal charges for his role in the protests. "We have to come together to fight more than just one pipeline to defeat the black snake." The health of the land and the water cannot be separated from the Indigenous communities that are so intimately connected with them—or from their self-determination in spiritual, cultural, and political terms.[38]

From the Marshall trilogy to the sacred land cases to Standing Rock, this chapter has identified and interrogated a secular contract that underwrites US settler sovereignty by valorizing Christianity and delegitimizing Indigenous traditions, even (or perhaps especially) when these traditions are set apart as religious. The legal management and delineation of religion in the United States, I have argued, presupposes settler sovereignty and facilitates the ongoing structural subordination of Indigenous ways of life. Those Native critics who have advanced the most radical demands for Indigenous nationhood and sovereignty, or challenged existing models of nationhood and sovereignty as colonial impositions, have thus been the least likely to emphasize the "religious" nature of their traditions or to phrase their demands in religious freedom terms.[39] Like Harjo and Rattler, they may be very much interested in prophecy, ceremony, and spirituality, but they have rarely found it useful (or even possible) to set apart "religion" as a category separable from other dimensions of life. Well beyond the circle of Native American activists and scholars, anyone engaged in the study of law, religion, and sovereignty in the United States must attend to their concerns.

NOTES

1 Carol Kuruvilla, "Standing Rock Protestors Burn Document That Justified Indigenous Oppression," *Huffington Post*, November 4, 2016, www.huffingtonpost.com; "Inter Caetera" is available online at "The Doctrine of Discovery, 1493," The Gilder Lehrman Institute of American History, www.gilderlehrman.org.

2 Daniel Engster, *Divine Sovereignty: The Origins of Modern State Power* (DeKalb: Northern Illinois University Press, 2001); Trevor Stack, Naomi R. Goldenberg, and Timothy Fitzgerald, eds., *Religion as a Category of Governance and Sovereignty* (Boston: Brill, 2015).

3 Thomas Blom Hansen and Finn Stepputat, eds., *Sovereign Bodies: Citizens, Migrants, and States in the Postcolonial World* (Princeton, NJ: Princeton University Press, 2005), 9–20; Ann Laura Stoler, *Duress: Imperial Durabilities in Our Times* (Durham, NC: Duke University Press, 2016), 176–77.

4 Natasha Lennard, "Still Fighting at Standing Rock," *Esquire*, September 19, 2017, www.esquire.com.

5 Giorgio Agamben, *Homo Sacer: Sovereign Power and Bare Life* (Stanford, CA: Stanford University Press, 1998); Andrew Norris, ed., *Politics, Metaphysics, and Death: Essays on Giorgio Agamben's Homo Sacer* (Durham, NC: Duke University Press, 2005).

6 Michelle Alexander, *The New Jim Crow: Mass Incarceration in the Age of Colorblindness* (New York: New Press, 2010); Mark Rifkin, "Indigenizing Agamben: Rethinking Sovereignty in Light of the 'Peculiar' Status of Native Peoples," *Cultural Critique* 73, no. 1 (November 19, 2009): 88–124, https://doi.org/10.1353/cul.0.0049.

7 Levi Rickert, "Standing Rock Sioux Tribe & Yakama Nation Sign Proclamation Calling for the United States to Revoke the Doctrine of Christian Discovery," *Native News Online.Net*, March 10, 2017, http://nativenewsonline.net.

8 My argument here draws on Holly Randell-Moon, "The Secular Contract: Sovereignty, Secularism and Law in Australia," *Social Semiotics* 23, no. 3 (June 2013): 352–67, https://doi.org/10.1080/10350330.2012.719732. See also Stack, Goldenberg, and Fitzgerald, *Religion as a Category of Governance and Sovereignty*; Jonathon S. Kahn and Vincent W. Lloyd, eds., *Race and Secularism in America* (New York: Columbia University Press, 2016).

9 Johnson and Graham's Lessee v. William M'Intosh, No. 21 U.S. (8 Wheat.) 543 (U.S. Supreme Court 1823). My analysis here follows Robert J. Miller, *Discovering Indigenous Lands: The Doctrine of Discovery in the English Colonies* (New York: Oxford University Press, 2010).

10 *Johnson v. M'Intosh.*

11 Ibid.; Joanne Barker, "For Whom Sovereignty Matters," in *Sovereignty Matters: Locations of Contestation and Possibility in Indigenous Struggles for Self-Determination*, ed. Joanne Barker (Lincoln: University of Nebraska Press, 2005), 1–31.

12 David Sikkink, "From Christian Civilization to Individual Civil Liberties: Framing Religion in the Legal Field, 1880–1949," in *The Secular Revolution: Power, Interests, and Conflict in the Secularization of American Public Life*, ed. Christian Smith (Berkeley: University of California Press, 2003), 310–54; Steven K. Green, *The Second Disestablishment: Church and State in Nineteenth-Century America* (New York: Oxford University Press, 2010).

13 Joseph Story, *The Miscellaneous Writings of Joseph Story . . . Ed. by His Son, William W. Story*, 2005, 260–61, http://name.umdl.umich.edu/agy0742.0001.001.

14 Patricia Seed, *Ceremonies of Possession in Europe's Conquest of the New World, 1492–1640* (Cambridge: Cambridge University Press, 1995).

15 Cherokee Nation v. Georgia, 30 U.S. (5 Pet.) 1 (1831).

16 Worcester v. Georgia, 31 U.S. (6 Pet.) 515 (1832). See also William Gerald McLoughlin, *After the Trail of Tears: The Cherokees' Struggle for Sovereignty, 1839–1880* (Chapel Hill: University of North Carolina Press, 1993); William Gerald McLoughlin, *The Cherokees and Christianity, 1794–1870: Essays on Acculturation and Cultural Persistence* (Athens: University of Georgia Press, 1994); Gregory D. Smithers, *The Cherokee Diaspora: An Indigenous History of Migration, Resettlement, and Identity* (New Haven, CT: Yale University Press, 2015).

17 Tee-Hit-Ton Indians v. United States, 348 U.S. 272 (1955).

18 Randell-Moon, "The Secular Contract"; Charles W. Mills, *The Racial Contract* (Ithaca, NY: Cornell University Press, 1997). For more on Australian settler colonialism and sovereignty, see Aileen Moreton-Robinson, *The White Possessive: Property, Power, and Indigenous Sovereignty* (Minneapolis: University of Minnesota Press, 2015).

19 David W. Daily, *Battle for the BIA: G.E.E. Lindquist and the Missionary Crusade against John Collier* (Tucson: University of Arizona Press, 2004); chapter 3 in Wenger, *Religious Freedom*.

20 US Office of Indian Affairs, *Annual Report of the Commissioner of Indian Affairs to the Secretary of the Interior for the Year 1883* (Washington, DC: Government Printing Office, 1883), xiv–xv; US Office of Indian Affairs, *Annual Report to the Secretary of the Interior*, 1883.

21 Kathleen Davis, *Periodization and Sovereignty: How Ideas of Feudalism and Secularization Govern the Politics of Time*, Middle Ages Series (Philadelphia: University of Pennsylvania Press, 2008); Willie James Jennings, *The Christian Imagina-*

tion: Theology and the Origins of Race (New Haven, CT: Yale University Press, 2010); Sylvester A. Johnson, *African American Religions, 1500–2000: Colonialism, Democracy, and Freedom* (Cambridge: Cambridge University Press, 2015); Theodore Vial, *Modern Religion, Modern Race* (New York: Oxford University Press, 2016); Mark Rifkin, *Beyond Settler Time: Temporal Sovereignty and Indigenous Self-Determination* (Durham, NC: Duke University Press Books, 2017).

22 US Office of Indian Affairs, *Annual Report of the Commissioner of Indian Affairs to the Secretary of the Interior for the Year 1883*, xi, xv. This paragraph draws on Tisa Wenger, "'A New Form of Government': Religious-Secular Distinctions in Pueblo Indian History," in *Religion as a Category of Governance and Sovereignty*, ed. Trevor Stack, Naomi R. Goldenberg, and Timothy Fitzgerald (Boston: Brill, 2015), 71–72.

23 Wenger, "A New Form of Government."

24 US Office of Indian Affairs, *Sixty-First Annual Report of the Commissioner of Indian Affairs to the Secretary of the Interior* (Washington, DC: Government Printing Office, 1892), 550–52, cited in Wenger, "A New Form of Government," 72–73.

25 Rebecca Anne Goetz, *The Baptism of Early Virginia: How Christianity Created Race* (Baltimore: Johns Hopkins University Press, 2012).

26 Wenger, "A New Form of Government," 80–81. A similar dynamic can be observed in other colonial contexts. See, for example, the case of the Moro people in the Philippines, described in Wenger, *Religious Freedom*, 82–100, where the US military government imposed new religious-secular distinctions as a way to facilitate colonial control.

27 Tisa Wenger, *We Have a Religion: The 1920s Pueblo Indian Dance Controversy and American Religious Freedom* (Chapel Hill: University of North Carolina Press, 2009); Tisa Wenger, "Indian Dances and the Politics of Religious Freedom, 1870–1930," *Journal of the American Academy of Religion* 79, no. 4 (December 2011): 850–78, https://doi.org/10.1093/jaarel/lfr061.

28 For relevant analysis, see Lee Irwin, *Native American Spirituality: A Critical Reader* (Lincoln: University of Nebraska Press, 2000); Carter Jones Meyer and Diana Royer, *Selling the Indian: Commercializing & Appropriating American Indian Cultures* (Tucson: University of Arizona Press, 2001); and Christina Welch, "Appropriating the Didjeridu and the Sweat Lodge: New Age Baddies and Indigenous Victims?," *Journal of Contemporary Religion* 17, no. 1 (2002): 21–38.

29 "'We Also Have a Religion': The American Indian Religious Freedom Act and the Religious Freedom Project of the Native American Rights Fund," *Announcements: Native American Rights Fund* (Winter 1979): 1, Native American Rights Fund Documents, www.narf.org/nill/documents/nlr/nlr5-1.pdf; Vine Deloria and James Treat, *For This Land: Writings on Religion in America* (New York: Routledge, 1999), 203–13.

30 Badoni v. Higginson, 638 F.2d 172 (10th Cir. 1980); Brown, "Native American Religions," 19–44; Brown, *Religion, Law, and the Land*, 39–60.

31 Brown, "Native American Religions," 28–32; Brown, *Religion, Law, and the Land*, 93–118.

32 Wenger, *We Have a Religion*; Michael D. McNally, "From Substantial Burden on Religion to Diminished Spiritual Fulfillment: The San Francisco Peaks Case and the Misunderstanding of Native American Religion," *Journal of Law and Religion* 30, no. 1 (February 2015): 36–64, https://doi.org/10.1017/jlr.2014.34.

33 My argument here is informed by Talal Asad, *Genealogies of Religion: Discipline and Reasons of Power in Christianity and Islam* (Baltimore: Johns Hopkins University Press, 1993); Markus Dressler and Arvind-pal Singh Mandair, eds., *Secularism and Religion-Making*, Reflection and Theory in the Study of Religion Series (New York: Oxford University Press, 2011).

34 Taiaiake Alfred, "Sovereignty," in *Sovereignty Matters: Locations of Contestation and Possibility in Indigenous Struggles for Self-Determination*, ed. Joanne Barker (Lincoln: University of Nebraska Press, 2005), 33.

35 Joanne Barker, *Native Acts: Law, Recognition, and Cultural Authenticity* (Durham, NC: Duke University Press, 2011), 11, 220–28. Other efforts to reformulate sovereignty in Indigenous terms include Gerald R. Alfred, *Peace, Power, Righteousness: An Indigenous Manifesto* (New York: Oxford University Press, 1999); Kevin Bruyneel, *The Third Space of Sovereignty: The Postcolonial Politics of U.S.–Indigenous Relations* (Minneapolis: University of Minnesota Press, 2007); Audra Simpson, *Mohawk Interruptus: Political Life across the Borders of Settler States* (Durham, NC: Duke University Press, 2014).

36 Vine Deloria, "Self-Determination and the Concept of Sovereignty," in *Economic Development in American Indian Reservations*, ed. Roxanne Dunbar Ortiz (Albuquerque: Native American Studies, University of New Mexico, 1979), 22–28.

37 Vine Deloria, *God Is Red: A Native View of Religion* (Golden, CO: North American Press, 1992), vol. 2; Deloria and Treat, *For This Land*.

38 Lennard, "Still Fighting at Standing Rock."

39 Wenger, *We Have a Religion*; Wenger, *Religious Freedom*, 101–42.

7

Protection

ROSEMARY R. CORBETT

On January 27, 2017, Suha Amin Abdullah Abushamma, a Sudanese citizen and doctor of internal medicine at the Cleveland Clinic, returned from visiting family in Saudi Arabia and was detained at John F. Kennedy (JFK) International Airport in New York. That day, the recently inaugurated president of the United States signed an executive order prohibiting entry to the country of anyone from Iran, Iraq, Libya, Somalia, Sudan, Syria, or Yemen. "The United States is my home," said Abushamma, bearer of a valid work visa. "My apartment with all my things except what I packed for my vacation, my car, my job, and my fiancé all are in the United States." Customs and border officials repeatedly denied her requests to contact an attorney and threatened her into resigning her work visa by telling her—incorrectly—that doing so was the only way to make it legal for her to enter the country later.[1]

The purpose of the travel ban, the new president claimed, was "to protect the American people from terrorist attacks by foreign nationals." The ban involved an initial ninety-day exclusion of those with valid visas and green cards (permanent residency permits), a 120-day suspension on entry of refugees from any area of the globe, and an indefinite suspension of refugees fleeing the civil war in Syria.[2] Upon resumption of the refugee admission program, preference would be for refugees who were religious minorities (i.e., non-Muslims) and facing persecution in said countries.[3] These restrictions, the president argued, were necessary to prohibit entrance to those who would engage in violence, particularly against women, or discrimination against and oppression of those of religions, races, or sexualities other than themselves.[4]

In the hours and days following issuance of the order, customs and border officials detained and deported hundreds of people bearing valid credentials. Many were prevented from contacting friends, family, or counsel. Many, such as Abushamma, were also lied to and forced into signing away their legal claims to entry. A supervisor told Abushamma "that an order that would allow me to stay in the United States would need to come from the Supreme Court, and that this would not happen. They told me that my lawyers could not do anything to help me in my situation and so I should just sign the form." Coerced, deceived, and deported, she was sent back to Saudi Arabia with no legal recourse for returning.

Social and legal backlash to the executive order came almost as quickly as the order's implementation. As word spread of the order's effects, activists and ordinary citizens began arriving at airports to protest the policy and demand the release of detainees. By the following afternoon, despite the New York Police Department's attempt to stop the flow of protestors, thousands of people had filled the parking garage outside JFK's terminal 4. Similar scenes unfolded at international airports across the country, and legal teams from civil rights organizations quickly followed, offering services to those with friends, family, or other associates trapped inside.

On Sunday, January 29, 2017, amid intense public outcry and media focus on the plight of detained refugees such as Hameed Khalid Darweesh—an Iraqi whose life was endangered because he had served as an interpreter for US armed forces[5]—the president rescinded the exclusion of green card holders. By the end of the following week, judges around the country faced cases questioning the legality of other provisions of the law, particularly its apparent targeting of Muslims. A stay on the executive order was issued in Washington State, over vocal objections from the Department of Justice. The Justice Department ceased defending the order, however, when, on March 6, the president signed a new one bearing the same name.[6] The new order was vastly longer and, among other things, removed restrictions on those with valid visas and green cards and exempted Iraqi citizens. Nevertheless, new social and legal challenges followed, with judges in Hawaii and Maryland soon issuing orders that halted implementation of the law in whole or in part.[7]

In subsequent months, various lawsuits and appeals proceeded through the federal court system until the Supreme Court agreed to review the law's constitutionality during their next session.[8] Before the court could convene for a full hearing on the second version of the travel ban, the president issued yet another rendition of it that September as a proclamation and, in so doing, removed Iraq from the list of countries affected.[9] To the third version he also added prohibitions on immigrants from Chad (another primarily Muslim country, which was later dropped) and on the immigration of most North Koreans and select Venezuelan officials. Believing these changes to be merely cosmetic ones meant to circumvent earlier charges of religious discrimination, federal district court judges in Hawaii and Maryland again issued orders prohibiting the September proclamation's implementation in whole or in part.

The social and legal challenges to the 2017 executive orders arose not just because of the orders' immediate effects, although those were severe. People—not least, refugees fleeing horrendous violence—were detained, deceived, and deported. (Eminent economist Jeffrey Sachs, writing in the *Boston Globe*, was one of many to make an analogy to Jews turned away in 1939.[10]) Economic impact included lost revenue due to disruptions in tourism and other industries, as well as the loss of tax dollars, all of which gave states standing to contest the orders, courts decided. Despite their immediate draconian effects, the orders might not have produced so severe a backlash had not opponents of the laws been previously primed by the president's campaign promise to enact a "complete and total" ban on Muslims entering the United States.[11] To many, this and other statements of intent to target a particular religious group seemed grossly illegal and possible evidence of the president's unsuitability to hold public office. Once the campaign promise became an actual order, legal and social challenges swiftly arose, not only because of the law's immediate human and economic cost but also because of brewing disagreements with the president. The legal challenges, in particular, arose from disagreements over which principle should take precedence: the executive prerogative to exercise protectionism in matters of immigration, or the First Amendment protections of religion guaranteed by the Constitution.[12]

The First Amendment to the Constitution, adopted in 1791 along with nine other amendments that collectively make up the Bill of Rights, protects citizens' rights of freedom of religion and speech, freedom to peaceably (nonviolently) assemble or to petition the government to ameliorate legal wrongs, and freedom of the press. With regard to religious protections, the amendment prohibits Congress from establishing a national church or other religious body and also protects the "free exercise of religion." Notably, as Tisa Wenger and Kathleen Holscher describe in other chapters of this book, Native Americans largely have been denied sovereignty and the right of self-rule, instead being designated as wards of the US government, partly on account of their traditions. Even after gaining citizenship, Native Americans still have been denied religious freedom protections repeatedly, raising the question of whether such protections have ever been applied equally. Other religious minorities of widely different stripes have also discovered the limitations of these early protections.

As religious minorities ranging from antebellum Mormons to dissenters of the state church of Massachusetts discovered, the religious freedom provisions in the Bill of Rights offered protection only from the federal government. They provided no protection to those facing discrimination from various state governments or from citizens within state jurisdictions. Religious minorities and dissenters who petitioned state courts for protection of religious practice during the first century of the new nation's existence found that such courts were not obliged, and many were not inclined, to enforce such federal laws. It was only during the late nineteenth century that federal agencies gained the ability to enforce protections in the Bill of Rights (such as the First Amendment's protection of free exercise) at the state level.[13] Simultaneously, however, with racist immigration protectionism running rampant in the years after the Civil War, Congress began rescinding protections of free religious exercise for non-Christians seeking to enter through the nation's borders.

As we shall see, the 2017 executive orders were not the first bans on Muslim immigration. Rather, a ban on Muslims and/or Muslim practices had been structured into American immigration law since before the creation of the federal immigration system. Like the 2017 executive orders, the initial exclusion—formulated in the Page Act of 1875—was not described explicitly as a Muslim ban by proponents and is not often treated as one by historians, although much like the 2017 orders, it laid the foundation for further prohibitions on Muslim immigration and prompts inquiries into the limits of religious freedom protections.

I will return to the 2017 orders below. First, to understand this early twenty-first-century contest between immigration protectionism and constitutional protections, it is illuminating to examine the nineteenth-century creation of protectionist federal immigration law and review the implications of Muslim bans then and since. These bans have sometimes been predicated on arguments about the need to protect Americans and their democracy from Muslims' ostensibly violent practices. Historically, immigration restrictions predicated on arguments about the need to curtail dangerous Muslim practices have faced few legal challenges— perhaps unsurprisingly, in that courts have generally interpreted the First Amendment protection of religious exercise as applying mainly to belief. Actual practice is where things get much more murky, with protections of free exercise long withheld from those whose traditions seem to contravene moral or social norms derived from Protestantism.[14] Nevertheless, Muslims *were* legally barred from entry on the basis of belief, not just practice, during a period that lasted nearly fifty years—proving that even protections of belief or conscience have not been observed during eras of intense protectionist rhetoric.

As we shall see, an historic overview of American bans on Muslim immigration reveals striking shifts in the racial characteristics of Muslims deemed dangerous to America's democracy and its citizens. These shifts not only testify to the instability of protectionist impulses, the malleability of racial and religious stereotypes, and the selectivity exercised in affording First Amendment protections, but they also direct our attention to how anti-Muslim protectionism in immigration law has buttressed claims to American exceptionalism, including the exceptional right to discriminate against members of other races, religions, or sexual orientations and the right to employ certain kinds of violence.

The First Amendment versus Federal Immigration Law

The US Constitution does not explicitly grant either Congress or the president powers to create or modify immigration restrictions. Because of this lacuna, and because of the need for new bodies to plow new fields, people new towns, and push out Native Americans on the country's western edge, Congress largely refrained from regulating immigration until the late nineteenth-century closure of the frontier. Before that, the legislature even incentivized migrants to come to the United States, although various states had their own restrictions on entry.[15] Under the Alien Enemies Act of 1798, Congress did briefly authorize the president to deport "all such aliens as he shall judge dangerous to the peace and safety of the United States," but that controversial law faced broad opposition and was allowed to lapse two years later.[16] After the Civil War, and spurred by Supreme Court intimations that only the federal government, not states, had the requisite authority to regulate immigration, Congress gradually manufactured a regime of explicitly race-based, and implicitly religious, immigration exclusions.[17]

It was not until after states ratified the Fourteenth and Fifteenth Amendments that Congress resorted to protectionism in immigration law. These Reconstruction-era amendments extended citizenship and the right to vote to almost anyone born in the United States. Rights previously held only by "free white persons" were now also conferred on freed slaves and the children of immigrants, although not on Native Americans.[18] Fearing lost privilege and the threat of free labor, nativist legislators and citizens quickly disenfranchised freed slaves with the use of poll taxes, literacy tests, and brutal violence. Similarly, legislators passed aggressive immigration restrictions—ostensibly to protect the nation from corrupting and violent elements.[19] According to the first such laws, passed in 1891, one practice American democracy needed protection from was that of polygamy—something long associated in American political rhetoric with Muslims.

As legal scholar Claire Smearman has demonstrated, a ban on immigrants associated with polygamy has "played a role in the development of United States immigration law from its very inception."[20] Seven years before passage of the Chinese Exclusion Act of 1892, the Page Law (or Act of March 3, 1875) was "the first federal immigration statute to declare a class of immigrants excludable."[21] The act prohibited entrance of female prostitutes and prohibited the forced entry of anyone from "China, Japan, or any Oriental country."[22] In other words, as proponents of the legislation insisted, the act prohibited enslavement, both in the form of women trafficked for sex work and in the coolie trade—the smuggling of Asian forced laborers—that had arisen in Europe and South America after the abolition of chattel slavery. With chattel slavery newly outlawed in the United States, American legislators burnished the nation's ostensible commitment to liberty by claiming to protect the country from the degrading influence of other forms of enslavement, particularly the supposed enslavement of women.[23]

The Page Act does not specify Muslims as an intended target, nor do legal scholars generally see this ban as having anything to do with Islam.[24] Rather, it is generally understood as being aimed at non-Muslim Chinese immigrants. Anti-Chinese sentiment in the US, fomented in California in the 1850s as Chinese and other immigrants competed for gold mining claims, among other things, had grown to epic proportions by the 1870s. In material terms, the connection to slavery was tenuous at best. Chinese immigration to the United States was primarily voluntary, not forced.[25] Of the Chinese women attempting to immigrate, many were not prostitutes but wives—often, polygamous ones.[26] Immigration officials, however, knowingly categorized any female romantic partners other than heterosexual monogamous spouses as prostitutes (i.e., in the terms of the day, enslaved sex workers). Thus the Page Law's protectionism was a red herring—one reliant on an analog between polygamy and slavery. That rhetorical analog reveals much about Americans' own anxieties and tendencies to use hyperbole to justify racial and religious discrimination in immigration law and elsewhere.[27]

Late nineteenth-century nativists were not the first to equate polygamy with slavery. Rather, a long tradition existed in American political writing of associating monogamous marriage with democracy and associating polygamy with the kind of violence and slavery that corrupted free morals. Monogamous, voluntary, hierarchical marriage mirrored and upheld the political system, many assumed. Just as a woman willingly signed away her individual civic and economic rights (such as they were) for her husband's protection, individual citizens transferred their votes and voices to their elected representatives. This system of coverture, in which wives were legally subsumed under their husbands, was based in English common law and buttressed by the Bible—or so argued leaders ranging from John Winthrop to John Adams.[28] Particular nineteenth-century familial and economic formations were, it was widely asserted, essential to the American way of life—a way of life diametrically opposed to that supposedly practiced by "Oriental" peoples in general and Muslims in particular.

Anti-Muslim Animosity and the "Imperialism of Virtue"

Early American leaders drew from a deep reservoir of Enlightenment theory when creating the philosophical and legal framework for the new nation. Essential to this tradition is the association of Islamic governance, particularly in the form of the Ottoman Sultan, with systemic despotism.[29] Thomas Jefferson, for example, invoked this tradition when libeling King George of Britain as an infidel despot who enslaved his subjects.[30] This modern European orientalist political theory, exemplified in Montesquieu's *Spirit of the Laws*, is crucial for understanding both American thinking about polygamy and American laws that regulate it. At the same time, however, ideas about polygamy and the threat Muslims posed were not simply inherited from the European continent. Rather, inhabitants of the newly formed American nation experienced political conflicts with real-time Muslim foes: North African rulers and pirates. In response, Americans adapted European narratives and created their own variety of orientalist political imaginary.

In 1777, the sultanate of Morocco was the first political entity to recognize the new American nation. Nevertheless, US relations with the so-called Barbary States (the Berber-inhabited territories of contemporary Morocco, Algeria, Tunisia, and Libya) were highly tumultuous due to Americans' refusal to pay tribute to ensure merchant ships' safe passage in and near the Mediterranean. In 1785, the Dey of Algiers declared war on America. Soon after, Virginia governor Patrick Henry detained three foreigners assumed to be spies. (After an inquisition turned up a few documents in Hebrew, the three were deported).[31] Two years later, John Jay, Chief Justice of the Supreme Court, warned New Yorkers that if they refused to ratify the Constitution and left the new nation militarily and politically weak under the Articles of Confederation, "Algerians could be on the American coast and enslave its citizens who have not a single sloop of war."[32] By the time Thomas Jefferson became president, the US had marshaled a naval force and deployed it in a series of conflicts between 1801 and 1815 over the matters of tribute and the capture of American sailors in Mediterranean waters.

As in Europe, two burgeoning literary genres reflected these tensions: the spy narrative and the captivity narrative. Central to both was the formulaic equation of polygamy with despotism and enslavement.[33] The narratives used the specter of polygamy as a parable for defending republicanism, constituting what American studies scholar Timothy Marr describes as an antebellum "imperialism of virtue" that compensated for Americans' military and political weakness.[34] While American sailors struggled to overcome their Muslim antagonists militarily, American writers triumphed over them narratively. In both kinds of narrative, heterosexual, hierarchical monogamy was celebrated as the marital form necessary for upholding virtuous democracy. Central to many captivity narratives was the drama, in particular, of American Christian women, who were rarely actual captives in the Mediterranean. In dire circumstances, would these women virtuously refuse to succumb physically to their violent Muslim captors and then lead them into true morality? Or would they falter, convert to Islam, and "live the slave of a despotic tyrant?"[35] American readers could not wait to find out. They voraciously consumed the gory details of these salacious narratives, as well as the images of bare-breasted women sometimes accompanying them.[36]

Spy and captivity narratives starring Muslim antagonists proved to American readers their superiority in the realms of religion and politics by showcasing the implications of violent despotism for women and other captives. As one "illiterate mariner" claimed in his journal-turned-travelogue-memoir, he had in Algiers suffered the "horrors of unspeakable slavery" at "the hands of merciless Mahometans . . . whose tenderest mercies towards the Christian captives, are the most extreme cruelties."[37] One might rightly imagine comparable tales told about the simultaneous horrors of slavery at the hands of American Christian captors. This did not trouble most slaveholders, who believed their own practices to be qualitatively different from those of Muslims and hardly evidence of despotism in the least. Rather than merciless, in fact, some argued that American slavery was a paradigmatic example of Christian mercy.[38] Comparisons to Muslims were meant to prove it.

While Americans were circulating stories about the superiority of Christian republicanism and the urgent need to protect women and democracy from the violent tyranny and despotism of "Turks" (Muslims of the Ottoman Empire) who would enslave them at home and abroad, they were simultaneously practicing a form of chattel slavery—including of African Muslims—among the most brutal of slaveholding systems in recorded history. But narratives about the need to protect citizens and the state from Muslims were not entirely fallacious. There were actual conflicts in the Mediterranean. Actual captives were taken, and these conflicts did demonstrate the weakness of the new nation. However, such narratives were extremely hyperbolic while also placing culpability for slavery not on white Americans but on those who supposedly practiced slavery incorrectly: those who had the temerity to hold white Christians captive. In such narratives, comparison to fantastical Muslim despotism allowed the new nation to be a beacon on a hill *including* in its slaveholding practices. Contemporaneous claims of American moral exceptionalism were not that Americans did not engage in slavery or violence but that such activities served a moral and redemptive purpose in the United States by subduing and disciplining subject populations through exercises of Protestant Christian stewardship and education.[39]

As the United States grew economically and politically over the subsequent century and began to match Muslim powers such as the mighty Ottoman Empire in eminence and strength, more Americans traveled abroad and came into contact with the ostensibly ruthless Muslim rulers of lore. Some abolitionists began to shame American slaveholders by characterizing them as morally inferior to Turks and Berbers who, some Americans now realized, treated their slaves in a relatively more humane fashion than did many Americans or had manumitted their slaves entirely.[40] Others maintained the orientalist emphasis but pulled in new targets by comparing Southern slaveholders with Mormons who had similar "harems." One Congressman even proposed that Mormon wives in polygamous marriages be protected by the Freedman's Bureau since they were essentially slaves.[41]

It was in the mid-nineteenth-century conflicts over Mormonism and Chinese immigration that these rhetorical framings of polygamy as slavery and despotism finally gained the force of federal law. The anti-Muslim animus behind such legislation is something legal historians have often minimized or missed entirely.[42] In 1862, Congress prohibited the practice of bigamy in territories such as Utah under the Morrill Act, thus overtly targeting Mormons. Anti-Muslim sentiments animated the ideas leading to passage of that law and of the Page Law in 1875, which prohibited the immigration of certain "Oriental" immigrants. Followers of Islam were not specified as targets of the legislation for two reasons. First, unlike Chinese immigrants, Muslims were not yet arriving to the United States in large numbers. Second, those who did were governed by Page Act restrictions, as most Muslims already fit in the racial category of "Oriental" according to popular conception. No one needed to state what seemed to contemporaries patently obvious: of course Muslims should be excluded.

Legislators would make their anti-Muslim sentiments more evident in drafting subsequent immigration legislation. As mentioned, Muslims were increasingly prohibited from immigrating to the United States by race-based exclusions, which were the basis for most legal restrictions during this period. Such exclusions do not disprove the importance of religion in immigration law, as one might imagine, because Americans almost invariably conflated race with religion in arguments about various people's suitability—or supposed lack thereof—for citizenship. One could tell a person's religion by their race, the reasoning often went, and could tell a person's level of civilization by their religion.[43] With some immigrants who were deemed Muslim on account of their race contesting such logic, lawmakers would soon specify the religious grounds for exclusion.

Muslim Bans: Barred on the Bases of Belief and Practice

Although American legislators would never specify Muslims as the intended target of immigration restrictions in the text of actual laws, they would specify in legislation that belief in a certain Islamic doctrine was grounds for exclusion. That doctrine involved polygamy. In 1891, polygamists had been included among those inadmissible to the United States under the new, and first ever, comprehensive immigration restrictions.[44] By 1907, in the midst of a high point in Syrian immigration (particularly of Syrian women), lobbying from American nativists led to the exclusion of any people who even "admit their *belief* in the practice of polygamy."[45] Not long after, US diplomats found themselves massaging relations with the dwindling Ottoman Empire over what both recognized as an effective ban on Muslim immigrants.

Because of objections raised by Ottoman diplomats, the commissioner general of immigration and the Department of State created a caveat they could apply when necessary. There is, they argued, a "well defined distinction between belief in a religion which tolerates a practice and belief in the practice itself."[46] In other words, so long as Muslims did not believe that Islam endorsed polygamy (i.e., that polygamy was Islamic), they were eligible to enter. Any Muslim who professed the acceptability of polygamy, was practicing polygamy, or had ever practiced polygamy would be denied.

This historic compromise seems to resemble others brought before US courts, in which the judiciary is called to navigate between preserving the First Amendment's religious freedom protections and abridging freedoms so as to protect the nation from seeming threats. As mentioned earlier, decisions in such cases tend to involve prohibitions on certain practices. The implication is that religion is primarily about belief, not practice, and that if courts do not abridge freedoms of belief, religious freedoms are not compromised. (Not incidentally, the Supreme Court first assumed the power to curtail religious practice in the 1879 antipolygamy case *Reynolds v. United States*, during which justices opined that the practice of polygamy belonged to the "life of Asiatic and African people"[47]). To treat these immigration restrictions and caveats as incidents of protecting faith but not practice, however, misses that the early twentieth-century compromise over belief in polygamy's legitimacy comprised a different development: that of defining the proper contours of protected faith itself. Protecting the nation from problematic religious *belief* in the morality of polygamy, and not just the practice of it à la *Reynolds*, was deemed more important than preserving First Amendment protections of religious freedom, and no legal challenge required courts to weigh in.

As a result of the polygamy provisions of the 1907 law, would-be immigrants from India, Turkey, and Syria, among others, were denied entry to the US just in the period between July 1908 and February 1910.[48] For some in Congress, such exclusions were not sufficient. Senator James Reed of Missouri, for example, offered a new framing of the antipolygamy statutes, which, he believed, would make it possible to effectively prevent the immigration of "all aliens not of the Caucasian race," "all members of the African or black race," and all "Turks and East Indians."[49] Although Reed's specific racial referents were not included in the expansive provisions of the Oriental Exclusion Act of 1917, his framing of polygamy was. Once again, the new law based exclusions not just on practice but on belief, with the provision that "polygamists, or persons who practice polygamy or believe in or advocate the practice of polygamy" would be barred from entry along with paupers, felons, and those diseased or insane.[50]

Many Muslim immigrants from targeted areas still gained entrance to the United States during these years, and some who managed to do so very likely reported belonging to a religion other than Islam. The case of Syria is especially interesting. Previously, because of the association of Syria with the Ottoman Empire and Islam, immigration officials considered Syrians part of "Turkey in Asia."[51] However, due to aggressive lobbying and legal campaigns by Syrian immigrants, the overwhelming majority of whom claimed to be Christian and who appealed to Christianity as proof of their whiteness and civilized status, Syria was omitted from the Oriental Exclusion Act of 1917's Asiatic "barred zones."[52] Further, for the purposes of the 1920 census, Syrians were counted as part of the "foreign-born white population."[53] Belief in Syrian whiteness would not last, however. The reassociation of Syria with Islam during the 1950s, as Syria allied with Egypt to form the United Arab Republic, would fuel potent nativist demands for restrictions once again—particularly once the racialized image of Muslims most commonly circulated in American popular culture transformed from the menacing Berber pirate or Turkish sultan to the roving Arab terrorist.[54]

Since 1891, the ban on polygamy has remained part of US immigration law with myriad implications. Although Congress amended the antipolygamy provisions under the 1952 McCarran-Walter Act and removed the ban on those who *believe* in polygamy, a ban on those who had previously practiced or advocated polygamy remained on the books until 1990. That year, Congress amended the exclusions, prohibiting entry only to those who intend to practice polygamy once in the country[55]—a prohibition that remains in effect and can, in effect, be applied retroactively.[56] With the 1952 Immigration and Nationality Act, Congress also formally conferred on the president the power to regulate immigration, paving the way for the executive orders issued in 2017, among others.[57]

When considering the 2017 executive orders in light of the history discussed here, it becomes clear that they are hardly the first American bans on Muslim immigration. While enforcement varied, Muslims were formally excluded from entering the United States on the basis of religious belief from 1907 to 1952, with the precedent for such exclusions passed as early as 1875 and the underlying ideology dating back to the nation's founding. When the prohibition on belief in polygamy was lifted in 1952 "without legislative comment," future historians were denied concrete evidence of the legislators' motivations for ending what, for half a century, had effectively been a Muslim ban.[58] One could easily imagine that the Cold War imperative of making Middle Eastern allies was a contributing factor to the revised polygamy provisions. Nevertheless, subsequent quotas established for immigrants from many Muslim-majority countries kept the actual number of immigrants quite low. As Harry Truman, who favored more liberal immigration policies, put it derisively when vetoing the legislation on June 25, 1952 (a veto that was overridden), "you Turks, you are brave defenders [against Communism] of the Eastern flank, but you shall have a quota of only 225!"[59]

At the very least, scholars of law and religion can regard 1952 as a year in which political protectionism was scaled back—for a time—to reflect First Amendment protections of religious belief. Religious practice would remain proscribed, limited by legislators' continued insistence that polygamy is a practice dangerous to both democracy and to individuals, particularly the women who are—it is universally presumed—subjugated by it. And yet, even that protectionism has proven to be superficial, at least in effect. As Smearman has amply demonstrated, the implications of antipolygamy laws have been particularly severe for women seeking protection from violence, as those who do experience violence in polygamous marriages are considered "inadmissible" due to their ostensible lack of "good moral character" and are thus barred from asylum, among other things. Those already in the US are ineligible to petition for naturalization under the 1994 Violence Against Women Act for the same reason.[60] For women fleeing the brutality of militants in Syria or elsewhere, the consequences could be equally dire, despite the 2017 orders' professed concern for victims of gender-based violence.

On December 3, 2017, the Supreme Court ruled that the September 2017 proclamation could stand until further review.[61] Then, on June 26, 2018, in a highly contested 5–4 decision, the court upheld the legality of the proclamation. Chief Justice John Roberts, writing for the majority, defended the president's broad powers to regulate immigration and exercise protectionism, regardless of his having made incendiary comments about Muslims and having vowed to ban Muslims, as a group, from entering the country.[62] In a scathing dissent, Justice Sonia Sotomayor cited the president's campaign rhetoric and subsequent comments as evidence of the obvious "anti-Muslim animus" behind the proclamation and as proof of its discriminatory and unconstitutional character.[63] Separately, Justice Stephen Breyer argued that the administration's blanket denials of travel-ban waiver requests also suggested anti-Muslim animus.[64] Particularly disturbing was a report from the Yale Law School and Center for Constitutional Rights documenting mass denials of requests from Yemenis fleeing a catastrophic US-supported bombing campaign in their home country.[65] Many, like some Syrians fleeing their own civil war, were already in possession of approved US visas when the ban went into effect, but they were consequently stranded.

The question of religious freedom protections was one the Supreme Court's majority actually refused to consider, despite acknowledging the president's anti-Muslim comments, because, in Roberts' words, the proclamation was "neutral on its face."[66] Slightly uncomfortable with that assertion of neutrality, Justice Anthony Kennedy, in a written concurrence agreeing with the majority, warned against violating the First Amendment's protection of religious freedom: "It is an urgent necessity that officials adhere to these constitutional guarantees and mandates in all their actions, even in the sphere of foreign affairs."[67] Meanwhile, Sotomayor noted the court's deep inconsistency in ignoring the president's anti-Muslim comments. The week before, she pointed out, the Supreme Court had reversed a lower court's ruling that deemed unconstitutional a white evangelical Christian's refusal to serve gay clients. The Supreme Court decided in favor of protecting his asserted religious right to discriminate against gay clients because members of the Colorado Civil Rights Commission who had originally reviewed his claim had made statements hostile to his expressed beliefs.[68] In other words, the court's rulings, taken together, suggested that evangelical Christians' religious freedoms should be protected from government maligning and interference, even when the expression of such freedoms includes discriminating against others, while even more obvious government discrimination against Muslims, including infringement of Muslims' religious freedoms, can be disregarded in deference to the president's opinion about the kind of threat immigrating Muslims might pose. Once again, as acknowledged by one of its own members, the Supreme Court had raised the issue of to whom the religious freedom protections of the First Amendment actually apply, and how.

Conclusion

The protectionism underlying older race- and religion-based immigration restrictions has proven to be superficial, inconsistent, hyperbolic, and diversionary. Not only did many Americans long use the specter of violent Muslim (or supposedly Muslim-style) enslavement as a foil for their own slaveholding practices and brutal repression of black Americans and others, minimizing or justifying American exercises of violence in the process, but the nineteenth-century antipolygamy crusades also deprived women of political enfranchisement, installing them back in "voluntary" hierarchical relationships with male relatives. In point of fact, the Edmunds-Tucker Act that prohibited polygamy in Utah also rescinded from women the ability to vote, thus ending women's direct political participation for more than a generation.[69]

Using the specter of external Muslim threats as grounds for claims of American Christian exceptionalism, and in so doing minimizing or justifying violence and discrimination *within* the nation, is not just a matter for historians. Provisions of the 2017 executive orders were ostensibly designed to protect vulnerable populations from the threats of violence and discrimination at the hands of foreign-born Muslims. They were crafted even at a time when rates of violence against religious, sexual, and racial minorities and against women—already at shockingly high rates in the United States—were on the rise and as the threat posed by white American militants, whom some within the Department of Homeland Security and FBI have long considered a greater threat to domestic safety than radicalized Muslims, continued to grow.[70]

Meanwhile, despite the 2017 orders' professed concern for victims of gender-based violence, the administration's Justice Department removed gender-based violence from the list of reasons under which immigrants could seek asylum in the United States in 2018. The Attorney General's stated reasoning for this change was that gender-based violence should be considered a "private" matter and not grounds for political asylum, even if governments routinely refuse to protect their female citizens or prosecute attackers.[71] Thus, in affirming the constitutionality of the travel ban, the Supreme Court allowed the president to claim to protect women from violence even as his administration rescinded protections from women fleeing violence. Simultaneously, even members of the court who upheld the president's ban felt impelled to warn against abridging religious freedoms with a law ostensibly meant, in part, to protect the safety and freedoms of vulnerable religious groups.

A generous reading of protectionist immigration laws, including the 2017 executive orders, might regard their language as aspirational rather than actual, reflecting not what the United States is in terms of protecting racial, religious, and sexual minorities and women but what many Americans hope for it to become. This aspirational quality was certainly evident in Civil War–era debates about ridding the US of slavery of any kind, including the assumed enslavement involved in polygamy and the so-called white slavery of prostitution. And yet this aspirational aspect does not preclude using immigration law to make Muslims a foil against which to project American Christian—especially Protestant—exceptionalism, in so doing minimizing or justifying violence and discrimination against various populations. If anything, the twinning of these purposes has extensive precedent. Historically, those who have promoted the idea of Christian America as the great protector against supposed threats of violence (by Muslims or others) have often done so while claiming the unique right to *exercise* violence, both at home and abroad, for the supposed purpose of moral and physical improvement. In the twenty-first century, that tradition continues.

NOTES

1 Abushamma's case is one of twenty-six included in a complaint submitted to the Department of Homeland Security by the Center for Constitutional Rights and the Kathryn O. Greenberg Immigration Justice Clinic at the Benjamin N. Cardozo School of Law after the first ten days of the executive order. All quotes from Jen Nessel, "Abuses by Border Patrol Related to Muslim Ban Order: Complaint Submitted to DHS Inspector," Center for Constitutional Rights Press Release (February 7, 2017). Disclosure: at the time of this writing, the author was a member of the board of directors of the Center for Constitutional Rights.

2 The White House Office of the Press Secretary, "Executive Order, Protecting the Nation from Foreign Terrorist Entry into the United States," January 27, 2017, www.whitehouse.gov/the-press-office.

3 Ibid., § 5(b).

4 Ibid., § 1.

5 Central Broadcasting Station and Associated Press, "Iraqi Immigrant Freed after Being Detained at New York Airport in Wake of Trump Immigration Action," CBS, January 28, 2017, http://multimedia.cbs.com.

6   The White House Office of the Press Secretary, "Executive Order Protecting the Nation from Foreign Terrorist Entry into the United States," March 6, 2017, www.whitehouse.gov/the-press-office.

7   While a federal judge in Hawaii issued an order that prevented the entire law from going into effect, the Maryland judge ruled only on the travel ban portion. See Alexander Burns, "2 Federal Judges Rule against Trump's Latest Travel Ban," *New York Times*, March 15, 2017.

8   In the meantime, the court upheld the travel restrictions for anyone without a "bona fide relationship" to a person or entity in the United States—a provision that still left room for interpretation and further lawsuits. Saba Hamedy, "Lawyers Express Concern with 'Bona Fide' Relationship Restrictions," CNN, June 29, 2017, www.cnn.com.

9   Donald J. Trump, "Proclamation on Enhancing Vetting Capabilities and Processes for Detecting Attempted Entry into the United States by Terrorists or Other Public-Safety Threats," September 24, 2017, www.whitehouse.gov.

10 Jeffrey D. Sachs, "The Muslim Ban and American History," *Boston Globe*, March 19, 2017.

11 "Trump Calls for 'Complete and Total Ban' on Muslims Entering U.S.," CBS New York, December 7, 2015, http://newyork.cbslocal.com.

12 I use the term "protectionism" in the general sense here of a policy of protecting something, such as the environment. (For example, the term "environmentalism" is a contraction of the original phrase "environmental protectionism.") Notably, the forty-fifth president also tried to link his proposed immigration protectionism, especially immigration over the United States' southern border, to economic protectionism (what is most commonly meant by "protectionism" now). This link was evident since 2016, before his election to the presidency, when the then-candidate tried to appeal to people of color alienated by his apparent racism by arguing that immigrants steal jobs from "hardworking African Americans and Hispanic citizens." See, for example, "The Latest: Trump Says Immigrants Taking Minorities Jobs," August 31, 2016, https://apnews.com.

    According to the 2017 executive orders, the list of countries from which immigrants were prohibited was ostensibly based not on the religion of said countries' inhabitants but on the "countries of concern" from which immigration was temporary limited under the Visa Waiver Program Improvement and Terrorist Travel Prevention Act of 2015. The list of countries identified in that act included Iran, Iraq, Sudan, and Syria and was expanded in 2016 to include Libya, Somalia, and Yemen. See The White House Office of the Press Secretary, "Executive Order, Protecting the Nation from Foreign Terrorist Entry into the United States" (January 27, 2017), § 3(c). Importantly, the 2015 act did not temporarily suspend immigration of anyone "from" those countries, as the 2017 executive orders did, but of any person who had "been present" in those countries at a certain period of time (thus changing it from an exclusion based on race, religion, or nationality to one based on geographic location and travel history). See Visa Waiver Program Improvement and Terrorist Travel Prevention Act of 2015, H.R. 158, 114th Congress (2015), § 3.

13 Sarah Barringer Gordon, *The Mormon Question: Polygamy and Constitutional Conflict in Nineteenth-Century America* (Chapel Hill: University of North Carolina Press, 2002).

14 See, for example, ibid.; Tisa Wenger, *We Have a Religion: The 1920s Pueblo Indian Dance Controversy and American Religious Freedom* (Chapel Hill: University of North Carolina Press, 2009); and Winnifred Fallers Sullivan, *The Impossibility of Religious Freedom* (Princeton, NJ: Princeton University Press, 2009).

15 See Michael LeMay and Elliot Barkan, eds., *US Immigration and Naturalization Laws and Issues: A Documentary History* (Westport, CT: Greenwood, 1999). LeMay and Barkan describe the antebellum period as an "era of unrestricted entry and unrestricted admission" (ix).

16 Kerry Abrams, "Polygamy, Prostitution, and the Federalization of Immigration Law," *Columbia Law Review* 105, no. 3 (April 2005): 665.

17 The Supreme Court had expressed the idea that the federal government should, alone, regulate immigration as early as 1849—a position it took definitively in the 1876 decision of *Chy Lung v. Freeman*. Congress failed to act on that authority until passing the Page Law in 1875 (Abrams, "Polygamy," 666–68). Although the Supreme Court then ruled definitively in 1889 that regulating immigration was within the plenary power of Congress, it was not until 1950 that the court declared "the exclusion of aliens" a "fundamental act of sovereignty" that "stems not alone from legislative power, but is inherent in the executive power to control the foreign affairs of the nation." See Chae Chan Ping v. United States, 130 U.S. 581 (1889) and Knauff v. Shaughnessy, 338 U.S. 537 (1950), respectively. With the 1950 decision, the court established that it was reasonable to infer that Article II of the Constitution implicitly imbues the president with powers over immigration under the commission to regulate foreign affairs.

18 As LeMay and Barkan point out, one of the first actions of the newly created Congress of the United States was to pass the Immigration and Nationality Act of 1790, limiting naturalized citizenship to "free white persons" of good character who had resided in the country for at least two years—a period lengthened to five years in an 1802 revision of the law and in an 1813 piece of legislation, the Five Year Residence Act (*US Immigration and Naturalization Laws and Issues*, xxxix). The Fourteenth Amendment overturned not just this legislation but also the 1857 *Dred Scott v. Sanford* decision, in which the Supreme Court ruled that American descendants of African slaves could not acquire citizenship. Birthright citizenship for children of immigrants was affirmed by the Supreme Court in 1898 after much contestation (see United States v. Wong Kim Ark, 169 U.S. 649). The primary exception to birthright citizenship in the US was Native Americans, who did not receive automatic citizenship until passage of the Indian Citizenship Act of 1924.

19 Literacy tests were later used as a tool to restrict immigration as well (LeMay and Barkan, *US Immigration and Naturalization Laws and Issues*, xxxiii).

20 Claire Smearman, "Second Wives Club: Mapping the Impact of Polygamy in US Immigration Law," *Berkeley Journal of International Law* 27, no. 2 (2009): 382.

21 Ibid., 394.

22 Act of March 3, 1875 (Page Law), Sect. 141, 18 Stat. 477 §1.

23 President Ulysses S. Grant, for example, supported the Page Act as a means of protecting Chinese immigrant women (Smearman, "Second Wives Club," 13n74). Other supporters of restrictions hoped to protect the nation not just from the practice of slavery (female or otherwise) but also from the races of people ostensibly so feeble-minded and weak as to end up in such a condition (Abrams, "Polygamy," 658–59).

24 As Smearman and others such as legal scholar Sarah Barringer Gordon have pointed out, the late nineteenth-century ban on polygamous immigrants reflected Americans' anxieties not just about infiltration by foreigners bearing customs that would despoil civilized morals but also domestic pollution and corruption from within in the form of Mormon polygamy—a concurrent debate that gave force to fears about Chinese practices. Smearman rightly devotes a great deal of time to contextualizing the Page Act in terms of anti-Mormon sentiments. The effect of anti-Mormon debates about polygamy in helping to make the federal Constitution binding on states is the entire subject of Gordon's book. Yet what both fail to recognize is that the debate about Mormon polygamy itself was so charged because of the history of American political contests with other sometimes polygamous (and often militarily superior) groups: Muslim polities. Reviewing this history makes it clear that although the first ban on polygamy was overtly directed at Chinese immigrants, it was never not about Muslims.

25 The 1862 Coolie Trade Prohibition Act was passed not to prohibit trafficking in Chinese slaves to the US, as that was not a relevant issue, but to prohibit Americans from trafficking slaves between China and Cuba. On this history, see Abrams, "Polygamy," 668–69.

26 Most were the second wives of male Chinese immigrants. First wives generally stayed in China, managing homes. As Abrams points out, even for women paid for sex, the term "prostitute" did not translate Chinese practices well, as those who engaged in such activities were not stigmatized and marginalized in the same ways they were in the United States. Rather, "prostitutes" commonly married laborers and enjoyed a measure of respectability in Chinese society. See Abrams, "Polygamy," 653–57.

27 As Gordon demonstrates, antebellum Republicans intertwined their antipolygamy and antislavery stances, using them metonymically, as it was "far less controversial to condemn Mormon patriarchs in Congress than to condemn slaveowning patriarchs" (*The Mormon Question*, 55).

28 Nancy Cott, *Public Vows: A History of Marriage and the Nation* (Cambridge, MA: Harvard University Press, 2002), 11–21; Gordon, *The Mormon Question*, 66–68.

29 Cott, *Public Vows*, 10, 18–23.

30 Timothy Marr, *The Cultural Roots of American Islamicism* (Cambridge: Cambridge University Press, 2006), 20.

31 Ibid., 37.

32 Ibid., 39.

33 The spy narratives that dramatized the terror of a Muslim informant in Americans' midst were modeled on another of Montesquieu's influential works, *Persian Letters*, in which Persian travelers in France write of their adventures and learn of developments back home. The tale largely pivots on the revolt within the harem of one traveler while he is away—a revolt meant to reveal the decrepitude and despotism inherent in polygamy (ibid., 46).

34 Ibid., 37–54.

35 Ibid., 51.

36 So popular were these captivity narratives that the most frequently circulated tale was reprinted a dozen times between 1800 and 1828. The narratives were often also so graphic that they simultaneously allowed the (generally male) reader to indulge in illicit fantasy, picturing himself as the rapacious despot but then ultimately identifying with triumphant Christian morality and republicanism. For this reason, Marr describes the narratives not simply as morality tales but as "picaresque pornography" (ibid., 45) and concludes that the genre "sometimes embodied the very form of licentiousness it was designed to regulate" (46). Quoting David S. Reynolds, Marr notes that such narratives allowed for a kind of satire and commentary that most writers could otherwise engage in "only at the risk of the writer's reputation" (46).

37 Ibid., 54.

38 For antebellum theological arguments in support of (and against) slavery and racial differentiation, see Mark Noll, *The Civil War as a Theological Crisis* (Chapel Hill: University of North Carolina Press, 2015); Paul Harvey, "A Servant of Servants Shall He Be: The Construction of Race in American Religious Mythologies," in *Religion and the Creation of Race and Ethnicity: An Introduction*, ed. Craig Prentiss (New York: New York University Press, 2003), 13–27.

39 On the constitutive relationship between Christian freedom and racialized repression, including in slavery as practiced in the United States, see Sylvester Johnson, *African American Religions, 1500–2000: Colonialism, Democracy, and Freedom* (Cambridge: Cambridge University Press, 2015).

40 Marr, *Cultural Roots*, 135–83.

41 Cott, *Public Vows*, 113n5.

42 Smearman and Gordon note in passing the ways opponents of Mormon and Chinese polygamy depicted the practice as a form of Islamic-inspired slavery (see, for example, Gordon, *The Mormon Question*, 35, 37, 112, 174). Despite the ubiquity of such rhetoric, they skim over the anti-Islamic themes and concentrate, in Gordon's case, on exploring how Mormonism "was frequently opposed with tools that had been deployed against Catholicism" (ibid., 11). Meanwhile, Smearman acknowledges the anti-Muslim animus connected to late nineteenth-century

antipolygamy agitation, but she argues that it originated as a racist impulse in the 1870s rather than recognizing it as part and parcel of American political rhetoric since the nation's founding (Smearman, "Second Wives Club," 391).

43 See, for example, Sarah Gualtieri, *Between Arab and White: Race and Ethnicity in the Early Syrian American Diaspora* (Berkeley: University of California Press, 2009); Jennifer Snow, "The Civilization of White Men: The Race of the Hindu in *United States v. Bhagat Singh Thind*," in *Race, Nation, and Religion in the Americas*, ed. Henry Goldschmidt and Elizabeth McAlister (New York: Oxford University Press, 2004), 259–80.

44 Act of March 3, 1891 (Immigration Act of 1891), Ch. 551 § 1, 26 Stat. 1084.

45 Act of February 20, 1907 (Immigration Act of 1907), Ch. 1134 § 2, 34 Stat. 898, 899 (emphasis mine).

46 Quoted in Cott, *Public Vows*, 139.

47 Reynolds v. United States, 98 U.S. 145 (1879) at 164. On the implications of the *Reynolds* decision for religious practice disputes, see especially Gordon, *The Mormon Question*, 119–32.

48 Cott, *Public Vows*, 139.

49 Quoted in Smearman, "Second Wives Club," 396.

50 Act of February 5, 1917 (Immigration Act of 1917), Ch. 29, § 3, 39, Stat. 874, 875–76.

51 Gualtieri, *Between Arab and White*, 74–77.

52 Ibid.

53 Ibid., 46 and 45, respectively.

54 On changes in racialized images of Muslims, it is illuminating to compare Marr's *Cultural Roots of American Islamicism* with Melani McAlister, *Epic Encounters: Culture, Media, and US Interests in the Middle East Since 1945* (Berkeley: University of California Press, 2005).

55 See Immigration and Nationality Act of June 27, 1952, Ch 477. § 212(a)(11), 66 Stat. 163, 182 and Immigration Act of 1990, Public Law No. 101–649, 104 Stat. 4978, § 601 (a).

56 A Canadian Mormon woman was denied naturalization, for example, when eight years after she immigrated to the United States, her husband married a second wife; see Smearman, "Second Wives Club," 401.

57 In passing the act, Congress also enabled the president to use proclamations (or executive orders) as a means to suspend the entry of any immigrants or immigrant groups for as long as he or she deemed necessary for protecting US interests (1952 Immigration and Nationality Act, Public Law No. 82–414).

58 Smearman, "Second Wives Club," 397.

59 Harry S. Truman, "Veto of Bill to Revise the Laws Relating to Immigration, Naturalization, and Nationality," June 25, 1952, https://trumanlibrary.org/publicpapers/viewpapers.php?pid=2389.

60 Smearman, "Second Wives Club," 400–407, 416–17.

61 Department of Justice appeals for determining the legality of the various orders did not go directly from district courts to the Supreme Court, of course, but

passed through circuit courts first. In contrast to their March ruling, when judges at the Ninth Circuit Court of Appeals prevented the first travel ban restrictions from taking effect, they ruled in favor of the president pending further review in November and partly reinstated the third version of the travel ban. Miriam Jordan, "Appeals Court Partly Reinstates Trump's New Travel Ban," *New York Times*, November 13, 2017.

62 Trump, President of the United States, Et Al. v. Hawaii, Et. Al. 585 U.S.___ (2018).

63 *Trump v. Hawaii*, 18 (Sotomayor J. dissenting).

64 *Trump v. Hawaii*, 1–8 (Breyer J. dissenting).

65 Center for Constitutional Rights and the Rule of Law Clinic, Yale Law School, *Window Dressing the Muslim Ban: Reports of Waivers and Mass Denials from Yemeni-American Families Stuck in Limbo* (New York: Center for Constitutional Rights, 2018), cited in Breyer's dissent at page 8.

66 *Trump v. Hawaii*.

67 *Trump v. Hawaii*, 2 (Kennedy J. concurring).

68 *Trump v. Hawaii*, 12 (Sotomayor J. dissenting). The other ruling Sotomayor made reference to was that of Masterpiece Cakeshop, Ltd. v. Colorado Civil Rights Comm'n, 584 U.S. ___, ___ (2018).

69 On the Edmunds-Tucker Act, see Gordon, *The Mormon Question*, 180–220. Not until thirty-three years later, with the passage of the Nineteenth Amendment, would legislators confer the legal right to vote on all women in the United States. Acting on such rights in the face of opposition was another matter entirely.

70 On law enforcement concerns about white militants, see, for example, Daryl Johnson, *Right-Wing Extremism: Current Political and Economic Climate Fueling Resurgence in Radicalization and Recruitment* (Washington, DC: US Department of Homeland Security Office of Intelligence and Analysis, 2009). This report reflects only concerns about recent incidents of racial terrorism, of course. The practice of using violence to terrorize nonwhite populations in general and to discourage them from engaging in collective organizing or political activity in particular is a centuries-old one in the United States, as is the history of using such tactics against women.

71 Katie Benner and Caitlin Dickerson, "Sessions Says Domestic and Gang Violence Are Not Grounds for Asylum," *New York Times*, June 11, 2018.

PART III

Management

To this point this volume's keywords have largely been the key terms of First Amendment jurisprudence, but in this section, our organizing keywords are drawn less from the law than from the study of religion. In relation to our featured terms—"noise," "sexuality," "Indigenous," and "the secular"—certain individuals and communities have been marked for special treatment. Simultaneously, these same knots have furnished valuable resources for mobilization, resistance, and fugitive ways of being. With religion sometimes as component, sometimes as complement, and sometimes as analogy, these chapters show us how the law is used to socially differentiate and manage suspect practices, bodies, and peoples.

In Ashon Crawley's contribution, this redirection of focus is also accompanied by a shift in style and tone. Drawing on his experiences in the Pentecostal churches of his upbringing, Crawley considers the fraught dialectic between spontaneous religious expressions and the concerted management of the very same. Returning to Pentecostalism's rapturous beginnings in turn-of-the-century Los Angeles, Crawley shows how a new kind of Holy Spirit, one with new syntax that made new kinds of noise, found itself immediately pitted against middle-class norms, rules of civic order, and the law. In Crawley's read, there is a queering power to these holy vibrations, an embodied ethics that gestures toward and enacts new ways of being. Not incidentally, this troublesome new noise was also irreducibly black. A holy sigh against rationalism, a fermata in industrial time, Blackpentecostal noise has from its inception represented a problem, an unruliness that demands discipline. This discipline has been exerted by various modes: by city councils passing noise ordinances, by agents of state and nonstate violence, and by soaring real estate markets that dislodge communities. Religious street festivals and black churches are two sites where joyful rituals of radical embodiment occasionally kick up blowback. Gay nightclubs like Orlando's Pulse are another.

If noise is one problem requiring management, sex is another. In her chapter, Heather White considers the legal regulation of sex within and alongside the legal regulation of religion. Contrary to what one might expect, White argues, the secularization of American law has led to far greater regulation of sexual activity and sexuality. With the gradual enfolding of the sex acts of gays and lesbians into the set of privacy rights enjoyed by heterosexual couples, the Supreme Court fashioned a legal regime governing sexuality, "disestablished sexual pluralism," which is akin to the legal regime that governs free exercise jurisprudence. Meanwhile, shifting from religion as analogy to religion as trope, White pinpoints how, in the jurisprudence, a species of Protestant biblicism served to manufacture a putative Judeo-Christian "consensus" about "sodomy." With this tool in hand, White tracks a shift from a legal regime that sought to manage and control specific deviant sexual practices to one that sought to manage and control a certain class of sexual deviants. During the moral panic of the Lavender Scare, what had functioned as a weird kind of anatomical fetishism targeting discrete forms of illicit penetration became a project of policing a new kind of "homosexual pervert."

Colonized bodies represent another kind of problem-subject in need of management. Spencer Dew looks at the entanglements between religion, law, race, and colonialism expressed in the self-described Taino people of Puerto Rico. As with the condition of having been assigned a "race," being designated "Indigenous" can alternatively hem people in or open up room to maneuver. In ways that align with and echo free-exercise jurisprudence, indigeneity has emerged both internationally and domestically as a privileged legal category, one that has the capacity to afford certain kinds of people with special exemptions from generally applicable laws. Not always, however—indeed, rarely—is this legal courtesy afforded to colonial subjects. By claiming an identity that many self-identified Puerto Ricans regard as newly invented, the Taino spark a scene of intramural contestation that both trades in and disrupts age-old imperialist fantasies—fantasies codified in law and enforced by the police—about the presumed social coherence of black and brown colonial subjects. Whether this symbolic benefit will manifest materially, however, remains to be determined.

If Crawley, White, and Dew are concerned with the people and practices that demand special legal management, in his chapter, Jason Bivins is concerned with the management itself. His focus is the knotty cluster of the secular, secularism, and secularization. As a force, Bivins argues, the secular consistently regulates religion in a way that obscures some of American democracy's more unruly elements. After winding his way through a thicket of theoretical passes, Bivins posits a notion of "legal secularism." According to him, this articulation of the secular is characterized by prominent if slippery presumptions about the space, sincerity, and inviolability of religion. Legal secularism presumes spheres to be separable and ideas to be detachable from the practical contexts that animate them. As a concept, as a political paradigm, Bivins's secular is trapped by its own contradictions. Much in the way that the secular delineates religion as an object while dubiously asserting that what it is doing is leaving that object alone, the secular creates a field of persons and imperatives that seethes with the very contradictions and tensions it promised to resolve.

8

Noise

ASHON CRAWLEY

We're talking about the emergence of a culture which is
largely a secret culture, a culture which has developed a lin-
guistic code in which public speech can hide two meanings.
If you're not a part of the culture, you can't hear. It's noise.
—Cedric Robinson[1]

I like a good noisy church. Having been born into and brought up in
a church—both building and congregation—that made lots of sound,
sound is how I came to understand the concept of community and
notions of the sacred. The sound was noise. Cold weather'd descend
and we'd walk into the building from the harsh air to be greeted by the
loud creak of the dark wood door. It was an old edifice with the original fixtures, a former Swedenborgian church. Arriving on a cold night,
we'd hear the *shhhhhsh!* of steam from the banging, clanging heating
system that made sounds like water percolating. The sound was music.
There was Sister Morgan's playing of the Hammond B-3, or my brother
Ronald's playing, or even my own. There was Elder Wilkins's riffs on
the guitar—get down, get out. There were the songs Daddy or Mommy
would sing.

On Thursday nights, if we arrived between 8:00 and 8:30—and we
almost always did because my father was the assistant pastor there—
saints would be on their knees praying with fervor, with quietude. Faint
sounds just above a whisper, barely audible, but there. Such quiet would
at times erupt into loud handclaps and speaking in tongues and declarations of *yes!* or *have your way!* or myriad other phrases of praise
and adoration. Though not always loud, the noise was continuous and
always full of conviction and intensity. Bowed down, knees bent, the
sound of the door would announce more and more arrivals. My youth-

ful head, weary because praying for a half hour on your knees is boring to a kid, would look up to see who it was. The Jacksons. Sister Streeter. Aunt Joyce and my cousins. Deacon Waller. The Benjamins. Whoever. Praying would recommence. Those moments, those minutes, with all that noise electrified my thinking and produced for me a way to consider worlds.

* * *

Only five seconds but it begins with noise.[2] Only five seconds but it's hard to be sure if it's the sound of a congregation before service begins or the sound after it ends, or the sound of family and friends at the Fourth of July barbecue or a Thanksgiving gathering. It's the noise. Before the beat drops, before the music commences, we hear the chatter, the murmur, of conversation. Noise—the often discarded material—is not thought to have thought, is not thought to be thought. At least, not often enough. Yet Marvin Gaye's "Give It Up" is a testament to noise as habit, as life, as love, as hallowed. Throughout its performance, noise remains. The conversation, the *yeahs* and *heys*, the yelps, the ungatherable mishmash of howls and talk. There remains, throughout "Give It Up," an imprecision that is written into the performance, an imprecision because sounds heard come to the audience as noise. We do not know who says what. Or why. We do not know why. But this noise, noise that precedes the performance, remains throughout its duration.

Dance, smooth move. Hand, clap. Drum, rimshot. Tambourine, smack. Churchy organ. Bass, slap. Whooooo! Yeah, yeah! Wait, wait!

Of course it's not the only song or performance that has noise as its basis. Indeed, total elimination of noise is an impossibility. Noise *ain't nothin' but*[3] vibration, and it is there, all around and in and through us, as unending pulse and movement. But this song, this performance, is about the flourishing, the flowering, of noise. It is about the making apparent of the necessity of noise. As such, it is an ethical demand, an ethical statement, about how we might be and think *otherwise*.[4] Such noise is a sign, a sound, of love. Noise, a refusal of individuation. Gotta give the noise up in order to receive noise, noise as the basis for being with, being together, being social. Music, in its finality, is but one way to organize noise. And black music is all about that noise. Black music lets noise happen, organizes with and in and sometimes against it. Black music is the gathering of the dark matter of noise, gathering and, rather than dispensing with the materiality as inconsequence, using it in the cause of being moved.

Sylvester understood the noise too.[5] Like Gaye, Sylvester's song attempted liveness through the making apparent the sound of noise throughout the performance of his hit "Over and Over." The *yeahs* and yelps and *whooos* heard throughout could easily be the foundation for Gaye's "Give It Up." It is also the foundation for black sacred sounding, black sacred practice. And isn't that the point of noise? That it cannot be easily discarded because it can find residence in various formations; it can be integrated because of its imprecision. Noise gathers itself in "Over and Over" as sung conversation between friends—"Find yourself a friend!" they sing over and over again, repetitiously. The noise spreads out, the noise *jes' grew*, and finds itself a friend. The noise is the foundation, the vibration before abstraction, before being formed into sound, into music.

* * *

Black flesh is its own kind of noise. Black flesh is a condition, a condition that before abstraction is the material fact of existence. The flesh is the grounds for existence. What does that mean? It means that before being named by parents, before being gendered by doctors, before birth certificates and Social Security numbers, before birth rites of Christianity or Islam or other traditions, before being *placed*, we are flesh. And this is a fact that we should not seek to escape but to love, and love hard. Flesh, like noise, is difficult to capture and individuate, because indeterminacy is written into the way flesh behaves and finds relation in the world. Accepting the flesh, the fact of one's flesh, is to accept noise as that from which life grows and that to which life returns.

Yet not everyone is pleased with noise, with the noise of flesh. Noise has the capacity to antagonize and exposes us to the vibration, the movement, the sound that the Western theological and philosophical traditions seek to still. This theological and philosophical tradition has racialized and gendered and sexed and classed ideas about what is, who is and can be, normal. One arena where normality is regulated is that of the law. In courtrooms and legal proceedings, it is determined not only what normal looks like but also how normal sounds.

For example, the law attempts to manage noise through noise ordinance violations, legal measures used to control the sounding out, the vibrational agitation, of blackness. Gastón Espinosa writes, "In June 1906, the Los Angeles Ministerial Association attempted to silence [William] Seymour and the [Azusa Street] revival. It filed a complaint with the Los Angeles Police Department against the 'negro revival' (thus injecting race into the complaint) on the grounds that it was disturbing the peace."[6] The police were hailed to control the noise of blackness. Though they decided against the request because the area was zoned as industrial rather than residential, this spiritual sound of black communities, this agitational sound of blackness, was considered, and still is today, a public nuisance, a sound and vibration that needed to be remedied.

The Ministerial Association sought to control the noise of Blackpentecostals, an interracial, interclass group gathered at a makeshift church on Azusa Street in Los Angeles. Blackpentecostal is a portmanteau joining black and Pentecostal together in the service of thinking about the mutual interrelation and articulation of concepts I explore more fully in *Blackpentecostal Breath: The Aesthetics of Possibility.*[7] The way I theorize blackness and Pentecostal-ness is that they constitute each other through reciprocal relationality. Not a racial class distinction, blackness here follows Fred Moten's concept of blackness as "the resistance of the object."[8] This group was known for their interruptive noise. These "holy rollers" were first announced in a *Los Angeles Daily Times* article titled "Weird Babel of Tongues," April 18, 1906.[9] Within such an announcement was the calling of attention to the sounds, the noises, the strange utterances, these people were making. Religious historian David Daniels states, "The early Pentecostal syntax of sound disrupted the Protestant soundscape. Volume, a lot of it, was valued. Particular religious noise became acceptable as part of the early Pentecostal sound within the Pentecostal syntax."[10]

Within mainstream Protestantism, to be a proper spiritual subject was to be closed and quieted consistently, to be deeply reflective and meditative *in opposition* to noisy. Noise was imagined to be the antithesis of reflection and meditation. But here are the Blackpentecostals, making noise in the service of deep reflection and meditation. Here are the Blackpentecostals, refusing to cease in the practice of noise, but rather practicing the enunciation, elevation, and celebration of noise. Here are the Blackpentecostals, using noise as a way of life, as spiritual tradition.

But the violation of noise ordinances was in no way exclusive to the Blackpentecostals. Even church bells had a history of agitation. "[I]n urban centers (beginning at the close of the 19th century), it became increasingly common for neighbors to complain bitterly about the sound of nearby chimes," says Isaac Weiner.[11] He continues, "Even more surprising, many of them turned to the law for protection and achieved some degree of success. In several cases, bell ringing became subject to careful regulation by the state."[12] Yet there is a difference between what Weiner records and the noise I'm after. Unlike the noise of church bells, what I'm after are the noises produced by the flesh itself: the shouts, the foot shuffles, the clapping hands, the murmurs, the exhortations. Though different in terms of quality and the object of emergence—bells and flesh are different—it turns out that the law attempts to quell and quiet both similarly. And this because the juridical apparatus considers blackness to be antithetical to and the rejection of property. I will explore this below.

Hear, for example, the "friendly advice" given to Methodists that were purportedly in "error" because of worship—noisy worship—with nonwhites. Of black noise, John Fanning Watson, in 1819, stated, "At the black Bethel church in Philadelphia, it has been common to check the immoderate noise of the people"; of the performance of enthusiastic public worship generally, he said, "It began in Virginia, and as I have heard, among the blacks."[13] The noise was nuisance, the noise was racialized, the noise was in and of and from blackness. Watson described the emotions that produce this noise as "extravagant."

The quality of the noise that troubled both Watson and the LA Ministerial Alliance ninety years later was not just its volume but also its intensity of affect and emotion, and the capacity for such intensity to be transitive, to travel, to affect others unsuspected who perhaps may be engulfed and changed. The black noise was an event horizon, like a gravitational field, and Watson wrote of the "error" of being seduced by and participating in black noisemaking to warn white Methodists of the possibility of being engulfed, taken over, by the noise. It would be approaching something like a sonic *becoming black* through spiritual practice. In order to remain a quiet and reflective Protestant—and to maintain whiteness—one should be wary of the noise, of the funk, of blackness. What is it about noise that unmoors and destabilizes the project of white supremacist capitalist patriarchy? What is it about noise that forestalls the project of settler colonialism and antiblackness? It seems to me that the possibility of being moved is what so worries, what so threatens to abolish the coherence of being a subject of settler colonialism and antiblackness, a subject that is unbothered by the conditions of violence and displacement as a structuring logic of the world.

Sometimes the violation of a noise ordinance was because the worship noise took place late into the night. Some critiqued the noise by hinting that the congregants could never be effective during the workday. Unlike the noise of church bells, there was no regularity nor synchronicity to the noise of the flesh. Unlike the noise of church bells, one could not set a clock to such flesh noise; one would not know when it would erupt, interrupt, disrupt in the cause and practice of worship. Unlike the noise of church bells, the noise of this movement was not given to sequence and order but a flouting of them, an antagonistic threat against them—and thus also against the political economy that demanded such regularity of time and space. The noise itself was the announcement of a shifting, and a critique, of Newtonian time and space and the labor this logic necessitated.

The noise of the flesh is not the announcement of, but a disordering and breaking with, modern time and space. This is not a claim about race as a biogenic fact but about the racialization that is the process of European thought. Cedric Robinson in *Black Marxism: The Making of the Black Radical Tradition* explored the ways in which racialization as a process was produced by European hierarchies and distinctions, a way to produce classes of people that could then be dispossessed. Racialization as racial capitalism, Robinson informs us, found its perfection or perhaps supersession or, even more precisely, its codification in law, with its expression against blackness.[14]

Noise, according to this logic, is racialized. Mark Smith notes, "If colonial elites agreed on what produced sound, they also agreed on who produced noise. Native Americans, African Americans (slave and free), and the laboring classes generally were among the greatest noisemakers in colonial America . . . African Americans, like Native Americans and other nonliterate groups, 'defied the surveillance of writing' and made

sounds that threatened to fracture the acoustic world of English settlers."[15] Noise, then, obstructed subjectivity as colonial elites sought to
imagine it and normalize it; noise obstructed the process of becoming
man in *his* fullness. To remove the noise, on the other hand, is to remove the excess; the solution to the problem of settler colonial dispossession and antiblack racism is to remove the funk. And while Smith
writes about the colonial era in particular, what he notices has purchase
on how noise works—what it makes and why some fear it and others
desire it—today.

Those of us rendered Other are the noise, carry the noise, flesh as
noise. Such flesh—through manifest destinies, through invisible hands
of economies, through rational man against the bestial backward black,
brown, indigene, impoverished—has to be discarded, removed from the
land, and forced to labor for the production of peace and quiet. Such
stilling of noise, such stilling of vibration, is purportedly for peace, for
clear thinking, for rest. It is a curious impossibility, noise abatement,
curious but no less desired as a means to create normalcy.

And because Protestantism does not just belong to the Christians
but is fundamental to the way Americanness is performed—what Max
Weber describes as an ethic—the opposition of noise to normal subjectivity is generalized. We find a strain of the opposition to blackness, to
black noise, throughout practices of land displacement and resource real-
location. The remediation of noise would then be considered an achievement of urban development, of mixed-use planning, of the modern city.
There is a silence, a removal of a certain black noise, and that silence is
evidence of the colonial logics ongoing in our time. This silencing of the
noise of the flesh is different from the silencing of the noise of industry, a
kind of noise that is produced in the service of the political economy that
sounds out the exploitation of the worker class. It might be noisy but it is
not noise, at least in my theory of black noise. It is noisy but not in need
of remediation. It is a kind of noise that is allowed through the practice
of law and by the proliferation of policing violence.

* * *

Saint John Coltrane African Orthodox Church in San Francisco, California, has the love. The love of flesh, the love of noise. It is a church
founded to spread the "sound baptism" that would then lead to a way to

love all, to do justice in the world and strive against inequity. The sounds heard, the vibrations felt, by the congregants and those walking past its doors is the noise of the ethics, of blackness, of love. "The church ends every Sunday mass with a meditation on Coltrane's 'A Love Supreme' and provides food and clothing to the needy."[16] Such a deep inwardness is an outpouring, a movement toward others, an ecstasy communal. Yet like lots of churches in urban epicenters, the noise constitutes a nuisance, a nuisance to new inhabitants that again produces a confrontation between the law and the noise. And the church is being displaced.

The church was recently in the midst of a campaign because of the astronomical raising of rent from $1,600 to $4,000 a month. This is because land in the Bay Area is at a premium and noisy, which is to say, black, spaces like the Coltrane church are an obstruction to the development of the land for the purpose of profit. But the church's removal means more than just a displacement from a building. The newly landed gentrifying citizenry's desired displacement of the church would mean the shuttering of the sound, of the noise, of blackness, of the sound and noise of black social life as worship, meditation, deep inward reflection. To get rid of the noise is to uproot a way of life, to radically alter the vibratory pattern of sound, noise, music.

What happens when white supremacist capitalist patriarchy shows up as the renunciation of the flesh, renunciation of the noise? Gentrification, which is imprecise shorthand to talk about the processes of displacement of communities through the making private of public goods, services, and land, is a racialized, gendered, classed process. The movements and flows of gentrification are against noise, the pulse of black, brown, and Indigenous flesh. Under the guise of desiring a space for all, the noise of black flesh worshipping has become a problem, an obstruction, for land development and revitalization. The law is called on to account for and control black flesh in story after story.[17]

Yet there is an example produced by blackness, the process and practice of liberation of which the resonance of black music is but one example: find your noise, let it flower, flourish, be free. Such noise queers us, makes us otherwise, allows us the space of non-normativity. And isn't the point of the work many of us self-proclaimed queer political actors do is to queer desire itself? Should that not be in operation for the ways we think about our flesh and worship spaces? Shouldn't this give way to noise? Shouldn't noise be celebrated as beyond the edge of the horizon? But when we lose our noise, what happens? When we not only do not desire its varied intensities of vibrant signs of life at various frequencies but also seek its fundamental undoing, a noiselessness—an impossible achievement, though a desire nonetheless—what is the trajectory of the loss?

Saint John Coltrane African Orthodox Church performs Coltrane's "A Love Supreme" every Sunday as a meditation. They allow for anyone that plays an instrument, anyone that has flesh, to participate through sound, through choreography. Some tap dance as a meditation. Some play horns or drums or chimes as a meditation. This is all a noisy enterprise. To listen to the noise, to hear into it—feel the weight and texture of its vibration—is an ethical demand, a plea to recalibrate our ethics. The Coltrane church, like the Blackpentecostal church of my youth, offers a liberation praxis of noise, a liberation theology that has a preferential option for the noise, for the flesh. Noise—like the flesh, like blackness—is not a possession; it cannot be owned. Noise can only be performed, can only be practiced, as a way of life. Noise, then, can be repressed, silenced, only through violence, through violation. Noise cannot be possessed but can be felt—its vibration—experienced by all.

So we have to think about the raising of the rent from $1,600 to $4,000 as part of a colonialist tradition of violent unsettlement, uprooting, displacement. We have to think about the displacement of the church as part of a long, ongoing project attempting to remove the noise of blackness from communities. And we have to think about the noisy flesh of homeless persons living in San Francisco, roundly criticized as "riff raff,"[18] how their noise does not register as a suffering that needs to be alleviated. We cannot think, in other words, of these various desires for remediation apart from each other; they are part of the same historical and contemporary settler colonial, antiblack political economic project.

You will lose your noise, you will lose your church, you will lose your flesh.

* * *

What if one retreats into rather than away from noise?

> The mass movement is taking place every day in town, we're here, all caught up in it. So it's not like now, when one would have to sit down and make a conscious decision to say, "I'm going to do this." Rather, you were

carried by a movement something like that in America in the sixties, the black and other movements which had begun earlier with the bus boycotts, in Montgomery, Alabama.[19]

Sylvia Wynter offered that about her time in Jamaica in the 1940s, how one was not necessarily intentionally a part of a movement but was carried by its currents. I think of Blackpentecostal performance practice like that, the noise and the joy, the fervor and the fury; somehow it carries those near it, in it, and it spreads. Blackpentecostalism is about the withdrawal, the retreat, into noise. And since such withdrawal and retreat are made in the direction and service of the purported incoherent, the unordered, the disorderly, it is a call to consider the flesh and the concept of embodiment through an epistemological shock and shudder, a shudder and shaking away from the desedimentation of European Man. This mode of personhood, of enfleshed—otherwise-than-embodied—experience is fundamentally about being vulnerable and open and available to being *carried*.

The Blackpentecostal church services I miss are the ones driven by joy, the kind when, walking in the service, you say, "I love this kinda carrying on," the noise, the praise, the exuberance. It's an exuberance that isn't embarrassed about the noise, the fleshliness, the excess. We called that kinda carrying on "getting happy" and in that announcement is a liberatory possibility. That one can get happy, seize hold of it, because they *give* or outpour or release praise, breaks the frame and enclosure that produce the Western categorization of the possessive individual, the subject, the citizen, what Wynter calls the overrepresentation of Man, the coloniality of being/power/truth/freedom.[20] Wynter discusses the genre of human called Man, and such a genre, I argue, has a sonic resonance, a resonance that is supposed to enact quietude and exact silence over the flesh—a kind of sonic proprietary muffle.

And so one must open up to being carried, carried away, carried away to get happy in the way Wynter describes it. Such a making-open to being carried and carried away, such a making-open to being happy and *getting* happy, is the announcement of a different modality through which life and breath movement is given and given away.

* * *

What might we say about the law and its relation to noise, not just in terms of ordinances but in terms of a kind of inhabitation of the flesh that exceeds the juridical? Here, I want to consider noise and joy and joymaking as an instantiation of the *lawless freedom* that is previous to the juridical. Lawless freedom, Winfried Menninghaus tells us, takes us to the terrain of Kantian ideals for imagination and understanding.

> "All the richness of the imagination," Kant cautions in the Critique of Judgement, "in its lawless freedom produces nothing but nonsense." Nonsense, then, does not befall the imagination like a foreign pathogen; rather, it is the very law of imagination's own "lawlessness."[21]

And if Kantian, so then noise is also about imagination and its deregulated, anoriginal—without origin—refusal to and of regulation. Perhaps the noise of Blackpentecostal joy and of the queerness to come helps us to consider a critique of the project of modernity, its dispensing with the flesh in the cause of understanding, which is another way to say modernity's fetishizing of binary logics of body from mind and the privileging of mind through the renunciation of an anoriginal fleshliness. How does the law, against lawless freedom, practice renunciation of flesh, which is also a dispensing with the noisiness of worlds?

Cheryl Harris talks about whiteness as property through the juridical apparatus.

> The racialization of identity and the racial subordination of Blacks and Native Americans provided the ideological basis for slavery and conquest. Although the systems of oppression of Blacks and Native Americans differed in form—the former involving the seizure and appropriation of labor, the latter entailing the seizure and appropriation of land— undergirding both was a racialized conception of property implemented by force and ratified by law.[22]

Seizure. Whiteness is constructed through the racialization of the Other and, after such racialization, the seizure, the theft, the taking of land and flesh in the proliferation of property as refused relation. But we might also say that whiteness as racial construct is *inaugurated* through the dual relations to land and flesh as available for seizure, theft and taking, and is an epistemological difference and break with relation to land and flesh that imagines theft as the grounding of—or, more precisely, the very possibility for—nonrelation. Whiteness is an epistemological structure that creates the concepts of likeness, kind, species through the religious, the juridical, the racial. Whiteness produces the occasion for the creation of these concepts only insofar as it wants to dispense with those that would inhabit their underside.

Harris asserts, "[t]he origins of property rights in the United States are rooted in racial domination." She continues,

> The hyper-exploitation of Black labor was accomplished by treating Black people themselves as objects of property. Race and property were thus conflated by establishing a form of property contingent on race—only Blacks were subjugated as slaves and treated as property. Similarly, the conquest, removal, and extermination of Native American life and culture were ratified by conferring and acknowledging the property rights of whites in Native American land. Only white possession and occupation of land was validated and therefore privileged as a basis for property rights. These distinct forms of exploitation each contributed in varying ways to the construction of whiteness as property.[23]

White possession and occupation of land and white theft of flesh pressed into servility (though the project of servility remains incomplete and impossible) are what *make* whiteness. Whiteness is an enclosure that makes itself through articulating its nonrelation to worlds. This possession and occupation necessarily has sonic resonances. Noise is what whiteness would come to create in order to dispense with it, noise is what whiteness announces in order to remediate it. But noise is a kind of lawless freedom, a refusal of the enclosure that is the basis for whiteness as seizure of land and flesh. Noise is the ephemera that is constantly made. Such noise is that which constantly escapes the logics of private property and, thus, whiteness. It is the unproprietary vibration that is the foundation and possibility for creaturely existence.

Noise names a category of stealth and escape: things—matter—can slip through cracks and loopholes and cramped spaces. As such, noise is the reminder to whiteness that ceaseless, unending, unrelenting resistance exists previous to the situation of seizure. And as reminder, then also nuisance. And as nuisance, then also the violence against it. It makes sense, in other words, that noise is against the law and codified in law as in need of remediation. It makes sense that noise is produced as a racial category that needs containment, enclosure, seizure. Whiteness attempts property relations by the removal of flesh from land, by the theft of flesh forced to work, by the desired tranquility and stillness of a noiseless world. I am not primarily talking about noise of white people versus noise of black people, though noise of black people becomes the enfleshment of the general worry about noise. To attend to noise is to attend to racialization. To *tend to* noise and to cultivate it as a practice, to think with noise, to allow noise to be, is to critically engage and practice a critique of modern racialization and its violence.

* * *

I like a good noisy church. And sometimes, that church is a nightclub. A space of gathering, a space of intellectual practice, against the imposition of normative ways to be human. A place of movement and restive refuge against the imposition of a violent world. Some religionists tell us we queer and trans* identified people are sinful, are shameful. This would be true, this concept of sinfulness, of even the place where I discovered the love and necessity of noise, that former Swedenborgian church. So we find other places, other sanctuaries. So we gather together in the cause of noise, to find our noise against the religious, cultural demand for noise being lost. The noise of hands held freely underground, outta the way, off and to the side. The noise of sweat and flesh gyrating and pulsating to the music. The noise of flirtations and hesitancies and desires held, desires felt, desires consummated.

Of course, I am thinking of Pulse nightclub in Orlando, the violence that infused the encounter, the violence that produced a demand for the silencing of queer potentiality, queer noise. Pulse was a gay bar and dance club, and on June 12, 2016, forty-nine people were murdered and fifty-eight people injured by Omar Mateen. The violence was a demand not dissimilar to desires for noise remediation, for the settler colonial logic of displacement. Pulse nightclub was a queer refuge, a space of inhabitation, a location wherein the noise of working-class queer of-color folks could gather, feel the weight and texture of the sounds of song, and move with and in and through such music.

The way I think about black spiritual noise helps me understand other histories of noise and ways other communities have and make noise as vibration, as a modality for celebrating their flesh. Celebrating flesh against settler colonialism and dispossession. It is important to note that the violence at Pulse took place on Latinx night, that the names of victims present a mosaic of peoples, many of whom were Puerto Rican. The violence they encountered is part of the history of settler colonialism. And the violence of that encounter, June 12, 2016, causes me to think about other sanctuaries that have ceased to exist: Chi Chiz, No Parking, Secret Lounge, Escuelita.[24] Lounges and bars and nightclubs displaced because of rising costs of living and increased police presence because of purported needs for safety from the gay bourgeoisie. Where can the noise be felt, heard, for queers of color? We have to think about the violent encounter at Pulse as part of a trajectory of displacement, a trajectory of violence.

Displacement, like noise late into the night, is also about the political economy, about labor and exploitation:

> This urban speculative economy is cleared through the destruction of the very communities, Black and Brown, that have historically known how to resist and survive the violence of capitalism by creating projects for collective survival and self-determination (from the original quilombos, to the underground railroad, to the Black Panthers' and Young Lords' survival programs).[25]

What we find, in other words, is that the noisemaking—living into the fact of the noise—is an antidote to the foundations of our modern political economy and its current neoliberal iteration. Noise is meditation, meditation against violation and violence. Noise is an ethics of otherwise possibilities, another modality, otherwise verve and vibration. Noise is the plural event, always more than itself. Noise, the plural event of hidden and secret gathering, the plural event of hidden and secret sociality—a sociality given through sounding out, sounding out while hiding itself.

NOTES

1 Majyck MJR, *Retracing Black Radicalism With Dr. Cedric J. Robinson(segment4)*, YouTube, accessed May 2, 2018, www.youtube.com/watch?v=kF5abUP1PDM.

2 kriptking, *"Got to Give It Up"—Marvin Gaye*, YouTube accessed May 2, 2018, www.youtube.com/watch?v=fp7Q1OAzITM.

3 Ashon Crawley, "Otherwise Movements," *New Inquiry* (blog), January 19, 2015, https://thenewinquiry.com.

4 Ashon Crawley, "Otherwise, Ferguson," *Interfictions Online*, November 2014, http://interfictions.com.

5 Simon Ter Hart, *Sylvester Over and Over*, YouTube, accessed May 2, 2018, www.youtube.com/watch?v=nvopeny62q4.

6 Gastón Espinosa, *William J. Seymour and the Origins of Global Pentecostalism: A Biography and Documentary History* (Durham, NC: Duke University Press, 2014), 66.

7 Ashon Crawley, *Blackpentecostal Breath: The Aesthetics of Possibility* (New York: Fordham University Press, 2016).

8 Fred Moten, *In the Break: The Aesthetics of the Black Radical Tradition* (Minneapolis: University of Minnesota Press, 2003).

9 "Weird Babel of Tongues: New Sect of Fanatics Is Breaking Loose; Wild Scene Last Night on Azusa Street; Gurgle of Wordless Talk by a Sister," editorial, *Los Angeles Daily Times (1886–1922)*, April 18, 1906.

10 David D. Daniels, "'Gotta Moan Sometime': A Sonic Exploration of Earwitnesses to Early Pentecostal Sound in North America," *Pneuma* 30, no. 1 (2008): 12.

11 Isaac Weiner, *Religion Out Loud: Religious Sound, Public Space, and American Pluralism* (New York: New York University Press, 2013), 20.

12 Ibid., 20.

13 John Fanning Watson, *Methodist Error, or, Friendly, Christian Advice, to Those Methodists, Who Indulge in Extravagant Emotions and Bodily Exercises* (Trenton, NJ: D. and E. Fenton, 1819), 22, 27.

14 Cedric J. Robinson, *Black Marxism: The Making of the Black Radical Tradition*, 2nd ed. (Chapel Hill: University of North Carolina Press, 2000).

15 Mark M. Smith, *Listening to Nineteenth-Century America*, illustrated ed. (Chapel Hill: University of North Carolina Press, 2001), 10.

16 Cy Musiker, "Little Hope for Saving Coltrane Church, Last Vestige of SF Jazz District," *KQED* (blog), February 17, 2016, www.kqed.org.

17 "United Pentecostal Church | 51 Mich. App. 323 (1974) | Happ3231332 | Leagle. Com," www.leagle.com; "Raleigh Church Cited for Noise after Years of Complaints," May 27, 2012, www.wral.com; "SC Church's Joyful Noise Too Much, Neighbors Say," www.thestate.com; Cheryl Hurd, "West Oakland Churches Respond to Noise Complaints," www.nbcbayarea.com; Sam Levin, "OPD Responds to Noise Complaints by White Man against Black Drummers at Lake Merritt, Sparks Concerns about Racial Profiling," www.eastbayexpress.com.

18 Justin Keller, "Open Letter to SF Mayor Ed Lee and Greg Suhr (Police Chief)," February 15, 2016, http://justink.svbtle.com/open-letter-to-mayor-ed-lee-and-greg-suhr-police-chief.

19 David Scott, "The Re-Enchantment of Humanism: An Interview with Sylvia Wynter," *Small Axe* 8 (September 2000): 126.

20 Sylvia Wynter, "Unsettling the Coloniality of Being/Power/Truth/Freedom: Towards the Human, after Man, Its Overrepresentation—an Argument," *CR: The New Centennial Review* 3, no. 3 (2003): 257–337.

21 Winfried Menninghaus, *In Praise of Nonsense: Kant and Bluebeard* (Stanford, CA: Stanford University Press, 1999), 1.

22 Cheryl I. Harris, "Whiteness as Property," *Harvard Law Review* 106, no. 8 (1993): 1715.

23 Ibid., 1716.

24 Duncan Osborne, "Gay Bar Calls It Quits, Saying It Was 'Targeted,'" *Villager* 80, no. 30 (December 23, 2010), http://thevillager.com; Michael J. Feeney, "Pioneering Washington Heights Gay Bar 'No Parking' Closes," April 15, 2014, www.nydailynews.com; Nathan James, "NYC's Secret Lounge Closes," March 25, 2014, http://gbmnews.com; "RIP Latin LGBT Dance Club Escuelita," March 2, 2016, www.papermag.com.

25 El Kilombo, "The Beginning of The End? Or, The End of The Beginning?," September 22, 2015, www.elkilombo.org.

9

Sexuality

HEATHER R. WHITE

For much of the 2010s, the defining legal question about sexuality and religion boiled down to gays and Christians fighting over cake. It began in 2012, when two men approached their local Lakewood, Colorado, baker to purchase a wedding cake. He refused on the grounds that his Christian faith opposed same-sex marriage. The couple sued. The Colorado Civil Rights Commission issued an injunction against the baker, citing him for a civil rights violation. The baker appealed. *Masterpiece Cakeshop v. Colorado* continued up through the court system to the US Supreme Court, gathering heightened significance with every step. As conservative pundit Dan McLaughlin interpreted this case for the *Federalist*, the central question was no less than "Can gays and Christians co-exist in America?"[1] This was not just about cake; it was about freedom. More specifically, the question was whether the American Constitution could protect both gay civil rights and the freedom of religion. Or did the law have to choose a side? Almost one hundred public interest groups filed amicus briefs, with arguments evenly split between the baker and the gay couple.

Amid these stark divisions, the much-awaited ruling of June 4, 2018, was something of a puzzle. On its face, it was a win for the baker—the court dismissed the penalty issued by the Colorado Civil Rights Commission. However, journalists and commentators of various ideological stripes quickly pointed out that the opinion also maintained adamant support for same-sex marriage and gay civil rights. Rather than a decisive precedent, the majority offered a narrow, procedural ruling. It chided the Colorado Civil Rights Commission for using disrespectful language about the baker's religious beliefs, and it closed with a plea for civility: "These disputes must be resolved with tolerance, without undue disrespect to sincere religious beliefs and without subjecting gay persons to indignities when they seek goods and services in an open market."[2] In content and tone, these words positioned the court as a neutral mediator between contending forces. And yet, in opting to duck the substantive legal issues, the justices may well have secured only one guarantee: this battle will appear in court again. As conservative Christians gird themselves to further defend religious freedom, LGBTQ advocates worry that this freedom might yield the license to deny things more consequential than cake.

The language of this ruling presents the Supreme Court—and the American legal system broadly—as a disinterested arbitrator between intractably conflicted parties. More than one pundit explained these deep divisions as an ancient inheritance rooted in traditional religious taboos against sex. "The cultural prohibition on homosexuality stretches back thousands of years, to the Law of Moses," argued *Washington Post* blogger Megan McArdle; "the relegation of women to separate spheres goes back so far that we cannot date it."[3] McArdle's point was about history: these long religious legacies unavoidably collide with modern feminist and queer struggles for gender and sexual rights. In this zero-sum bid for freedom, the task of allocating constitutional protections would inevitably short one of the contending parties.

This chapter argues for a different way of seeing the relationships among sexuality, religion, and law. The law is not a neutral mediator. Constitutional rights are not fixed quantities. Religion and sexuality are neither natural enemies nor singular and timeless entities. Rather than picking a side in the battle between religious and sexual freedom, we should first investigate how they came to be defined as sides. That is to say, the question that this chapter seeks to answer is not "How should the law choose between sexual and religious freedoms?" A more fundamental curiosity, and the driving inquiry for this chapter, is how this oppositional relationship between religion and sexuality came to be a defining aspect of modern law and politics.

Rethinking Sexuality and Religion

Examining the assumed relationship of opposition begins with rethinking what counts as sexuality and religion. Not only conservative Christians but also many everyday Americans, attribute the emergence of the modern sexual system to secularization, the perceived decline of religion in American culture. However, this declension narrative obscures a more complex history. Feminist and queer lifestyles stand in as ready symbols of sexual change. And yet, the traditional family as imagined by conservatives is no less a twentieth-century innovation. Breadwinner husband, stay-at-home wife, and their children: this household of only two generations is searchingly rare in the history of human societies. And despite its status as a (white, middle-class) civilizational norm, it has continued to be a demographic anomaly among American families. Through the twentieth century, this domestic ideal emerged alongside a new sexual ideology: heterosexual pleasure and happiness, the key to healthy marriage. The term "heterosexuality," along with "homosexuality," was coined in the late nineteenth century by medical specialists in the fledgling field of psychiatry. These terms encapsulated innovative ways of identifying and classifying human sexual behavior, with transformational consequences for the cultural meanings of marriage. That same-sex couples may now be legally married is one obvious sign of these changes. More far-reaching, however, is the reinvention of modern marriage around heterosexuality, with erotic attraction and sexual compatibly at the heart of marital happiness and stability. This innovation, moreover, has fit perfectly with traditionalist visions of marriage and family. In short, the rise of traditional "family values" politics is perhaps the most foundational—although least obvious—expression of sexual change in modern American culture.[4]

The courtroom has been an important arena for debating these changing sexual norms. At the same time, the legal discourses largely echo the cultural narratives of secularization. The story that lawyers and judges tell is about the unraveling of moral regulation from the fabric of the law to make the law neutral—secular—while freeing sex to be a matter of private choice. The notion that public law should not infringe on private morality—or perhaps more accurately, private *immorality*—was slowly and unevenly established by a series of landmark Supreme Court decisions, which reviewed and overturned a body of morals legislation that had codified and enforced Anglo-Protestant norms for sex and marriage.[5] While some of these laws had roots that extended to the nation's founding, many of them were relatively new, originating in morals reforms of the nineteenth and early twentieth centuries. This succession of overturned morals laws, when viewed as a linked trend, conveys a distinct trajectory of secularization. By the early twenty-first century, these rights formally included the right to purchase and view obscene materials; the right to access contraception regardless of marital status; the right to terminate a pregnancy before twenty-one weeks; the right to engage in nonmarital, interracial, and/or same-gender sex; and the right to marry the partner of one's choice, regardless of race or gender.[6] The terms in which these rights have been won, moreover, echo and amplify the secularization story. Religion and sex have vied against each other with very clear stakes: less religion in the law equates to more sexual freedom.

A closer look at these cases, however, shows that something called religion or morality never operated in isolation. It had to be distinguished and disentangled from other social forces of regulation. The ruling in *Eisenstadt v. Baird* (1972), a textbook example of the secularizing logic, illustrates these obscured entanglements. This case overturned a Massachusetts law that barred unmarried persons from accessing medical forms of contraception. Moral regulation was an overt rationale for the law: by banning single people from accessing contraception, the law deterred immoral, nonmarital sex. The justices refuted this rationale: "Such a view of morality is not only the very mirror image of sensible legislation; we consider that it conflicts with fundamental human rights. In the absence of demonstrated harm, we hold it is beyond the competency of the state."[7] The ruling sidestepped the question of whether morality was always an illegitimate concern of law, and it maintained that protecting health and preventing harm were indeed rightful interests for the law. The ruling established that a particular kind of immoral sex—nonmarital, heterosexual, and otherwise procreative intercourse— did not pose any form of public harm that justified a ban on contraception. To define this issue as one of *private* morality, the justices had to unthread the moral rationale from bodily health and social harm. Thus quarantined, this particular form of immorality could be entrusted to the consciences of its sexual subjects, namely, unmarried heterosexual couples. Their private affairs were none of the law's business.

This process of isolating morality or religion as "one great central mechanism destined to say no" relies on assumptions about power and control that philosopher Michel Foucault calls the "repressive hy-

pothesis."[8] While religion—however one might recognize and identify it—may well be a source of legal prohibition, Foucault and others
would remind us that regulation—moral or otherwise—is also embedded within complex structures of bodily management. This reminder
about the complexity of what Foucault calls "biopower" is not merely a
theoretical point.[9] The twentieth century brought a whole nest of new
mechanisms for managing the sexual body: massive technological innovations, successive new media for communication and connection,
an array of federal programs—such as welfare and criminal justice—
for managing populations, medical procedures for diagnosing physical
and mental health, scientific methods for aggregating data and setting
standards of normalcy, and a consumer market filled with endless goods
for self-improvement. This is certainly not an exhaustive list of the innovative modern techniques for managing and regulating twentieth- and
twenty-first-century sexual bodies. Amid these changes, the focus on
religion as the preeminent force of sexual control obscures important
modern transformations in both sexuality and religion.[10]

A complete picture of these transformations is outside the scope of
this chapter; we shall follow one thread in these developments by focusing on the strange career of sodomy laws. Tracing twentieth-century
developments in sodomy laws shows that the imagined past of the religious regulation of sex does not actually reflect the historical facts. The
imagined past is of ancient taboos dating from the Law of Moses, which
have slowly come under challenge in a modern secular age of sexual
freedom. What we find instead is a whole series of modern transformations that have generated new notions of religious tradition as well as
consolidated new sexual and gender identities. The Judeo-Christian tradition of homosexual regulation, no less than gay identity, is a twentieth-
century innovation.

Christian Sodomy

"That utterly confused category": this is Foucault's famed description
of sodomy.[11] The term did not originate in the Law of Moses, nor does
it appear in either the Hebrew or Greek scriptures. It was coined in
the ninth century as a shorthand reference to the "sin of Sodom." The
author of this neologism, according to religion scholar Mark Jordan,

was Benedictine reformer Peter Damian, who added a Greek ending to the proper noun "Sodom." Thus, *sodomia* or "sodomy."[12] While the word itself was a medieval invention, references to the "sin of Sodom" may be found in various parts of the Hebrew Bible and the Greek New Testament. The lengthiest and most detailed of these references appears in the book of Genesis, which recounts a series of events that take place as God decides to destroy the ancient city of Sodom. The reason for this destruction: the city's sin. The Genesis account is circumspect about the nature of this wickedness. Various interpreters focus on one part of the story, which euphemistically alludes to a threat of gang rape by the men of the city upon two angels, visitors arrived to warn the city's one righteous resident, Lot, about the imminent destruction. But the story has no shortage of loathsome wickedness, and even Lot and his family come out tarnished. Lot's wife turns into a pillar of salt when she looks back at the city as the family flees, and his daughters subsequently orchestrate an incestuous seduction of their father in order to "preserve his seed" after the death of their mother.[13] Other scriptural allusions to Sodom do not help pinpoint the nature of its sin. Ezekiel 16:49–50 (KJV) identifies multiple forms of wickedness: "pride, fullness of bread, a consequent abundance of idleness, neglect of the poor and needy, haughtiness, and the commission of abomination before God."[14]

The instability of Sodom's sin lent elasticity to this parable of divine retribution. In the discourses of medieval and early modern European Christians, this pliability made sodomy talk useful as a multipurpose polemic against perceived enemies of the faith. This slander encompassed the homoerotic, but it was never a singular target. "Sodomy" and "sodomites" operated as sexual slander that succinctly linked sybaritic ritualism and bodily monstrosity. Its targets included idolatrous papists, infidel Moors, pagan American Indians, and barbaric Hindus, among others.[15] These forms of sexual slander conflated bodily, ritual, and racialized alterity with sodomy as the expression of an anti-Christian idolatry.

The definitions for "sodomy" in Anglo-American law were similarly elastic. English statutes deliberately refrained from definition; as sixteenth-century jurist Sir William Blackstone influentially noted, the "infamous crime against nature" was "a crime not fit to be named."[16] Case law specified sodomy to be anal intercourse by a man; the penetrated body might be that of a man, woman, child, or beast. Women could commit sodomy only by "lying with a beast."[17] Legal scholar William Eskridge argues that sodomy laws, together with laws prohibiting fornication, adultery, and seduction, constituted the disciplinary norms of Anglo-American legal regulations against sexuality: "Adultery and fornication laws insisted that sexual activities occur only within marriage; sodomy and seduction laws insisted that the sex be procreative."[18] Sodomy, as a legal prohibition, included but was not limited to same-sex behavior. When focused on unnatural and criminal sex, it could be interpreted to include even the relations between wife and husband.

The vagueness of sodomy laws also rendered them malleable to new perceptions of the natural and the unnatural. Changes to these laws not only illustrate the elasticity of sodomy offenses; they also exhibit the naturalizing reasoning by which justices and lawyers imputed timelessness to innovative legal interpretations.[19] In the United States, in the late nineteenth and early twentieth centuries, judges and legislators began to broaden the interpretation of sodomy law to include oral sex as well as anal penetration.[20] By the 1920s, regulating oral sex had become a widely accepted application of the law, but for nearly two decades prior, justices had to provide careful accounts of their legal reasoning. A 1914 case from Nevada typified the naturalizing logic with which justices decided cases involving oral sex:

> In the order of nature the nourishment of the human body is accomplished by the operation of the alimentary canal, beginning with the mouth and ending with the rectum. In this process food enters the first opening, the mouth, and residuum and waste are discharged through the nether opening of the rectum. The natural functions of the organs for the reproduction of the species are entirely different from those of the nutritive system. It is self-evident that the use of either opening of the alimentary canal for the purpose of sexual copulation is against the natural design of the human body. In other words, it is an offense against nature. There can be no difference in reason whether such an unnatural coition takes place in the mouth or in the fundament—at one end of the alimentary canal or the other. The moral filthiness and iniquity against which the statute is aimed is the same in both cases.[21]

The court concluded that it was reasonable to determine that the "crime against nature" should be defined more broadly as "all unnatural acts of carnal copulation between a man with a man or a man with a woman, where a penetration was effected into any opening of the body other than those provided by nature for the reproduction of the species." The definitional authorities cited—and challenged—in this ruling were legal commentaries, which at this time all uniformly insisted that a penetration of the mouth was not sodomy.[22] The judge resorted to an anatomical logic, which expanded the commonplace understanding of "against nature" to include the mouth as well as the anus.

The Nevada court defined "sodomy" with a reasoning that focused entirely on body parts and contact points. It mattered not if the other involved party in this crime was a man, a woman, a child, or a beast. Nor did it matter if the act was consensual or forced.[23] This was typical of contending opinions on whether "sodomy by the mouth" was in fact sodomy, which worked through a logic of body parts that only incidentally addressed the gender of the bodies involved. Notably missing from this anatomical logic is an organizing grid of same and other gender. Heterosexuality and homosexuality were simply absent as categories that might somehow mark the boundaries between natural and unnatural.

Also absent in the courts' reasoning: overt reference to anything recognizably religious. There is no easy way to interpret this absence; the silence contrasts markedly with contemporaneous nineteenth-century and early twentieth-century debates about the religious intent of laws addressing other kinds of moral offenses, such as Sabbath breaking and blasphemy. Both supporters and critics of these laws acknowledged their anchors in Christian teachings, even as legal authorities began to justify them legally on secular grounds. However, no similar debates were taking place about sodomy laws. Quite possibly, sodomy laws appeared effectively neutral rather than overtly sectarian, which is to say that their Christian and Anglo-Protestant influences remained culturally invisible.[24] The absence of overt reference to religion at the turn of the twentieth century also contrasts with a form of reasoning that became increasingly common through the middle and end of the century. An emerging appeal to a Judeo-Christian tradition worked to justify and naturalize further interpretive changes to American sodomy laws.

Judeo-Christian Homosexuality

The United States emerged from World War II as a global military leader with a new Judeo-Christian national identity. This new pluralist moniker reflected a measure of civic inclusion for American Jews in the wake of the Nazi Holocaust. Even more, it strategically represented America's global political brand during the rising Cold War with Russia, as politicians and social critics championed homegrown faith and freedom as cultural weapons against godless communism.[25] "Judeo-Christian" communicated a cultural heritage and shared moral tradition, which placed the ordered domestic lives of the traditional—heterosexual—family at the heart of American nationalism. It was in this context that homosexuality became a newly explicit focus of US law and policy. At this critical moment of expanding federal power, historian Margot Canaday argues, federal officials created "the straight state."[26] These new policies utilized psychoanalytic measurements for sexual health to determine who could enter the country, collect state benefits, serve in the military, and be eligible for government employment.[27] This convergence of tri-faith pluralism, psychoanalytic medicine, and federal power was remarkably innovative. And yet, as historian George Chauncy describes it, this new mix of sin, sickness, and crime looked like "the residue of an age-old, unchanged social antipathy toward homosexuality."[28]

Biblical narratives helped authorize and naturalize these new policies as the expression of ancient tradition. Lawmakers and public officials often invoked the destruction of Sodom and the perversity of the Roman Empire, referenced in the biblical accounts in Genesis 19 and Romans 1, respectively, to warn against civilizational ruin brought about by sexual permissiveness.[29] "The Biblical description of homosexuality as an 'abomination' has well stood the test of time," announced a Florida legislative committee in a 1964 brief that advocated for a statewide purge of homosexuals employed in public schools and in the civil service.[30] The laws and practices that targeted homosexuals, however, were not the remains of long-standing religious taboos. Legal historian William Eskridge shows how the purview of sodomy laws shifted over the course of the twentieth century. By 1961, Eskridge argues, sodomy was "a thoroughly homosexualized term."[31] Not only did sodomy laws and their enforcement more narrowly target same-sex behavior; they also expanded the kinds of physical contact that could be prosecuted. As a further component of the legal stew, nearly a third of US states, between 1935 and 1950, added nebulously defined "sexual psychopath" laws. Initially justified as a net for violent sex predators, the laws in practice resulted in broad targeting of gender and sexual behavior thought to result from psychological maladjustments.[32] These laws drew authority from religious censure but targeted homosexuality in uniquely modern ways.[33]

It was this web of "homosexualized" sodomy laws that came under scrutiny in *Bowers v. Hardwick*, a case that came before the US Supreme Court in 1986. The defendant in *Bowers* was a gay man who was arrested and charged in 1981 in Atlanta for an act of consensual oral sex that took place in his own bedroom. Georgia was one of twenty-five states that continued to outlaw sodomy, in resistance to a trend toward repeal that began quietly in 1962 with Illinois. The first handful of states to strike down sodomy laws did so by adopting the legal reforms of the Model Penal Code, a set of modern reforms developed by the American Law Institute in 1962. These efforts initially proceeded quietly, without significant political resistance and with the prominent support of mainline Protestant clergy. By the late 1970s, however, sodomy law repeal began to encounter significant pushback. It became increasingly visible and politicized in local political battles between gay rights activists and a coalescing movement for traditional moral values.[34] By the mid-1980s, advocates for sodomy law repeal looked to the courts as a solution to gridlocked legislative battles, and they watched hopefully as the lower courts ruled in favor of the defendant. Sponsored by the American Civil Liberties Union, the case seemed to offer a textbook example of how the law violated citizens' rights to privacy, a right with considerable precedent in recent rulings. The appeal of the case to the US Supreme Court promised the possibility that sodomy laws would be struck down in the remaining American states and territories where they were still in force.[35]

Gay rights advocates responded with dismay when the ruling, declared on June 30, 1986, upheld the enforcement of these laws to target same-sex behavior. The majority ruling, closely split 5–4, held that the US Constitution did not confer the "right to engage in homosexual sodomy."[36] This phrase—"homosexual sodomy"—provided the conceptual foundations for a ruling that thoroughly reinterpreted sodomy laws through a homosexual-heterosexual binary. With this "heterosexual reasoning," as legal scholar Janet E. Halley terms it, the court distinguished homosexuality from the kind of sexual behavior to which prior rulings granted the right to privacy.[37] Those earlier cases, argued Justice White for the majority, pertained to "family, marriage, and procreation" and bore no resemblance "to the right asserted in this case." This language made a coded distinction between heterosexual and homosexual sex. The rights granted to the former did not naturally extend to the latter.

In differentiating heterosexual from homosexual sex, the court also ignored the specific language of the Georgia sodomy law. The full text of the law prohibited "any sexual act involving the sex organs of one person and the mouth or anus of another." The law, in theory, prohibited oral or anal sex without respect to the sex of the participants. By asserting a difference between heterosexual and homosexual sex in general and heterosexual and homosexual practices of sodomy in particular, *Bowers* introduced a distinctively modern definition for sodomy laws. Legal scholar Janet Halley argues that the ruling "set the stage for a peculiar act/identity incoherence in American law." The reasoning in the case erased the ways that existing sodomy laws defined this sex act by anatomical contact, without regard for the gender of the partners. The *Bowers* ruling, in contrast, identified the sex act as homosexuality. This change also implicitly specified a class of people—homosexuals—as those whose behaviors were rightfully regulated by the law. As Halley interprets this shift in the law, sodomy became the "behavior that defines the class" of homosexuals.[38]

Religion was an important prop for this heterosexual reasoning. Justice White, in the majority opinion, argued that sodomy laws have "ancient roots." A concurring opinion by Justice Burger elaborated on these roots, explaining, "Homosexual conduct [has] been subject to state intervention throughout the history of Western civilization. Condemnation of these practices is firmly rooted in Judeo-Christian moral and ethical standards." As evidence, Burger cited passages from scripture as well as the writings of medieval Catholic theologian Saint Thomas Aquinas. With this religious foundation established, Burger warned that repealing sodomy laws would "cast aside millennia of moral teaching." The language of Judeo-Christian conveyed a notion of civilizational foundations rather than narrow sectarianism. Thus, the court established religion regulation as a rightful interest of the law, as religion scholars Janet Jakobsen and Ann Pellegrini note, "with the recasting of specific religious laws as general moral ones."[39]

This argument outraged the dissenting justices. Justice Harry Blackmun, writing for the dissent, singled out Burger's supporting opinion as a view that perhaps unwittingly undermined the majority ruling. "The legitimacy of secular legislation depends . . . on whether the State can advance some justification for its law beyond its conformity to religious doctrine." Burger's appeal to scripture and theology, Blackmun argued, showed that the only animating rationale for sodomy laws was religious intolerance.

However, in this back-and-forth over "Judeo-Christian moral standards," neither side of this argument addressed the veracity of these historical claims about religion and its long tradition of censoring something called "homosexual sodomy." Even if the justices disagreed about whether morality and religion had a rightful place in the law, it seemed that both sides believed in the historical fact of this moral tradition as a rightful foundation of the law under scrutiny. This oddly shared faith in the regulatory power of religion granted a patina of tradition to the modern reinvention of sodomy laws.

Conclusion

Homosexuality, as this chapter has demonstrated, is a remarkably recent category in American law. It became an overt subject of legal regulation during the middle decades of the twentieth century. However, the regulations enforced under this term did not announce themselves as innovations. Instead, legislatures and courts drew descriptive recourse to religion—in the form of a Judeo-Christian moral tradition—in ways that imputed timelessness to new forms of sexual regulation while also stabilizing and naturalizing new categorizations of human sexual behavior. In other words, the changes to sodomy laws demonstrate something that defies the linear progress toward secularization. What we find is not old moral punishments gradually loosened and religious taboos unraveled from the secular interests of law. What we do find is the consolidation of new forms of moral regulation even as courts and legislatures work to separate religion—as private morality—from the neutral and rational application of the law. In the case of sodomy, this trend paradoxically coincided with the instating of new religious influences—in the form of a seemingly neutral Judeo-Christian legal tradition—as sodomy laws increasingly targeted homosexuality as a category of regulation. One important consequence of these innovations was to establish heterosexuality as the form of sexuality granted the right to privacy even as homosexuality continued to be subject to public moral regulation.

In 2003, the US Supreme Court overturned *Bowers*, thus repealing the remaining laws against homosexual behavior in thirteen American states and colonies. Remarkably, a closer look at this history was an important part of the justices' reasoning in *Lawrence v. Texas*. In his majority opinion, Justice Anthony Kennedy repeatedly cited the historians' amicus curiae and its argument about "the historical contingency of the 'homosexual' as a suspect class."[40] He also subtly suggested that this historical reassessment "causes some doubt" about Justice Burger's sweeping narrative claims about Judeo-Christian condemnation.[41] So, the justices got their history straight. But did this altered view of the history change the justices' evaluations of religious sanctions against homosexuality? Kennedy's comments in another part of the same ruling suggest otherwise, as he notes that "condemnation [against homosexual conduct] has been shaped by religious beliefs, conceptions of right and acceptable behavior, and respect for the traditional family. For many persons these are not trivial concerns but profound and deep convictions accepted as ethical and moral principles to which they aspire and which thus determine the course of their lives."[42] The ancient religious tradition of antihomosexual prohibition does not need historical accuracy in order to count in the courts as genuine religion. What matters, ultimately, is interiorized sincerity—the "profound and deep conviction"—with which people believe it.

NOTES

1 Dan McLaughlin, "Can Gays and Christians Coexist in America? Part I," *Federalist*, June 8, 2018, http://thefederalist.com/2015/06/08/can-gays-and-christians-coexist-in-america-part-1.

2 Masterpiece Cakeshop, LTD v. Colorado Civil Rights Commission 16–111 (2017), 18, www.supremecourt.gov/opinions/17pdf/16–111diff2_e1pf.pdf.

3 Megan McArdle, "The Tension between Anti-Discrimination Laws and Freedom of Religion," *Washington Post*, June 6, 2018, www.washingtonpost.com.

4 On the history of twentieth-century marriage and family, see Rebecca L. Davis, *More Perfect Unions: The American Search for Marital Bliss* (Cambridge, MA: Harvard University Press, 2010); Robert O. Self, *All in the Family: The Realignment of American Democracy since the 1960s* (New York: Hill and Wang, 2014).

5 On the history of nineteenth-century and early twentieth-century Protestant moral regulation, see Steven Green, *The Second Disestablishment: Church and State in Nineteenth-Century America* (New York: Oxford University Press, 2010); Gaines M. Foster, *Moral Reconstruction: Christian Lobbyists and the Federal Legislation of Morality: 1865–1920* (Chapel Hill: University of North Carolina Press, 2002).

6 On contraception for married couples: Griswold v. Connecticut, 381 U.S. 479 (1965); contraception and right to privacy for nonmarital heterosexual sex: Eisenstadt v. Baird, 405 U.S. 438 (1972); obscenity and pornography: Stanley v. Georgia, 394 U.S. 557 (1969); abortion: Roe v. Wade, 410 U.S. 113 (1973); interracial nonmarital sex: McLaughlin v. Florida, 37 (1964); same-gender sex: Lawrence v. Texas, 539 U.S. 558 (2003); interracial marriage: Loving v. Virginia, 388 U.S. 1 (1967); same-gender marriage: Obergefell v. Hodges, 576 U.S. __ (2015).

7 Eisenstadt v. Baird, 405 U.S. 438 (1972), https://supreme.justia.com/cases/federal/us/405/438/case.html.

8 Michel Foucault, *The History of Sexuality, Volume I: An Introduction*, trans. Robert Hurley (New York: Pantheon, 1978), 12.

9 Ibid., 140.

10 See Gillian Frank, Bethany Moreton, and Heather Rachelle White, eds., *Devotions and Desires: Histories of Sexuality and Religion in the Twentieth-Century United States* (Chapel Hill: University of North Carolina Press, 2018).

11 Foucault, *History of Sexuality*, 101.

12 See Mark Jordan, *The Invention of Sodomy in Christian Theology* (Chicago: University of Chicago Press, 1997), 29, 43.

13 Genesis 19:1–36.

14 For a history of interpretation, see also Jordan, *Invention of Sodomy*, 30–32; Michael Carden, *Sodomy: A History of a Christian Biblical Myth* (New York: Routledge, 2004).

15 See, for example, Jonathan Goldberg, "Sodomy in the New World: Anthropologies Old and New," *Social Text* 29 (January 1, 1991): 46–56; H. G. Cocks, *Visions of Sodom: Religion, Homoerotic Desire, and the End of the World in England, C. 1550–1850* (Chicago: University of Chicago Press, 2017), 133–60; Tisa Wenger, *We Have a Religion: The 1920s Pueblo Indian Dance Controversy and American Religious Freedom* (Chapel Hill: University of North Carolina Press, 2009), 218–19; George Aaron Baron, "Sodomy," in *Encyclopedia of Religion and Ethics*, ed. James Hastings (Whitefish, MT: Kessinger Publishing, 1921), 672–74.

16 Sir William Blackstone, "Chapter 15: Of Offenses against the Person of Individuals," *Commentaries on the Laws of England (1765–1769), Book 4*, www.gutenberg.org.

17 William N. Eskridge Jr., *Dishonorable Passions: Sodomy Laws in America, 1861–2003* (London: Penguin Books, 2008), 2.

18 Ibid., 2.

19 For a similar analysis of changes to early modern British sodomy laws, see Cocks, *Visions of Sodom*, 106–32.

20 Ibid., 50–52.

21 *Ex parte Benites*, 37 Nev. 145, 140 Pac. 436 (1914), www.lexisnexis.com.

22 See, for example, Joel Prentiss Bishop, *Commentaries on the Criminal Law, Fourth Edition, Vol. II* (Boston: Little, Brown, 1968), 1174. For historical context on Bishop, see Stephen A. Siegel, "Joel Bishop's Orthodoxy," *Law and History Review* 13, no. 2 (Autumn 1995): 215–59.

23 According to commentaries cited above, "consent" simply meant that the other involved person could be tried as an accomplice, with the requirement that the act must have been witnessed by a third party. With this high burden of proof, consensual sodomy charges were rare.

24 On debates over Sabbath breaking and blasphemy and similar morals offenses, see Green, *The Second Disestablishment*.

25 On the history of "Judeo-Christian" as a category, see Kevin Schulz, *Tri-Faith America; How Catholics and Jews Held Postwar America to Its Protestant Promise* (New York: Oxford University Press, 2011); Tisa Wenger, "Freedom to Worship," in *The Four Freedoms: FDT's Legacy of Liberty for the Unites States and the World*, ed. Jeffrey Engle (New York: Oxford University Press, 2015), 73–110.

26 Margot Canaday, *The Straight State: Sexuality and Citizenship in Twentieth-Century America* (Princeton, NJ: Princeton University Press, 2009).

27 See David Johnson, *The Lavender Scare: The Cold War Persecution of Gays and Lesbians in the Federal Government* (Chicago: University of Chicago Press, 2004); Heather White, *Reforming Sodom: Protestants and the Rise of Gay Rights* (Chapel Hill: University of North Carolina Press, 2015).

28 George Chauncey, *Gay New York: Gender, Urban Culture, and the Makings of the Gay Male World, 1890–1940* (New York: Basic Books, 1994), 353; John D'Emilio, *Sexual Politics, Sexual Communities: The Making of a Homosexual Minority in the United States, 1940–1970* (Chicago: University of Chicago Press, 1983), 13, 147.

29 See, for example, Carleton Simon, "Homosexuals and Sex Crimes" (paper presented before the International Association of Chiefs of Police at Duluth, Minnesota, September 21–25, 1947), 1.

30 Report of the Florida Legislative Investigation Committee, *Homosexuality and Citizenship in Florida* (Tallahassee, 1964), 9, http://ufdc.ufl.edu/UF00004805/00001?m=hmh (November 14, 2014).

31 William Eskridge, *Dishonorable Passions: Sodomy Laws in America, 1891–2003* (New York: Viking Press, 2008), 75.

32 Ibid., 94–108.

33 For further analysis of religion and debates over sodomy laws, see White, *Reforming Sodom*, 61–3, 71–96.

34 Eskridge, *Dishonorable Passions*, 136–228.

35 Ibid., 229–37.

36 Bowers v. Hardwick, 478 U.S. 186 (1986).

37 Janet E. Halley, "Reasoning about Sodomy: Act and Identity in and after *Bowers v. Hardwick*," *Virginia Law Review* 79 (1993): 1721–80.

38 Ibid.

39 Janet Jakobsen and Ann Pellegrini, *Love the Sin: Sexual Regulation and the Limits of Religious Tolerance* (New York: New York University Press, 2003), 32.

40 See Kathryn Lofton's chapter, "Friend," in this volume.

41 Justice Kennedy, Opinion of the Court, Lawrence v. Texas, 539 U.S. 558 (2003), 11.

42 Ibid., 10.

10

Indigeneity

SPENCER DEW

On July 25, 2005, a group of Indigenous activists began a seventeen-day occupation of the Caguana Ceremonial Park in Utuado, Puerto Rico. The activists claimed this archaeological park as their ancestral sacred land, and they demanded that the US government recognize their legal rights to access and use the site. During the occupation, activists camped in one of the plazas and "peacefully performed their ceremonies," courting media attention.[1] They repeatedly voiced their arguments for legal rights, framing these rights in terms of the US Constitution, federal Indian policy, and the rights of Indigenous peoples under international law. Several of the activists undertook hunger strikes, emphasizing their understanding of what was at stake in this protest—the life or death of their culture.[2]

The Caguana Park, a government-run National Historic Landmark, is a popular tourist attraction and heritage site as well as an educational facility. It features the remains of multiple ritual ball courts dating from before the European conquest of the New World, along with stone monoliths from the same period and rocks carved with elaborate petroglyphs. The park also features a museum displaying various artifacts from archaeological excavations at that site and elsewhere. Additionally, a botanical garden cultivates representative native plants, with a focus on those used for food by the Indigenous people of Puerto Rico, the Taínos.

The Taínos were the native people met by Christopher Columbus in his "discovery" of the island of Puerto Rico.[3] Yet while the consensus of historians and anthropologists holds that the Taíno population of Puerto Rico was wiped out in the wake of European arrival, the occupiers of the Caguana site declared the opposite. Indeed, they used their occupation to publicly declare their identity as Taínos. Their action served to call attention to the existence of a contemporary Taíno population. "The Taíno people live," they insisted.[4] As a living Indigenous people, the occupiers held, contemporary Taínos deserved the legal rights accorded to other Indigenous peoples. In their protest, Taínos at Caguana demanded rights, for instance, to "the repatriation of ancestral remains and sacred objects and to the protection, preservation, conservation, administration, management and access to their sacred ceremonial and burial sites."[5]

Contemporary Taíno understand their identity as simultaneously racial and religious, an inheritance as well as a spiritual path that locates the individual within a community and ancestral lineage, orients the individual in history, and gives meaning and value to life.[6] The contemporary Taíno movement represents a religio-racial movement in the sense described by Judith Weisenfeld in her study of similar communities of African Americans in the early twentieth century. A religio-racial group is organized explicitly around an "understanding [of] individual and collective identity as constituted in the conjunction of religion and race."[7] Critics of the movement dismiss contemporary Taínos as advancing only a belief in indigeneity rather than representing an authentic Indigenous identity as descendants of the ancient Taínos. Yet even this debate, and the anxiety about the category of indigeneity at its core, reveals something of the deep entanglements of American religion, race, and law. For the examination of such entanglements, contemporary Taínos serve as a useful case study.

Contemporary Taínos mobilize their claims to Indigenous identity as legal claims. They seek recognition, by the state, of special rights, opportunities, and accommodations offered to Indigenous people under federal US law. This move simultaneously differentiates contemporary Taínos from other Puerto Ricans while calling attention to the tenuous legal location of Puerto Rico—an American colony with only partial rights granted to its population, who are nonetheless US citizens.[8] Taíno claims of distinct Indigenous identity destabilize a popular consensus among Puerto Ricans about Puerto Rican identity, which reveals the colonial politics at play in *racialization*—the imposition or claiming of a racial identity on or by a people. In addition, contemporary Taíno activism, focused on publicizing claims to indigeneity in the hopes of achieving governmental recognition of this identity, reveals two uncomfortable aspects of contemporary American law. On the one hand, Taíno attempts at accessing the legal benefits of Indigenous status show the way federal US law unequally privileges some populations over others, making certain accommodations and protections available to those people labeled Indigenous while denying such accommodations and protections to other populations similarly affected by colonialism. On the other hand, Taíno appeals to the government for recognition as Indigenous emphasizes an ongoing colonial dynamic of the imperial state controlling the act of racially labeling populations.

Indigeneity as a Privileged Legal Category

One occupation leader, Elba Anaca Lugo, described the Caguana protest as "part of a larger national campaign to raise public awareness about issues of national patrimony and Indigenous rights" for contemporary Taíno people.[9] These activists understood their claim to indigeneity to be a particularly privileged sort of legal move. Indigenous people, when recognized by the American state, are entitled under law to special rights. The Caguana protestors articulated some of these, demanding that the government "End the Destruction and Desecration of our Sanctuaries and Sacred Places, Archeological Sites, Coaibays (Cemeteries), Ancestral Remains, Sacred Funerary and Ceremonial Objects, and Ceremonial Centers Now!" The occupiers requested specific legal protection for their "practices and beliefs" as an Indigenous community, "the Indigenous Taíno People of Borikén (Puerto Rico)."[10]

As a legal category, "indigeneity" emerged in the twentieth century as part of a global turn toward acknowledging and seeking to redress the destruction wrought on native peoples by colonialism. As "living descendants of preinvasion inhabitants of lands now dominated by others," law scholar James Aya writes, Indigenous peoples were widely considered to deserve special protection.[11] Under the assumption that without legal intervention, Indigenous cultures could be lost forever, nations created laws offering Indigenous peoples special exemptions from otherwise generally applicable laws. These new laws also sought to preserve populations considered to be in danger of cultural annihilation. They offered a modicum of reparation or recompense for histories of deep injustice inflicted by the state and ongoing inequality in terms of resources and opportunities. So, for instance, Indigenous peoples were allowed, via law, hunting and fishing rights denied to other citizens. Indigenous peoples were granted the ability to establish limited political autonomy or sovereign control over a territory, whether in the form of the right to move freely across borders or the right to manage a reservation. Legal measures offered reparations in the form of economic development activities and special tax status in acknowledgment of the economic disadvantages suffered as the result of colonization. To help preserve traditional practices, laws allowed for Indigenous control over education and extended protection for religious activities.

The special protections afforded Indigenous people under the law are rooted in an understanding that such individual cultures are unique, even as the category of indigeneity is used to unite disparate communities around the world. Such people—from the Sami of Scandinavia to the Māori of Polynesia, the Hopi of North America to the Adivasi of South Asia—"share common problems related to the protection of their rights as distinct peoples," as one United Nations document puts it.[12] Indigeneity as a legal status implies a common legal struggle on an international level, one that transcends specific political and legal systems. To claim such a legal status, therefore, is necessarily to locate oneself and one's people as part of a transnational community and a global, pan-Indigenous struggle. Many of the shared legal and political goals of this struggle are framed as natural rights in the 2007 *United Nations Declaration on the Rights of Indigenous Peoples*.[13] It is these rights that are understood by Taíno activists as "inherent rights."[14]

At the same time, contemporary Taíno recognize that to be subject to American law regarding indigeneity—federal Indian law—they must first be "acknowledged" by the state *as* Indigenous. In the United States, this process of recognition has changed over time, but in its most recent iteration it requires a community—a "tribe" in American law—to prove that it has existed as a distinct and politically organized community since 1900 with a governing document and restrictions on membership and evidence of existence as a community from historical times.[15] To be acknowledged, a given community must petition the Office of Federal Acknowledgment of the Bureau of Indian Affairs, part of the governmental bureaucracy created to administer America's Indigenous peoples. Acknowledgment as Indian is necessary to secure a variety of legal protections and privileges, including special laws accommodating Indigenous religious practices such as those covered under the 1978 American Indian Religious Freedom Act. This law, according to the expanded and amended version of 1994, applies only to those who are Indians according to federal law and "recognized as eligible for the special programs and services provided by the United States to Indians because of their status as Indians."[16]

The same language canonizing federal recognition as essential for status as Indian/Indigenous is used in the 1990 Native American Graves Protection and Repatriation Act (NAGPRA), which allows for the protection and repatriation—return to the descendants—of funeral sites and objects.[17] This law has had major ramifications for museums; many museums have removed from display or returned to contemporary tribes artifacts and remains taken by past archaeological excavation or tomb-raiding expeditions. The Caguana protestors cited NAGPRA in their demand for access to the park's ceremonial sites as well as in their call for the removal of Taíno remains and grave goods from the park's museum. Yet federal Indian policy has never been applied on the territory of Puerto Rico due to the distinct status of Puerto Ricans as only semicitizens of the United States.[18]

Racialization and Puerto Rican Identity

Contemporary Taíno discourse emphasizes existential statements—that the Taíno continue to live, exist, survive. Such statements are phrased in direct rebuke of claims of Taíno extinction. They reject popular narratives of history as works of colonial aggression, as attempts even at cultural genocide. "The true genocide is to say that we do not exist, that we are extinct," one contemporary Taíno writes, "Do they not see that I am here?"[19] As scholar of Native American religious history Gregory Smoak has argued, "Expression of and control over one's identity has been a key form of resistance among subject peoples."[20] The case of contemporary Taínos exemplifies such resistance. Indeed, some of the criticism of this movement is rooted in the degree to which contemporary Taíno identity appears to be self-determined.

Contemporary claims of Taíno identity are contested by both academic experts and many Puerto Ricans. Critics argue that such claims to indigeneity lack "authenticity."[21] Historians point out that the revival of Taíno identity within Puerto Rican communities dates largely to the last three decades.[22] Critics of contemporary Taínos refer to them as "neo-Taínos," a name that emphasizes critics' belief that the Taíno culture of today is a recent adoption and ongoing invention—a contemporary religious and social movement claiming an affiliation with Taíno history and employing Taíno symbols. "Neo-Taíno" marks the contemporary movement as distinctly new, differentiating contemporary Taínos from authentic, historical Taíno identity. The very term conveys a rejection of Taíno claims.[23]

Among other Puerto Ricans, contemporary Taíno claims to indigeneity are a source of anxiety. On the one hand, while contemporary Taíno consider themselves Puerto Ricans, their calls for rights "inherent" in Indigenous identity distinguish them from their fellow citizens. Indigeneity offered them legal recourse unavailable to the "non-Indigenous" survivors of European colonialism.[24] This unequal access to legal remedies is particularly jarring when considered from the vantage point of other colonized peoples. At the same time, as contemporary Taíno activism calls attention to Puerto Rico's status as a colony, so too the Taíno legal struggle for the specific and special rights of Indigenous people highlights the inequality inherent in a system that offers protections and privileges to only one protected category. Moreover, contemporary Taíno claims to identity pose what one academic critic called "a threat to political unity" among Puerto Ricans by destabilizing popular Puerto Rican conceptions of identity.[25] Yet accusations that contemporary Taínos are accused of fabricating—of simply making up—their identity, reveals how constructed categories of identity are. Indeed, contemporary Taíno claims to Indigenous identity reveal the often hidden politics behind identity claims, showing how certain (racial) identities are incentivized just as others are stigmatized.

Race, while a category imagined within and dependent on specific social contexts, continues to exert influence on society because it is assumed to be natural, to be an identity preexisting human labels rather than a fiction linked to such labels. Moreover, racial categories have real social consequence because they are legal fictions. The work of Ian Haney-López and other scholars of law and society have shown that racial categories are created in part and policed by law and the legal system.[26] "Racialization"—the process of creating and imposing categories of race—plays an essential role in the project of empire and colonization. Settlers use race as an administrative device, dividing, devaluing, and controlling populations. In this way, racialization is a tool of power, a weapon of the colonizers, who locate native people, for instance, below themselves in terms of hierarchy and even evolutionary trajectory. Moreover, racial divisions can fracture potential political resistance among the colonized.[27]

But racialization can, itself, be a strategy for resistance. Marginalized minority groups sometimes seize new identities, aware of the political ramifications of such an act. The reclamation of the imposed label of "Indian" by Native Americans, which facilitated political organization across tribal divisions, is one example of this.[28] The "ethnic turn" of various African American religious movements in the early twentieth century, rejecting the label of "Negro" in order to claim American citizenship, stands as another example.[29] Some South Africans made similar moves in the apartheid era, seeking legal classification as something other than "black."[30] While contemporary claims to Taíno identity involve much more than political machinations, they do, all the same, reveal race to be constructed and illustrate the ways race, as a legal category, has real consequences.

In the Puerto Rican context, one response to the racialization that came with colonization was a counter-racialization imagining a unified Puerto Rican people. This Puerto Rican national myth, called *la gran familia puertorriqueña*, "asserts that Puerto Rico is somehow a racially heterogeneous (*mestizo*), inclusive, and equal nation."[31] Essential to a sense of Puerto Rican identity, this myth is part of a racialization that identifies Puerto Ricans as a distinct people, unlike other Latino/a populations. Images of this understanding of Puerto Rican identity have been proliferated in various forms by Puerto Rican governmental and cultural institutions as well as by nationalist activists. An iconic example is the mural "Tres Razas y Una Cultura," which is in the town of San Germán. This painting illustrates the "gran familia puertorriqueña" myth, presenting Puerto Rico as a Spanish face framed by and emerging from silhouette faces of Native and African faces.[32] This postcolonial racialization, then, reified the stigma of earlier racial categories, with the Indigenous and black African populations of Puerto Rico presented as less significant than the (colonizing) population of European heritage. While these ancillary ancestors of Puerto Rican identity stare off to the side, existing only in the past, the Puerto Rican present and future, marked by European characteristics, show that Puerto Rico has "overcome racial difference" via "harmonious synthesis" that privileges Spanishness.[33]

Taíno claims to indigeneity—and thus to racial difference—take exception to this myth of a united Puerto Rican "race" while simultaneously highlighting the subsidiary role this narrative affords to Indigenous identity. When contemporary Taínos locate their struggle within the history of colonization, they are criticizing the racial hierarchy imposed by that process. As one contemporary Taíno writes, "Since the presence of the colonizing forces in the American Hemisphere, Indigenous societies have been forced into one European construct or another. Our ancestral ways have been deemed inferior, at times even demonic, and were forcefully replaced with the ways of the Europeans."[34] This, contemporary Taínos claim, led to popular conceptions of Puerto Rican identity and to the erasure of their existence from history books.

At the same time, contemporary Taíno claims to identity destabilize the notion of identity as given or inherited, revealing racialization to be a process requiring popular participation. Racialization depends on belief, and contemporary Taíno claims to racial difference are linked not to discovered genealogy but to conscious decision, not to historical circumstances as much as to *feeling*. The adoption of Taíno identity follows a felt sense of coming into consciousness of the truth of that identity. One converts to one's innate Taíno-ness. As one contemporary Taíno describes it, "There was something inside of me that knew who I was and wanted to come out."[35] Taíno identity is, in anthropological terms, understood as "a dormant yet realizable identity," one to be accessed on the level of individual emotional experience and acceptance.[36] While family genealogy and genetic evidence are discussed by contemporary Taínos, neither of these holds the power that felt affiliation does.[37] One knows that one is Taíno because one feels this to be true.[38] That which is felt, however, is not merely a sense of pride in or connection with the Taíno culture. Contemporary Taínos speak of feeling a sense of inherited pain, an "intergenerational trauma" that marks them as Indigenous.[39] Rather than accepting the racial myth of a unified Puerto Rico, with its nationalist features and general denial of colonialism's brutal and ongoing legacy, Taíno racialization emphasizes the sufferings of colonialism, foregrounding colonial oppression as central to one's sense of self.

Taíno Identity and Colonialism

The occupation of the Caguana archaeological park began on July 25, a Puerto Rican holiday. First called "Occupation Day" as a remembrance of the initial seizure of the island by the US military in 1898 as part of the Spanish-American War, in 1952 the holiday's name was changed to "Constitution Day" in commemoration of the Puerto Rican Constitution of that same year. Even as the new name frames the territory's status as "commonwealth" as a break from colonial ownership, the reality is that Puerto Rico is still radically subject to US sovereignty. Puerto Rican citizens are only partial citizens of the US, unable, for instance, to vote for the US president or to elect voting representatives to Congress. Puerto Rico exists under the American flag but without the full benefits of citizenship, a territory that in the language of the Supreme Court was "foreign in a domestic sense."[40] The Taíno action at Caguana, the occupation of a site that had been claimed and coopted from its original use and ownership on a day that, in turn, had been claimed and coopted from its original commemorative purpose, thickly referenced Puerto Rico's colonial status. Occupiers linked the erasure of Taíno existence from Puerto Rican history with the occlusion of ongoing American colonial occupation of Puerto Rico from contemporary Puerto Rican popular memory.

Contemporary Taínos insist on their identity as both Indigenous and Puerto Rican—as Boricua, the original Taíno word for the island. Simultaneously, however, Taíno Puerto Rican identity cannot be discussed outside the context of compounded colonization. As one contemporary Taíno writes, explaining her identity as a doubly colonized person:

> I am Taino; Boricua, from the American colony known today as Puerto Rico, and I am an American citizen. This means I am of an Indigenous American People colonized by Spain in 1492, and since 1898, we are a colony of the United States of America. We were colonized not once, but twice. And for those unfamiliar with American history, Puerto Ricans are natural born American citizens since 1917, when the US was running out of soldiers to fight their wars.[41]

This history lesson helps explain her identity. To be Taíno today means to exist under layers of colonial subjugation.

Moreover, to claim Taíno existence today is to testify to such colonization. The occupiers of the Caguana park understood this, approaching their role as, in part, living reminders of Puerto Rico's history of colonization. Insistent that they, the Taíno people of Puerto Rico, had survived waves of colonial exploitation into the present day, the occupiers embraced their function as a return of the repressed: a disruptive public reminder of Puerto Rican colonization past and present.

Recognition and the Power of the Imperial State

As an act of protesting regulations considered to be unjust and, in the process, calling attention to wider injustices, the occupation at Caguana evoked the American tradition of civil rights protests. As a seizure of a historically and symbolically important site, this action paralleled in particular the occupations carried out by the American Indian Movement.[42] The ultimate goal in the Caguana action was to influence the government to change its treatment of a minority group. Taíno activists understood the government—the federal US government, the ultimate authority in Puerto Rican politics—to have the ability to grant access to sacred sites, order the return of bodily remains and grave goods, and establish for the Taíno a new regime of heightened legal protections. The occupiers courted media attention in the hopes that public awareness could push governmental action, but it was such state action—specifically, the act of recognizing contemporary Taínos as Indigenous—that was necessary for the social transformation the activists sought.[43] As one of the Caguana occupiers put it, "Until there is official recognition of our people, classification of our ceremonial sites as historical landmarks will not result in the same protection that it may provide for other Native Americans. Taíno sacred, ceremonial and burial sites, artifacts and ancestral remains will continue to be the subject of further desecration."[44] Without state recognition as an Indigenous people, contemporary Taínos cannot be subject to and thus benefit from federal Indian law.[45]

As is true of Indigenous communities worldwide, the Taíno at Caguana recognized their dependency on and asymmetrical relation to the power of the state. Speaking a language they believed the courts and government of the United States would respect, the activists demanded some rights accorded all citizens and others reserved especially for Indigenous peoples. These activists—like Indigenous activists worldwide—sought to make use of the settler state's legal system to extract reparations from that same system. The legal privilege afforded to Indigenous identity allows for select colonized communities to seek some benefit, some amelioration, through the same law that has supported and upheld imperialism.[46]

This dynamic of seeking—of needing—recognition by the apparatus and authority of the state perpetuates the dynamic of imperial control over colonized populations, as many Indigenous activists and postcolonial scholars argue. This dynamic is itself a form of "coloniality," a conception and practice imposed on colonized people by the imperial state.[47] As scholar of indigeneity and the law Thalia Anthony has argued, recognition "conceals the unlawful nature of the state's authority" as predicated in the conquest and "violent dispossession" of territory from Indigenous people now reduced to suppliants before that same state's authority.[48] Indigenous peoples surrender one level of sovereignty in cooperating with the process of recognition, presenting themselves as subjects of the colonial state petitioning for special status. Even the "sovereignty" they may receive as a result of recognition is a partial sovereignty dependent on the grace of and remaining always under the authority of the settler state. As the state crafts policy to provide partial recompense and protections to Indigenous people, it retains and reexerts the colonial power to define categories and determine a community's legal status.

Contemporary Taínos point out that the Bureau of Indian Affairs Office of Federal Acknowledgment states that "federal recognition is granted only to those US tribes [that] reside within the US continental 48 contiguous and Alaska"; thus the colonial status of Puerto Rico precludes legally recognized indigeneity for any Puerto Ricans.[49] Contemporary Taínos point to this "loophole in the law," the exemption of Puerto Rico from federal Indian policy, as further proof of the problems of imperial power over colonized people. That the state has no mechanism through which to recognize Taíno existence is seen as part and parcel of the deeper history of claiming that the Taíno are extinct, and the stakes of such refusal are tantamount to a sentence of extinction for Taíno in the future.[50]

In response to this bind of double colonialism—realizing both that federal recognition by the colonial power is essential for the changes they desire and that as partial citizens of an American colony they are not fully subject to the benefits of American law—contemporary Taínos respond by seeking self-determination however possible. As one blogger writes, while "the trauma of colonialism leaves those colonized with a gaping wound that remains with us for life, the only element I have any control over is myself."[51] Individual declarations of identity, daily behavior, modes of public presentation and dress—these, at least, are actions that can be taken without approval by the state. Similarly, the hunger strikes carried out by some of the occupiers emphasized this sense of self-determination, even to the edge of death. In the face of the vast power of the state, Taíno activists demonstrated their control over their own bodies, their own lives, turning those lives and bodies into a symbol of Indigenous resistance to colonialism.

Conclusion: Indigeneity, Religion, and Law

Within the contemporary Taíno community, the 2005 occupation of Caguana is referred to as "El Grito Indigena Taíno de Caguana," the Indigenous Taíno *Grito* of Caguana. *Grito* means "cry" but also "uprising." Perhaps predictably, the *grito* ended with a brutal exertion of state power. Armored police, including members of a SWAT team, stormed the archaeological park and arrested the unarmed protestors.[52] The cry of the Taíno activists, their claims to rights of access and use of the site both through the First Amendment to the Constitution and through the special rights accorded to Indigenous people, were rejected. In fact, the occupiers were later the subject of a court injunction barring them from visiting the Caguana site outside of the park's normal operating hours.[53] They could come as tourists, buying a ticket to look around or visit the museum, but their demands for foundational rights, rights of access to and use of as well as inherited ownership of cultural objects and remains held at the park, were denied.

Contemporary Taínos provide an important case study for thinking about indigeneity and the law. As they struggle for reparations and privileges under the law as Indigenous, Taínos reveal the inequality of a system that ignores other oppressed minorities and colonized peoples in favor of one category of people. As they advance their individually felt sense of identity, the Taíno reveal the socially constructed, politically interested nature of racial categories—and they reveal that such categories are also legal categories, policed by law, with legal benefit or detriment. Taínos' efforts to achieve official recognition of their special status likewise reveal the continuing colonial dynamics of state control over who counts as authentically Indigenous, and who gets the double-edged benefits of this recognition.

Indigeneity, in turn, matters as a term for thinking about American law and religion because it designates a privileged status, an attempt to offset the damages of colonialism by offering protection and accommodations for ancient cultures and their practices. Such practices are often, as in the Taíno case, inextricable in many ways from religion; they are matters of ritual, of sacred claims to objects and sites.[54] Indigeneity overlaps with religion, and it also mirrors it. Both legal categories are linked to special rights—special in the sense of deserving extra attention by the courts and special in the sense, too, of being unequal. Winnifred Sullivan, arguing that religious freedom is "impossible" to achieve within the courts, argued both that the category is impossible to equitably define in judicial proceedings and that according special rights to religious practices in contrast to nonreligious practices codified unequal treatment of citizens.[55] The Taíno case shows that these two criticisms apply to the category of indigeneity. Contemporary Taíno claims to Indigenous identity are widely contested, and Taíno hope in the transformative potential of official recognition of indigeneity is predicated on the special privilege, the unequal treatment, legally offered to those thus recognized.

While contemporary Taíno identity cannot be reduced to legal or political activism, such work is widely understood to be an essential aspect of this identity. To be a contemporary Taíno is necessarily to be, to some degree, an activist (or "warrior," as some Taínos put it, fighting for ancestral rights in the legal and political sphere). Contemporary Taínos proclaim their Indigenous identity and work toward having their claims of identity recognized by legal and political authorities.[56] This struggle is undertaken through protests and petitions to government officials, through published declarations and public demonstrations of Indigenous culture, and through affiliation and participation with already-recognized Indigenous communities.[57] For instance, Taínos have participated in pan-Indigenous events on the mainland, joining other Native American groups for observations such as the Day of Mourning commemoration in Plymouth and the Indigenous Peoples' Sunrise Gathering on Alcatraz Island, both held yearly on November 23.[58] In these events, the existence of contemporary Taínos and their call for legal recognition is given a public voice as part of a broader critique of colonialism.

Law, as approached by Indigenous communities, serves as a structure of their historical and contemporary oppression and as a potential tool for resistance and the transformation of social reality. Law inspires and facilitates Indigenous *gritos* in both senses of laments over injustice and hypocrisy under and in the law *and* of uprising in the hope for new possibilities through legal appeal. Turning to legal appeals and legal language, marginalized communities can express their desires for altered social circumstances—specific benefits, access to sites, return of ancestral remains, for instance. Law's promise resides simultaneously in its affiliation with, even influence over, the power of the state and in its association with ethical ideals. "The government must obey the law, and the law calls for justice" is one way to formulate a popular *grito* advanced by Indigenous communities worldwide, as they seek to have their indigeneity recognized and thus accorded legal rights and accommodations. Such a *grito* is, as scholars of religion should quickly note, a statement of faith, a cry articulating a deeply held belief in law as a transcendent and transformative force, one that even the colonizing state must respect and obey. In this, too, the discourses and practices of indigeneity point to the entanglements of religion and law.

NOTES

1   "Caguana," Sacred Land Film Project, 2018, http://sacredland.org.
2   Katherine Stapp, "Rights—Puerto Rico: The Taino's Last Stand," Inter Press Service News Agency, August 8, 2005, www.ipsnews.net.
3   The standard work of history on the ancient Taíno is Irving Rouse, *The Taínos: Rise and Decline of the People Who Greeted Columbus* (New Haven, CT: Yale University Press, 1992).
4   Roberto Mucaro Borrero, "Boriken Taíno Reclaim Caguana Ceremonial Center," *The Voice of the Taino People Online* (blog), July 25, 2005, http://uctp.blogspot.com.

5 "Caguana," Sacred Land Film Project.

6 Email quoted in Gabriel Haslip-Viera, *Race, Identity, and Indigenous Politics: Puerto Rican Neo-Taínos in the Diaspora and the Island* (New York: Latino Studies Press, 2014), 243.

7 Judith Weisenfeld, *New World A-Coming: Black Religion and Racial Identity during the Great Migration* (New York: New York University Press, 2016), 5.

8 See, for instance, José Trías Monge, *Puerto Rico: The Trials of the Oldest Colony in the World* (New Haven, CT: Yale University Press, 1997).

9 Roberto Mucaro Borrero, "Taíno Occupation of Sacred Ceremonial Center Continues," *The Voice of the Taino People Online* (blog), July 26, 2005, http://uctp.blogspot.com.

10 Borrero, "Boriken Taíno Reclaim Caguana Ceremonial Center."

11 Stephen James Ayana, *Indigenous Peoples in International Law*, 2nd ed. (New York: Oxford University Press, 2004), 3.

12 United Nations (website), "Indigenous Peoples at the UN," no date, www.un.org.

13 United Nations, *United Nations Declaration on the Rights of Indigenous Peoples*, September 13, 2007, www.un.org.

14 Borrero, "Boriken Taíno Reclaim Caguana Ceremonial Center."

15 25 CFR 83.11, "What Are the Criteria for Acknowledgment as a Federally Recognized Indian Tribe?" Cornell Law School Legal Information Institute, no date, www.law.cornell.edu.

16 For the text of the act, see www.congress.gov/103/bills/hr4155/BILLS-103hr4155ih.pdf.

17 For the text of the act, see www.gpo.gov. For a discussion of its implementation as well as its mobilization by Indigenous communities, see Greg Johnson, *Sacred Claims: Repatriation and Living Tradition* (Charlottesville: University of Virginia Press, 2007).

18 On semi-citizenship status, see Elizabeth Cohen, *Semi-Citizenship in Democratic Politics* (Cambridge: Cambridge University Press, 2009).

19 A Taíno named Katsí, quoted in Sherina Feliciano-Santos, *An Inconceivable Indigeneity: The Historical, Cultural, and Interactional Dimensions of Puerto Rican Taíno Activism* (PhD diss., University of Michigan, 2011), 30. See also "El Taíno Vive," a video article by Rubén Urrutia in Puerto Rico's major daily newspaper, *Nuevo Dia*, October 10, 2010, www.elnuevodia.com.

20 Gregory E. Smoak, *Ghost Dances and Identity: Prophetic Religion and American Indian Ethnogenesis in the Nineteenth Century* (Berkeley: University of California Press, 2006), 153.

21 See, for instance, Miriam Jiménez Román, "The Indians Are Coming! The Indians Are Coming! The Revitalization of Taíno Identity in Contemporary Puerto Rico," *Taíno Revival: Critical Perspectives on Puerto Rican Identity and Cultural Politics*, ed. Gabriel Haslip-Viera (Princeton, NJ: Marcus Wiener Publishers, 2001), 55–82.

22 Whereas Taíno activists would say that it was only the vocal, politically engaged organization of their community that began at this time. See Lynne Guitar,

Pedro Ferbel-Azcarate, and Jorge Estevez, "Ocama-Daca Taíno (Hear Me, I am Taíno): Taíno Survival on Hispaniola, Focusing on the Dominican Republic," in *Indigenous Resurgence in the Contemporary Caribbean: Amerindian Survival and Revival*, ed. Maximilian C. Forte (New York: Peter Lang, 2006), 41–67.

23 Gabriel Haslip-Viera, "Introduction: Competing Identities: Taíno Revivalism and other Ethno-Racial Identity Movements among Puerto Ricans and other Caribbean Latinos in the United States, 1980–Present," in *Taíno Revival: Critical Perspectives on Puerto Rican Identity and Cultural Politics*, ed. Gabriel Haslip-Viera (Princeton, NJ: Marcus Wiener Publishers, 2001), 13. Forte is correct when he says that the *Taíno Revival* volume "strongly suggests that contemporary Taíno are pathological, self-deluding holders of a false consciousness that blinds them to their true nature"; see Maximilian C. Forte, "Introduction," *Indigenous Resurgence in the Contemporary Caribbean: Amerindian Survival and Revival*, ed. Maximilian C. Forte (New York: Peter Lang, 2006), 5.

24 A non-Indigenous politician, Victor Vassallo Anadón, has introduced legislation calling for all Puerto Ricans to be reclassified as Indigenous and thus convert Puerto Rico, as a whole, into a reservation. A symbolic gesture of protest rather than a practical political goal, this move nonetheless calls attention to the inequality of privileging indigeneity under law. The people of Puerto Rico, Anadón argues, would be better off classified as Indians than remaining in the limbo of semi-citizenship imposed upon them by the US government. See Haslip-Viera, *Race, Identity, and Indigenous Politics*, 277.

25 Robert Pool, "What Became of the Taíno?," *Smithsonian Magazine*, October 2011.

26 Ian Haney-López, *White by Law: The Legal Construction of Race*, 10th anniversary ed. (New York: New York University Press, 2006), 83.

27 For a comprehensive argument of how racialization is a tool of empire, see Sylvester Johnson, *African American Religions, 1500–2000: Colonialism, Democracy, and Freedom* (Cambridge: Cambridge University Press, 2015).

28 See Smoak, *Ghost Dances and Identity*.

29 See, for instance, Sylvester Johnson, "The Rise of Black Ethnics: The Ethnic Turn in African American Religions, 1916–1945," *Religion and American Culture* 20, no. 2 (Summer 2010): 125–63; for attention to the Moorish Science Temple of America, see Weisenfeld, *New World A-Coming*; Tisa Wenger, *Religious Freedom: The Contested History of an American Ideal* (Chapel Hill: University of North Carolina Press, 2017).

30 Joane Nagel, *American Indian Ethnic Renewal: Red Power and the Resurgence of Identity and Culture* (New York: Oxford University Press, 1996, 1997), 24.

31 Devyn Spence Benson, "Race and Radicalism in Puerto Rico: An Interview with Carlos Alamo-Pastrana," *Black Perspectives*, August 2, 2016, www.aaihs.org.

32 For an image, see Mural "Tres Razas y Una Cultura" (San Germán, Puerto Rico), August 10, 2018, http://this-is-not-taino.tumblr.com.

33 Isar P. Godreau, *Scripts of Blackness: Race, Cultural Nationalism, and US Colonialism in Puerto Rico* (Urbana: University of Illinois Press, 2015), 128. Puerto Rican

"racial syncretism has amounted to an inclusive ideology of exclusion that hides the unequal valorization of its racial components under the trope of racial mixture," writes Arlene Dávila in "Local/Diasporic Taínos: Towards a Cultural Politics of Memory, Reality, and Imagery," in *Taíno Revival: Critical Perspectives on Puerto Rican Identity and Cultural Politics*, ed. Gabriel Haslip-Viera (Princeton, NJ: Marcus Wiener Publishers, 2001), 69.

34 Nanu, "Ayaca e' Iguana: Decolonizing Indigenous Diets," *Taino Woman Comes Dancing . . . in the Spirit of Hatuey*, March 10, 2018, https://tainowoman.com.

35 Ermelinda Cortes, *We Are Still Here, The Taino Lives!*, YouTube, 2017, www.youtube.com/watch?v=P_joZcD8ybA.

36 Dávila, "Local/Diasporic Taínos," 33.

37 Haslip-Viera quotes a Taíno who argues, "We Taino as a people, validate the DNA evidence, not the other way around . . . the journey of self-discovery . . . is not about culture, not genes, for genes say little about us as a people"; see *Race, Identity and Indigenous Politics*, 56.

38 Contemporary Taínos, in describing their discovery of their Taíno identity, frequently link the experience to powwows and pan-Indian events as well as to individual research and study on the internet. As one Taíno argues, "dressing up in regalia" is an important ritual move for "recalling what was lost" and embodying Indigenous identity on an emotional level. Likewise, Taíno dancing and the music of the traditional *guiro* functions to both bring out and confirm indigeneity. 12Roundtable, *Contemporary Culture, State of Taino Movement, Embrace of the Serpent*, YouTube, April 16, 2016, www.youtube.com/watch?v=bqJEEkGmyZo. See also Michelle Tirado, "I am Taíno: Exploring the Indigenous Roots throughout the Caribbean," *Indian Country Today*, April 2, 2013, https://indiancountrymedianetwork.com; Forte, *Indigenous Resurgence in the Contemporary Caribbean*, 253–69.

39 "Taino: We Are Still Here!" Arawayakan Indigenous Radio, 2015, www.blogtalkradio.com. See also Ana Velez, "Still Here: A Taino History Lesson," *Brown Girls Out Loud*, August 7, 2017, https://browngirlsoutloud.com.

40 On the so-called Insular Case determining Puerto Rico's legal status, see Bartholomew H. Sparrow, *The Insular Cases and the Emergence of American Empire* (Lawrence: University of Kansas Press, 2006); Christina Duffy Burnett and Burke Marshall, eds., *Foreign in a Domestic Sense: Puerto Rico, American Expansion, and the Constitution* (Durham, NC: Duke University Press, 2001). A general history of Puerto Rico under American rule is César J. Ayala and Rafael Bernabe, *Puerto Rico in the American Century: A History since 1898* (Chapel Hill: University of North Carolina Press, 2007).

41 Nanu, "Decolonizing Public Spaces: One Taino's Perspective," *Taino Woman Comes Dancing . . . In the Spirit of Hatuey*, March 10, 2018, https://tainowoman.com.

42 Two resources on these American Indian Movement (AIM) actions are from AIM itself: Laura Waterman Wittstock and Elaine J. Salinas, "A Brief History of the American Indian Movement" (www.aimovement.org) and from the Civil Rights

Digital History Project, "The American Indian Movement" (https://digilab.libs. uga.edu). For a detailed, book-length treatment of one major direct action, see Troy R. Johnson, *The Occupation of Alcatraz Island: Indian Self-Determination and the Rise of Indian Activism* (Urbana: University of Illinois Press, 1996).

43 Thus requests were made for the public to write letters to government officials and sign a petition in support of granting access to and repatriation of objects and remains from the Caguana park; see "Caguana," Sacred Land Film Project. See also "A Letter to the Puerto Rican People," *Jatibonicu Taino Tribal Nation of Borkan*, www.taino-tribe.org, calling specifically for Puerto Ricans to "speak with their local politicians, Camara Representative, Senators and also with the Governor of Puerto Rico to move to officially recognize the Jatibonicu Taino tribe of Boriken."

44 "Caguana," Sacred Land Film Project.

45 Thus, while Indigenous communities often make appeal to international law— and international legal bodies and agencies—the value of such appeals is largely rhetorical. "International law and policy can strengthen the negotiating position of Indigenous peoples on national and local levels," but the decision of who can be considered Indigenous remains an administrative power of the state. See Christina Allard, Elsa Reimerson, and Camilla Sandströp, "Contrasting Nature, Contrasting Rights—Concluding Remarks," in *Indigenous Rights in Modern Landscapes: Nordic Conservation Regimes in Global Context*, ed. Lars Elenius, Christina Allard, and Camilla Sandström (London: Routledge, 2017), 216–31.

46 On law as "the West's perfect instrument of empire" through the facilitation of essential administrative functions, including categorization by race, see Robert A. Williams Jr., *The American Indian in Western Legal Thought: The Discourses of Conquest* (New York: Oxford University Press, 1990), 93. But as Williams also argues, the law of empire is always also available, on its own terms, for use as resistance against these imperial effects.

47 James Tully, *Public Philosophy in a New Key*, vol. 1 of *Democracy and Civic Freedom* (Cambridge: Cambridge University Press, 2008), 244–45. See also Glen Sean Coulthard, *Red Skin, White Masks: Rejecting the Colonial Politics of Recognition* (Minneapolis: University of Minnesota Press, 2014).

48 Thalia Anthony, *Indigenous People, Crime and Punishment* (New York: Routledge, 2013), 200.

49 Tribal Government of the Jatibonicu Taino People of Puerto Rico Facebook Page, "Someone Had Asked the Question," March 18, 2015, www.facebook.com/Jatibonicu.Taino/photos/a.281112888581901.86781.190511170975407/1053456821347500/.

50 Hwaa Irfan, "The Taino of the Caribbean: The People Who Are Not Supposed to Exist," *Hwaairfan's Blog* (blog), https://hwaairfan.wordpress.com. There is even hope for an international system that will replace the federal system. See the reply by Tyrico Carapana Tacarigua to the "Federal Recognition for Taino?" discussion board, May 20, 2012, http://indigenouscaribbean.ning.com.

51 Nanu, "Ayaca e' Iguana."

52 Roberto Mucaro Borrero, "Occupation Ends in Arrests but Taíno Claim Victory in Boriken," *The Voice of the Taino People Online* (blog), August 13, 2005, https:// uctp.blogspot.com.

53 "Caguana," Sacred Land Film Project.

54 For a discussion of religious claims as legal claims, see Johnson, *Sacred Claims.*

55 Winnifred Sullivan, *The Impossibility of Religious Freedom* (Princeton, NJ: Princeton University Press, 2005).

56 Roberto Mucaro Borrero, "Grito de Caguana—Next Court Date—April 25 1:30pm," *The Voice of the Taino People Online* (blog), April 10, 2006, https://uctp. blogspot.com.

57 See, for instance, "The Declaration of the United Confederation of Taino People," press release, January 4, 1998, www.hartford-hwp.com.

58 "48th Day of Mourning/Remembrance features Taíno Speakers," *The Voice of the Taino People Online* (blog), November 24, 2017, http://uctp.blogspot.com; "UCTP Representative Addresses Gathering on Alcatraz Island," *The Voice of the Taino People Online* (blog), November 25, 2017, http://uctp.blogspot.com.

11

The Secular

JASON C. BIVINS

Law is supposed to clarify. It is made of decisions and refers to its past rulings using terms like "settled case law." It consults precedent as a matter of procedural obligation. It strives for transparency, fairness, and consistency of thinking, which is often comparative and analogical. Law is public. Law is shared, and pursues egalitarianism in its application and effects. Since the Constitutional Convention of 1787, American law has strived for such clarity in relation to religion, particularly regarding religion's appropriate relation to, and treatment by, ostensibly nonreligious institutions. Religion, however, is not a simple or stable category; thus, it is not always conducive to the kind of clarity law seeks.

On the one hand, there is simply the manyness of religions, especially in the United States. Even during the founding era, beyond Protestant sectarianism lay an array of philosophical orientations, folk and ethnic religious identities, fraternal organizations, agrarian and lay "magical" traditions, not to mention a vast array of Indigenous cultures and growing immigrant populations, though few in colonial America were prepared to recognize all of these expressions as constituting religion in the formal sense. And yet, on the other hand, there was no clear, shared understanding of what just such a formal sense might look like. Was religion a form of community membership and self-definition? Was it a set of ritual obligations? Or was it, as many of the framers of the US Constitution seemed to believe, a matter of interior reflection, one's disposition in the face of creation? Beyond this, what was the proper scope of religion's influence: Should it shape policy and public institutions, or should it merely produce the kind of character or temperament appropriate to good citizenship?

In early American reckonings with such issues, we find terms like "establishment" and "articles of worship" and even "separation," rather than "secular." But, as is commonly known, after scant engagement with religion in the Constitution itself, these vexing questions came into play during the framing of the First Amendment. The establishment clause of that amendment remains heavily debated, but at the very least it introduced a distinction between laws that either do "establish" religion, and therefore aren't permissible, or do not "establish" religion, and therefore are. This distinction is in some sense germinal to later colloquial understandings of secularism as the absence or the opposite of religion. That characterization is only partly true, and below we will see that the secular is a good deal more complex than this. This amendment, intended to clarify, wrought great complexity.

At the time that the Constitution was written, "secular" was often understood as a synonym for "cyclical," referring to periods of astronomical or economic change, for the Latin *saeculum* means "generation" or "age." Some might even assume it refers to the line adapted from Virgil that is still on American paper money: *novus ordo seclorum*. It could simply have meant, as it did beginning in early modern Europe, some reality not explicitly tied to a religious institution or practice—worldly, in other words. From this tangle of assumptions and meanings, no clear orientation is possible. But the tangle has meaning for us in terms of contemporary American law and religion.

"Secular" is not the same as "secularism." The assumption now obtains that the secular is simply the opposite of religion. Perhaps it is the substance of the "wall of separation" that Thomas Jefferson wrote about in his 1802 letter to the Baptists of Danbury, Connecticut, an image that the Supreme Court later in the nineteenth century acknowledged was possessed of constitutional authority.[1] Or perhaps it was the chief characteristic of all that lay on one side of the wall, the "state" as opposed to the "church." But secularism is not so simple, and this complexity is not the only family resemblance it shares with religion, the category with which it is regularly contrasted.

Consider the following episode as a way of entering this climate of complexity and entanglement. It begins with what I judge to be bad reading. In the 1972 Supreme Court case *Wisconsin v. Yoder*, members of Old Order Amish families were being compelled to comply with a Wisconsin state law that required children to attend public schools until the age of sixteen. The Amish families, who preferred to live simple lives close to

nature, did not denounce public schooling as a whole but wanted to with-
draw their children at the age of fourteen, at which point, they claimed,
their children needed to be isolated from the sort of worldly influences
that might counteract their religious development. The court wanted to
know whether the state law amounted to an "excessive burden" on the
Amish's "free exercise" of religion and, if so, whether an exemption from
the "secular" law was warranted in the name of preserving this most important register of freedom. As part of its long-standing reckoning with
the rights of religious traditions, and the scope of these rights, the court
had to determine what distinguished a religious belief from a nonreligious one and how best to recognize and substantiate these distinguishing markers. Justice Warren Burger concurred with a lower court finding
that "respondents' religious beliefs were sincere" and that their admirable
devotion to simplicity and nature were backed up by "heavy obligations"
and "conduct . . . regulated in great detail."[2] Those were, apparently, the
salient qualities that a religion possessed. It was not enough to have
beliefs; they had to be "sincere." One's religious "obligations" had to be
"heavy." And conduct, presumably a religious community's behavioral
codes or institutional patterns, must not be loose.

But cannot secular beliefs and organizations also be heavy, sincere,
and rigid? In order to sharpen the pattern recognition, Burger turned to
another nature lover: Henry David Thoreau. Justice Burger judged that
Thoreau usefully demonstrated the distinction between "religious faith"
and a "mode of life." While more or less anyone can cobble together a
mode of life, Burger supposed, a mode of life only merited special constitutional protections if it and a "religious faith" are "inseparable and
interdependent."[3] If they are not, he reasoned, we are left with "a matter
of personal preference" rather than "deep religious conviction, shared by
an organized group, and intimately related to daily living."[4] What Burger
called "secular considerations" can resemble religious ones in their opting for strange life-ways, as exemplified by Thoreau's renunciation of
social norms and his isolation in the woods, but they are "philosophical
and personal" if judged to be something other than "deep" or "shared"
or "intimately related" to everyday life. For all of Thoreau's concern for
the "fountainhead" of truth in *Civil Disobedience* and his rhapsodies in
Walden, he was identified with the "purely secular"; Thoreau was the
other of the Amish.

This kind of distinction illustrates some of legal secularism's content and uses. Defined as religion's opposite, the secular is also a conceptual language and a repertoire of descriptions used by law to establish and maintain what culturally normative religion actually is. But law's generic religion is quite Protestant in its basic assumptions about religion's interiority, its individualism, and its public authority. By insisting on a generic religion that is actually quite particular, the legal secular enables the kinds of conflagrations about public religion that it believes it is actually soothing. In this chapter, I set out to remap and redescribe the secular so as to uncover and explore its involvement in several political entanglements central to American democracy. I focus on three components of secularism's hidden and explicit makeup, each of which resonates with a component of the famed *Lemon* test, the court's most widely used test to distinguish the secular from the religious. First are assumptions about the proper sphere of the religious, framed via a reading of *Good News Club v. Milford Central School* (2001). Second are legal constructs of a static and inviolable "religion," which I complicate using *Mozert v. Hawkins County Board of Education* (1987) and related cases. Third is the centrality of religious "sincerity" at the heart of the legal secular, posited most influentially by *United States v. Seeger* (1965). Tracing the convoluted pathways and competing understandings of the content, scope, and desirability of the secular reveals how it consistently regulates religion in a way that masks some of the more mercurial and unmanageable features of American democracy.

"Secular Force" and "Barbarism"

Conventional narrations of legal secularism in America generally focus on the steady march from the "first disestablishment" of the constitutional era, in which structural and philosophical foundations were laid, to the "second disestablishment" of the nineteenth century, when the conceptual and practical implications of the former wrestled steadily with the realities of American religious pluralism. This periodization, and the jurisprudential discourse that took shape between the 1930s and the 1980s, is undeniably important. But even leaving aside the currently often-muddled state of legal secularism, the inevitability presumed in this narrative ignores examples of secularism's contestation emerging in a different period.

Robert G. Ingersoll (1833–1899) was one of the most renowned American orators of the late nineteenth century. "The Great Agnostic" was a veteran, a jurist, a Republican, and a "free-thinker." Ingersoll played no small part in producing a powerful understanding of the secular. Repelled by the fate of his clergyman father, who once accompanied Presbyterian circuit-rider Charles Finney on a European revival and was defrocked for holding "liberal views" judged to be "inconsistent with his ministerial character," Ingersoll attacked blasphemy laws, defended dissidents, and, in lectures like "The Great Infidels," assailed religious traditions he considered impediments to progress and moral uplift.[5] While Ingersoll admired African American Christians, his antipathy for organized religion was both targeted ("Mormonism must be done away with . . . by education") and diffuse ("Abject faith is barbarism; reason is civilization").[6] For Ingersoll, it was the law that could regulate other American institutions, and it ought properly be calibrated for the flourishing of "true education" and the conquest of its enemies, fear and superstition.[7] Of particular concern were schools, especially the influence of anti-Catholic literature sponsored by nativists who believed only Protestant-guided schools could defend the innocent against "Jesuitical conspirators."[8] Rejecting educational parochialism, Ingersoll endorsed common schools as incubators of the secular: "Every child should be taught to doubt, to inquire, to demand reasons."[9]

One of Ingersoll's most consistent critics was the Reverend W. H. Platt (1821–1898), author of, among other texts, *Legal Ethics, or, The Unity of Law*; *God Out and Man In, or, Replies to R. G. Ingersoll*; and 1877's *Influence of Religion in the Development of Jurisprudence*. In the latter, Platt, "formerly of the Mobile [Alabama] bar," aimed to contest Ingersoll's vision of the secular and to forestall the broader social transformations advocated by this vision. While general laments of this sort have always been commonplace in American religious discourse, Platt wrote with a longer historical view and produced a narrative positing a different kind of inevitability. He described a "secular force" taking shape in Roman jurisprudence, one that bred first "class-legislation," later "the natural *instinct* of equality of all men," followed inevitably by the collapse of "principles of enduring law" and by "the decay of religion."[10] Egalitarianism itself was thus the enemy of religion; in Platt's vision, it enshrined a secularism backed up by degraded law.

Somewhere between Ingersoll, the nativists, and Platt, then, we find alternate wellsprings of the American secular. Alternatively, the secular is conspiracy, reason contra "barbarism," and the evaporation of legal and religious principles in the acids of the modern. This brief interval is cited as a provocation to think of the legal secular not as part of what theorist of the secular Charles Taylor calls a "subtraction narrative"— that is, defined by the increased removal of religion—but as a contest, aspiration, and experience that prefigures contemporary cultural controversies.

Secularisms

The secular can be understood as a condition—institutional, experiential, discursive—in which people are confronted with questions about what precisely makes religion religious. As some argue, the very production of religion as a singular category is a product of the secular's emergence in the sixteenth and seventeenth centuries. Before that, the thinking goes, one was either a Christian or not, a Muslim or not, a heathen or not. At the very least, the emergence of the secular has enabled the establishment of boundaries (and the generation of categories) facilitating recognition and naming, and subsequently a political obsession with locating the "proper" place for religion. Here precisely is where the secular's influence on law is most evident, since this singularity and emplacement have enabled the secular to shape religion in ways that regulate directly and indirectly how religious thinking, speech, and conduct are experienced. But as I show below, this regulation is always conceptually and materially unattainable, since religion refuses to cooperate.

Charles Taylor famously historicizes secularism as a development within Latin Christendom.[11] Amid "a steadily increasing emphasis on a religion of personal commitment and devotion" the conditions of belief and nonbelief changed. Modernity's "porous selves" thus came to experience religion in a context wherein its ubiquity could not be assumed.[12] While with premodern selves and societies religion was simply a social and epistemological given, now it was an option. José Casanova distinguishes between "'the secular' as a central modern epistemic category, 'secularization' as an analytical conceptualization of modern world-historical processes, and 'secularism' as a worldview and ideology."[13] By these terms, Casanova means that secularism refers, respectively, to an identifiable quality that language or institutions possess; a belief that human history will see steady detachments of religions from public institutions; and an ascendant vision of the good life that is absent religion. Casanova's distinctions are useful insofar as they enable us to identify the contextual specifics of the secular's production, reception, and institutionalization. These, I would add, train our attention to the interrelation of background assumptions, juridical norms, and the lived experiences of religions negotiating the secular.

In terms of religion and law in the United States, Winnifred Fallers Sullivan and others have noted the impossibility of settling fundamental issues and questions. Background assumptions about what makes religion religion, and law law, sustain this condition. One of liberalism's primary aims has historically been to guarantee the rights of conscience and religious belief, thus presumably safeguarding an inchoate religious pluralism. Here religion, as a general category of protected belief, is thought to be one of many legal bulwarks against the infringement on citizens' rights. This understanding of religion embodies specifically liberal conceptions of citizens, defined as disinterested, rational individuals. This understanding of citizenship implies that persons are best protected by a political order that is minimalist and morally neutral, read as secular.

These conceptions, of course, have been hotly contested by scholars and citizens. The assumption that religion is an individual phenomenon is challenged on the grounds that this conception privileges belief over action. So, too, is the idea that religion is best expressed in nonpolitical spaces, those clearly demarcated from the public realm of the state. Uncontroversial, however, is the determinative role played by these generally liberal conceptions in shaping American legal discourse. Several key court cases have enshrined elements of this liberal conceptualization. *Everson v. Board of Education* (1947) held that the state had to be neutral in its relations with nonbelievers and believers alike, thus foregrounding the regular association of secularism (i.e., nonreligion) with neutrality.

Torcaso v. Watkins (1961), carving out a broader space for religious plu-ralism and tolerance (of the sort that secular regimes are thought best to protect), acknowledged the legitimacy of nontheistic traditions (and in a footnote even posited that "Secular Humanism" was a tradition). Build-ing on earlier case law, *Lemon v. Kurtzman* (1971) proposed a three-prong test for determining the constitutionality of policies seeming to engage religion: that they have a "secular legislative purpose," that their primary legislative effect "neither advances nor inhibits" religion, and that they constitute no "excessive government entanglement" with religion.[14]

At first blush, the secular of Supreme Court case law appears distinct from an experience or condition of the sort that Casanova identifies. Tacitly or not, there seems to be an assumption that legal secularism is different: because of its sphere being ostensibly restricted, because of the discursive qualities of law, because it is thought to be reactive to rather than constitutive of a political atmosphere. Yet this same legal literature is marked by tension and circularity. These qualities are not quite as ro-bust as in the Ingersoll-Platt tilt, but the clear ambiguity in many legal decisions, and the hand-wringing of justices over the merits of neutrality in public speech and institutions, reveal the instability of the law's ver-sion of the secular. In *Walz v. Tax Commission of the City of New York* (1970), Burger wrote, "The Court has struggled to find a neutral course between the two Religion Clauses, both of which are cast in absolute terms, and either of which, if expanded to a logical extreme, would tend to clash with each other."[15] In *Wolman v. Walter* (1977), Justice Pow-ell bemoaned the "loss of analytical tidiness" in consideration of such clashes.[16] And in *Committee for Public Education and Religious Liberty v. Regan* (1980), Justice White observed, "Establishment Clause cases are not easy, they stir deep feelings."[17] If there is a through line detectable in all this, from the chaotic nineteenth century to Burger's strange use of Thoreau in *Yoder*, it is that the legal secular is, from the start, marked by fluid and unstable assertions about space, sincerity, and inviolability. In this, at least, Reverend Platt was correct: the secular operates by force.

Space

Secular law depends explicitly on a particular cartography of space. The various "spheres" presumed by liberal constitutional governance not only posit specific institutions—like courts themselves, or schools—as paradigmatically public but also reify assumptions that such institutions are, as public spaces, value neutral, free of what the *Lemon* test calls "excessive government entanglement." These very convictions about the blank quality of state or public space, though, use language and concepts that allow secularity to be contested. In 2001, the Alliance Defense Fund (ADF, now the Alliance Defending Freedom), an organization dedicated to protecting religious speech in the public sphere, challenged a school's constraint of pro-life speech on the grounds that such speech was not appropriate for secular spaces. The ADF petitioned that "we want the pro-life club to have the same rights that are allowed other clubs."[18] The ADF's success in *Good News Club v. Milford Central School* (2001) relied on their simultaneous appropriation and denial of liberal rights talk, grounded in their emphasis on key liberal fundaments like "presenting all sides" of an argument, "equal treatment," and "fairness." ADF lawyers argued that if people are "honestly stating their interpretation" of a religious matter, the depth and sincerity of this feeling is politically, institutionally inviolate.

Fascinatingly, though, the religious advocacy in this case consistently depended on one of the fundaments of legal secularism: the assumption that religious viewpoints are detachable, mobile, and thus eligible for dialogue. A lower court initially held that "the kinds of activities proposed to be engaged in by the Good News Club were not a discussion of secular subjects . . . from a religious perspective, but were in fact the equivalent of religious instruction itself."[19] The key word here is "perspective," which— one assumes—contrasts with a more substantive, ontological version of the secular as *Yoder* would have it. In a footnote, Justice Clarence Thomas observed that "the exclusion of the Club on the basis of its religious perspective constitutes unconstitutional viewpoint discrimination."[20] It is a fascinating moment in which the secular's unwritten juxtaposition— between the immersive, way-of-life constitution of religion at the heart of much jurisprudence and the detachment of "perspectives"—creates an entanglement that sustains controversies like those in this case.

This presumed detachability of viewpoints is an essential background assumption of the spheres-based conceptual logic of the legal secular, one that is intended to safeguard the institutional and public conditions for "conversation" or "tolerance." Without clearly demarcated spheres and viewpoints, what would there be to tolerate? While the secular aims on one reading to cleave the obviously religious from the obviously secular, as enshrined by the *Lemon* test's injunction to avoid "excessive government entanglement," it also makes possible their commingling by providing critics a language to criticize the government for withholding equal *access*. The ADF's challenges to public education reveal the secular as a space within which the religious can demand the right to speak *as* the religious precisely via the secular's claims that public institutions are obligated to afford all viewpoints equal access. Insistence on the integrity of "this constitutional principle" ironically mimics liberalism's concern with the integrity of the separate spheres and zones of public interaction, where no citizens should be excluded "because of the religious nature of their speech" from even those institutions identified explicitly as secular.[21] In *Good News Club*, we see a secular whose spheres are both porous and impregnable. Its focus on observable and identifiable content and on the locatable thingness of religion is not just liberalism's; it is also common to the way secularism construes religion: both socially embedded and interior, both a form of speech and a comprehensive way of life.

Friction

The both/and-ness of secularism's spaces—both fluid and separately posited—is characteristic, too, of the assumption that law is somehow able to leave religion as it is. Beyond mere disestablishment, this is a presumption that the secular's achievements are frictionless. This resonates with, and possibly emerges from, the *Lemon* test's assertion that proper law and policy possess a "secular legislative purpose" that does not excessively burden the religious. A family of cases involving the circulation of texts demonstrates that this desired outcome, like that of secular space, undermines itself.

In *Mozert v. Hawkins*, several Protestant fundamentalist families in Hawkins County, Tennessee, sought "injunctive relief and money damages" on the grounds that a new series of textbooks violated their children's free exercise rights.[22] The central claim was that exposure to ideas in the books compelled them to make choices antithetical to their religious beliefs and undermined the religious education they pursued outside the public schools. Although the parents initially sought released-time education and other compromises, the Hawkins County Board of Education insisted that it had a responsibility to use state-endorsed curricular materials to provide citizens the basics of education. In 1984, the district court granted one of the families' nine allegations. The court asserted that the *Mozert* families had not clarified which sections of the Holt reader taught—objectionably, as the plaintiffs alleged—that "one does not need to believe in God in a specific way" in order to achieve salvation. Though the court judged the state's curriculum to be neutral in relation to different religions and nonreligions, in language echoing the 1947 case *Everson v. Board of Education*, it nonetheless held in favor of the plaintiffs in a limited sense.[23]

Brought to the circuit court of appeals in 1985, the case invoked two separate understandings of secular. School authorities insisted that the Holt text was secular in the sense of creating no offense or friction upon being read, while the *Mozert* families—now represented by the Moral Majority and the Concerned Women for America—invoked the texts' secularity as constituting evidence of their *non-neutrality*. As they saw it, the nonreligious was, in fact, antireligious. The text's introduction was cited as evidence of discrimination, since it praised the series' shift from a focus largely on Judeo-Christian themes to "mindful[ness] of the richness of our diversity."[24] *Mozert* lawyer Michael Farris (who would go on to found the Home School Legal Defense Association) claimed that this statement, combined with the series' inclusion of Buddhist and Muslim materials, constituted discrimination against Christianity via its demotion. The court found the appellants' views "sincerely held" and admitted that their sense of offense was genuine, but it judged the texts to be "neither advocating a particular religious belief nor expressing hostility to any or all religions."[25] No burden was found in exposing students to these ideas; contrarily, the court asserted that as part of a broader state-sponsored education, public schools had an obligation (a "compelling government interest") to introduce these ideas.

After remand back to the district court, which held to and broadened its initial ruling, the final appeal to the circuit court resulted in a more forceful opinion. "Mere exposure" to competing religious ideals, the court ruled, were consistent with the broader purpose of state education and could not create an unconstitutional burden on religion. This well-known case is often cited as an example of the legal assertion of the priority of some kinds of religion (those strong enough not to be offended, for example) over others.[26] Aside from such constructions of religion, *Mozert* and similar cases suggest that law's secularity often turns on, and is beset by, experiences of friction around "secular legislative purposes."

In *Brown v. Woodland Joint Unified School District* (1994), an elementary school's use of a teaching aid, *Impressions*, which included readings representative of "a broad range of North American cultures and traditions," was cited by an Assembly of God family as violating their children's free exercise rights.[27] Through compulsory reading about Wicca, the *Brown* families claimed, their children were being forced to *practice* "witchcraft."[28] Although the families admitted that the school adopted and used *Impressions* for a "secular purpose," they claimed—using the language and the distinctions of the *Lemon* test—that the primary *effect* of this adoption advanced Wicca while inhibiting Christianity. The court concluded that participating in reading did not constitute an anti-Christian "ritual."[29] And in *Counts v. Cedarville School District* (2003), Arkansas parent Billy Ray Counts sued a library system that, for religious reasons, had restricted children's rights to read *Harry Potter*. This successful suit was an assertion of the secular as linked to, even constituted by, a constitutional right to have "access" to "information."[30]

Several commonalities emerge from this cluster of cases. Such rulings about the secularity of information—its legislative and educational function—are consistently a feature of the secular's legal logic. In them, a particular experiential quality emerges as central: friction in relation to the religious, which now rides the currents of information. The secular's ostensive purpose in each of these cases is to convey freestanding, frictionless information to citizens in the making. Education, like other spheres in the American political imagination, is understood as a place both defined by neutrality and dedicated to producing it: it understands itself to make no claims on particular religions or nonreligions and it aims to impart to students a civic knowledge that produces no negative effects on religion (particularly no "offense") through contact with or exposure to particular components of this knowledge. Yet we see in this range of cases that the secular's purpose creates precisely these effects, these experiences of friction, by foregrounding the very categories (like neutrality and secularity) thought to insulate the secular from such friction. Any secular legislative purpose, then, provokes questions about secularism.

Sincerity

The secular creates persons as well as purposes. *United States v. Seeger* (1965) famously articulated the centrality of sincerity to claims for religious exemption from legal obligation. This decision examined conscientious objection to military enlistment. To guard against endless exemptions, law must distinguish between legitimate and illegitimate claims, and the category of "sincerity" was employed to this end. Exemption could be justified if related to "belief in an *individual's* relation to a Supreme Being involving duties beyond a human relationship but not *essentially* political, sociological, or philosophical views or a *merely* personal moral code."[31] Since the Universal Military Service and Training Act "does not exempt nonreligious conscientious objectors," the secular is defined by identifying the exemptions that do not count, and by illuminating a sincerity whose ostensive emotional depth is otherwise inscrutable.[32] Observing that legitimate exemption must be "based on belief in a Supreme Reality," which yields "an obligation superior to one resulting from man's relationship to his fellow man," the district court initially denied Seeger's claims because he could not unambiguously embrace the existence of a Supreme Being.[33] The district decision, though, left an opening in its acknowledgment that Seeger's belief was "sincere, honest, and made in good faith."[34]

The Supreme Court sought to clarify what makes such a belief "truly held" and "sincere." Recognizing the limits of language, the court judged that while questions could be raised about the relation of the defendants' beliefs to normative definitions of religion, "these are inquiries foreclosed to Government."[35] Yet this very judgment that what matters is interiority establishes, albeit indirectly, the assertion that "for purposes of exemption certain systems of belief are by their very nature superior to others."[36] So while the court's insistence conforms to the later injunction that secularity "neither advance[s] nor inhibit[s]" religion, the secular also works by linking its taxonomy of the religious to an identification of which emotions power will leave alone. For it is through *Seeger*'s sincerity that, in Winnifred Sullivan's estimation, we see emerging the assumption that "religion that is internal, chosen, and believed—religion that is about conscience—could and should be free without threat to the public order."[37] More than simply setting up occasional religious exemptions in the secular, sincerity—as an affective quality of the secular—governs the relation between authentic and inauthentic religion.[38]

Though the court professed its inability to pursue certain lines of inquiry, its recognition of sincerity actually advances a particular kind of religion as "universal" and "natural."[39] The court's very disavowal of meaning making and value production is what allows the priority of sincerity in religions to advance uncontested. In substituting "sincerity" for the slippery and capacious "conscience," *Seeger* links authentic belief with the juridical power to name, to identify, to bestow legitimacy. Sincerity is the secular's medium of judgment, prioritizing certain expressions of religion and thus exacerbating one of the cultural controversies it pledges to settle.

Conclusion

Consider once more all of the elegant phrases that make the legal secular, and its chronicles. They are like posters covering up the holes in Jefferson's porous wall. There is Justice Black's identification of services "separate and so indisputably marked off from the religious function," a thing readily identifiable, on which turns the state's duty "to be neutral in its relations with groups of religious believers and nonbelievers."[40] There is the injunction to favor neither the religious nor the nonreligious, articulated in a rigorously liberal language of neutrality that haunts discourse about what constitutes religion and its proper place in the spheres of public and private life. From *Everson* through *Torcaso* and *Lemon*, it is assumed that pluralistic society is kept harmonious by keeping separate the spheres of religion and nonreligion (even while allowing for occasional accommodations and exemptions).

The framing of the secular I have essayed here is focused not abstractly on the discursive or taxonomic difficulties that religion ostensibly presents to law, nor simply on the fuzziness of the line separating the religious from its counterpart, but on its role as a medium of sustained political conflict.[41] Because it is experiential, and because its experiences are partly generated by its own languages, the secular resists mere propositional analysis. So in terms of its political implications for religions, I find it productive to locate where the secular emerges in law's cultural and political activity.[42] More than simply a principle or a rule to be applied, the secular is the substance and the context of struggles about precisely what *defines* the secular. It is produced through, sustained by, and results in its own assertions about proper place, sincerity, and frictionlessness.

These tensional categories resonate with broader political divides in American democracy: confusions about the link between religious identity and political action, debates about what counts as meaningful civic education, arguments about effective political representation in a multireligious country, and others. The conceptual consistency of the secular as a category matters, but so too does the specifically political quality of the elements I have named, consideration of which might facilitate a fuller understanding of how the secular is experienced and enacted. For the secular cannot easily deflect questions about its own political management of religious life, evident in its assumptions about the inner life of citizens, the designated spheres of religious participation, and the effects of juridical power. Precisely because the secular permits endless redescription—it is everything to everyone, from the blank space of the Leviathan state to the aspiration of philosopher-sages, and always at risk from religious enthusiasts—it is the medium for the very tensions it promises to resolve.[43]

NOTES

1   Reynolds v. United States, 98 U.S. 145 (1879).

2   Wisconsin v. Yoder, 406 U.S. 205 (1972).

3   Ibid.

4   Ibid.

5   Rufus R. Wilson, "'Bob' Ingersoll: A Sketch of the Life of America's Most Noted Agnostic," *Elmira Telegram*, March 16, 1890; Robert G. Ingersoll, *The Works of Robert G. Ingersoll, in Twelve Volumes, Vol. 3* (New York: Dresden, 1915).

6   Roger E. Greeley, ed., *The Best of Roger Ingersoll: Selections from His Writings and Speeches* (Amherst, NY: Prometheus Books, 1977), 73, 32.

7   Ibid., 103.

8   William G. McLoughlin, *Revivals, Awakenings, and Reform: An Essay on Religion and Social Change in America, 1607–1977* (Chicago: University of Chicago Press, 1978), 99.

9   Greeley, *The Best of Roger Ingersoll*, 31.

10 W. H. Platt, *Influence of Religion in the Development of Jurisprudence* (San Francisco, 1877), 10.

11 Charles Taylor, "Western Secularity," in *Rethinking Secularism*, ed. Craig Calhoun, Mark Juergensmeyer, and Jonathan Van Antwerpen (New York: Oxford University Press, 2011), 31–53.

12 Ibid., 37.

13 José Casanova, "The Secular, Secularizations, Secularisms," in *Rethinking Secularism*, ed. Craig Calhoun, Mark Juergensmeyer, and Jonathan Van Antwerpen (New York: Oxford University Press, 2011), 54.

14 Lemon v. Kurtzman, 403 U.S. 602 (1971).

15 Edward McGlynn Gaffney Jr., "Biblical Religion and Constitutional Law," in *The Bible in American Law, Politics, and Political Rhetoric*, ed. James Turner Johnson (Philadelphia: Fortress Press, 1985), 81–106.

16 Ibid., 83.

17 Ibid.

18 Alliance Defending Freedom, "Alliance Defense Fund Proceeding with Suit against St. Michael-Albertville School District," www.adflegal.org.

19 Good News Club v. Milford Central School District, 533 U.S. 98 (2001).

20 Ibid.

21 Alliance Defending Freedom, "Good News Club v. Milford Central School District," www.adflegal.org.

22 Bob Mozert, et. al. v. Hawkins County Public Schools, 647 F. Supp. 1194 (E.D. Tenn. 1986).

23 Ibid.

24 Bob Mozert, et. al. v. Hawkins County Public Schools, 765 F.2d 75 (1985).

25 Ibid.

26 Nomi Maya Stolzenberg, "'He Drew a Circle That Shut Me Out': Assimilation, Indoctrination, and the Paradox of a Liberal Education," *Harvard Law Review* 106, no. 3 (January 1993): 581–667.

27 Douglas E. Brown; Katherine E. Brown v. Woodland Joint Unified School District, 27 F.3d 1373 (1994).

28 Ibid.

29 Ibid.

30 Counts v. Cedarville School District, 295 F. Supp. 2d 996 (W.D. Ark. 2003).

31 United States Supreme Court, United States v. Seeger (1965) No. 50, http://caselaw.findlaw.com.

32 Ibid.

33 Ibid.

34 Ibid.

35 Ibid.

36 Robert L. Rabin, "When Is a Religious Belief Religious: *United States v. Seeger* and the Scope of Free Exercise," *Cornell Law Review* 51, no. 2 (Winter 1966): 247.

37 Winnifred Fallers Sullivan, "Religion Naturalized: The New Establishment," in *After Pluralism: Reimagining Religious Engagement*, ed. Courtney Bender and Pamela E. Klassen (New York: Columbia University Press, 2010), 95.

38 See also Ben Adams and Cynthia Barmore, "Questioning Sincerity: The Role of the Courts After *Hobby Lobby*," *Stanford Law Review Online* 67 (November 2014): 59–66.

39 Ibid., 91.

40 Everson v. Board of Education, 330 U.S. 1 (1947).

41 In legal studies, see Caroline Corbin, "Secularism and U.S. Jurisprudence," in *The Oxford Handbook of Secularism*, ed. Phil Zuckerman and John R. Shook (New York: Oxford University Press, 2017), 467–81; Paul W. Kahn, "The Jurisprudence of Religion in a Secular Age: From Ornamentalism to *Hobby Lobby*," *Law & Ethics of Human Rights* 10, no. 1 (May 2016): 1–30; Christine L. Niles, "Epistemological Nonsense—the Secular/Religious Distinction," *Notre Dame Journal of Law, Ethics & Public Policy* 17, no. 2 (2012): 561–92; Laura Underkuffler-Freund, "The Separation of the Religious and the Secular: A Foundational Challenge to First Amendment Theory," *William and Mary Law Review* 36, no. 3 (March 1995): 837–988.

42 Here I have been influenced by Benjamin L. Berger, "The Cultural Limits of Legal Tolerance," in *After Pluralism*, ed. Courtney Bender and Pamela E. Klassen (New York: Columbia University Press, 2010), 98–123.

43 In this sense, then, the secular is an explicit product of liberalism. See Jason C. Bivins, *The Fracture of Good Order: Christian Antiliberalism and the Challenge to American Politics* (Chapel Hill: University of North Carolina Press, 2003).

PART IV

Limits

As we have by now hopefully established, how religion is conceptualized relative to the law matters tremendously and helps to shape which American citizens (and noncitizens) are afforded material well-being and which are slotted for premature death. In this final section, our contributors press at the limits of the law. In different ways, they each confront the incapacity of law for resolving our society's most intractable political conflicts while also pointing to future horizons for the study of law and religion in the United States.

In the section's first chapter, the fourth wall crumbles and the scholar of religion finds herself as a character in the story. Kathryn Lofton writes about amicus briefs. These "friend of the court" briefs are increasingly prevalent in Supreme Court proceedings, written both for the jurists tasked with passing legal judgment and for the overlooking public, which stands at the ready to voice its approval or approbation. Amicus briefs are many things: a stage for corporations to perform civic virtue and a forum for social movements to build strength. Where the rubber meets the road, however, in terms of what gets heard and what gets ignored, amicus briefs showcase the disjuncture between the sorts of insights scholars of religion have to offer and those that jurists are looking for. To put it bluntly, our critical preoccupations—indeed, the very ones that animate this book—are decidedly *not* what Supreme Court justices care about. As Lofton cautions, scholars of religion looking to unmask unacknowledged Christian normativities or settler colonialist logics are subjecting themselves to a quixotic fantasy that has little relation to the game being played in prime time. If it's knowledge about religions that they want, the cool kids of the bar will befriend religious organizations; they will *not* befriend us. Scholars of religion determined to try to forge these friendships anyway need to think deeper, Lofton argues, and leverage a wider range of insights afforded by our collective field of study, insights that pertain not solely to technical matters like belief and ritual but also to broader anthropological concepts like parent and association, which, to date, the jurisprudence has left largely untheorized.

For Sylvester Johnson, personhood is one such concept. In his chapter, religion represents at once a tradition and a heuristic for thinking about the legal and political designation of personhood. Who (or what) is (or isn't) a person? Over the course of US history, the boundary between person and thing has been variously adjudicated. Is a slave a person? Is a fetus? Over such limit cases have wars been fought and political alignments maintained. Johnson zeroes in on the extension of personhood to two entities of contested humanity: corporations and intelligent machines. Corporate personhood arose in the wake of emancipation, and the personhood of machines is presently arising in the arena of artificial intelligence. The future is here and it is weird. The world of self-driving cars and machine-enhanced supersoldiers is upon us, and the law is beginning to adapt so as to encompass the posthuman. By bringing religion and race into this conversation, Johnson invites us to think about the Christian colonial logics by which the distinctions between people and things have historically been drawn, and the ways that anti-blackness is baked into the legal rituals of American jurisprudence.

In the end, do we expect too much of law? If, as our contributors have shown, the law frequently functions as a tool by which uneven power relations are perpetuated, it is also a vessel of collective hope, a sacramental arena in which our fallen world might yet be redeemed. In this volume's final chapter, Vincent Lloyd points out that as a concept, hope is at once a species of American religion and a species of American politics. Indeed, hope represents a core tenet of American civil religion. Lloyd is not against hope, but absent the willing suspension of disbelief afforded by this civic faith, he sees little reason for us to pin our hope on the law. Those engaged in the struggle against injustice, he argues, are better served by turning to and cultivating alternative sites for potential remediation. Historically, whether in catastrophic decisions such as *Dred Scott* or in victories like *Brown*, the law does not deliver what we hope it will deliver. Pivoting from social movements to jurists, Lloyd explores the rhetoric of hope within the jurisprudence itself. What he discovers is that when Supreme Court justices hope, their hope is placed in the figure of the child or in future generations where the world has been transformed. In the figure of the child, where the justices see the possibility of redemption, Lloyd sees a weak sort of secularist faith that doubles down on existing social relations at the precise moment it professes its longing for their transformation. The implication here is that those who want to eradicate injustice need to hope harder, dream bigger. Perhaps in communities of worship, perhaps as marshalled in the streets, what power hope possesses resides beyond the courthouse steps.

12

Friend

KATHRYN LOFTON

What kind of friend to the Supreme Court are scholars of religion? The simple answer is: not a very helpful one. If we take as our data Supreme Court decisions from the last twenty years and whether they cite amicus briefs filed by scholars of religion, then the verdict is clear: scholarship on religion has had no apparent effect on what the court thinks. Although scholars of religion have spent significant time paying attention to the work of the court, in their decisions addressing religious subjects the court apparently pays little to no attention to the commentaries of scholars of religion.[1]

Could it be otherwise? *Should* it be otherwise? The first question presses us to think about whether scholars of religion have information that the court wants; the second asks whether scholars ought to be useful to the court at all. It might seem obvious that the answers should be an eager "yes" and "yes," that scholars should work to get information they need to help governmental offices do their best thinking about religion. Yet the work of the court and the work of scholars are not the same thing, and—as we shall see—the kind of information legal authorities want about religion and the kinds of information scholars of religion provide are not easily coordinated. How, then, can scholars of religion work to be more useful to legal authorities, insofar as such use would be indicated by citation in decisions? This chapter answers this question through a study of the amicus brief as a genre and the role scholars have generally played in the authorship of such briefs.

To begin, let us take a wider lens and reflect on how scholars of religion have generally discussed court cases involving religion. The findings of this research are not diverse or conflicting. Time and again, scholars have observed the Christian bias of the Supreme Court. What this means is that, according to this scholarly bibliography, the court repeatedly explains non-Christian religions through comparisons to Christianity. Despite the promise of individual religious free exercise enshrined in the Constitution, dominant sociological communities of American culture—specifically, white Protestants—have had a controlling hold on the interpretation of what right religion is and which religious groups might pose a threat to the security of the nation. In decision after decision, jurists assume Christianity is the template for all religions and that they can figure out what is or is not properly religious on the basis of whether a behavior can be compared usefully to Christianity.[2] This normalization of Christianity by legal authorities has had significant consequences on the structuring of religious life in the Unites States.[3] There is a healthy historiography that has looked at how a variety of communities have had to explain themselves through Protestant norms in order to argue for their specific sectarian organizational and expressive freedom.[4] Although the majority of this chapter won't focus on this pattern of Christian predominance, I mention it because this kind of analysis is what has pervaded recent scholarship on religion and law in the US, and the information that it produces—information about the Protestant bias of the court, and the Protestant bias of the American public more generally—is definitely *not* the kind of information the court finds useful. This may be, at first blush, a bummer to realize at the conclusion of this volume, which has offered many essays that reflect this scholarly pattern.

In order to explore what kind of friend the scholar of religion might otherwise be to the court, let's take a step back and understand the genre by which scholarship is offered in friendship to the court, namely, through the amicus brief. The phrase "amicus curiae" is Latin for "friend of the court." In common usage, the phrase is shortened to "amicus." An amicus—sometimes an individual, sometimes a nonprofit organization, sometimes a corporation, sometimes a figure of government, sometimes a group of professionals like clergy—submits a written essay to a court, called an amicus brief. This brief, prepared by an attorney, provides judges with new information or a different perspective from what the parties provided in their suit to the judge. The history of amicus briefs reveals the relative consistency of its intent, albeit with significant variability in its manufacture, its abundance, and its politics.[5] Throughout the history of the amicus brief, its purpose has been to provide information the court does not have. For example, the premodern amicus provided courts with neutral information beyond its formal notice or specific expertise. The major point of the amicus brief was to prevent an obvious and indisputable error—a manifest error—that could warrant reversal on appeal. The amicus brief is, therefore, historically understood as a fact-checking tool.

In the earliest historical examples of amicus briefs, they were the result of the court's solicitation: the earliest briefs explained technical law to those jurists unfamiliar with that law. In the modern period, the amicus brief is not requested by the court, but is submitted by an assumed expert who gives a fuller understanding of the case. Consistent to the genre is the sense that a brief that would be helpful to jurists is one that prevents a manifest error. As such, the positive contribution of the amicus is not in service to a position *toward* the case but instead a data point necessary for thinking accurately *about* the content of the case. Amicus briefs might examine policy issues; they could support the grant of discretionary review; they might supplement a party's brief or endorse a position; they could provide a historical perspective or a technical assistant; they often hope to provide political pressure.

Within this variety the constant feature of a useful brief is one that offers information the court needs to understand the specifics of a case thoroughly. A good amicus brief tells the court something that the parties haven't because they can't or won't. Very often a good brief includes discussion of facts that are not entered into evidence in the prior legal proceeding. A brief that is unhelpful is one that tells the court something that the parties already have or is altogether irrelevant to the specific contours of the court's charge. I should underline that I am using the language of "helpful" and "unhelpful" to indicate whether a brief serves the jurists making the decision. The measure I have used for whether a brief is considered helpful is its citation in a jurist's decision. Of course a brief could be helpful but not cited; that is, a jurist could gain information from a brief and then not cite it. I lean into this language of helpful precisely because there is a common-sense view that briefs that serve such informational ends are useful to jurists, whether or not they are cited.

In a survey of former US Supreme Court law clerks on the hallmarks of briefs used in decisions by the court, a majority of the clerks said that amicus briefs are most helpful in cases involving either highly technical or specialized areas of law *or* complex statutory and regulatory regimes.[6] The good brief in such cases helps to translate a technical area or regulatory complexity into legibility relative to the case's particulars. Some prominent briefs have used social science research (especially from the fields of criminology or sociology), such as citing how many confessions given to police are probably false, how impaired the impulse control of a twelve-year-old is, or how racist the outcomes from all-white juries are. But the key element of the good brief, a brief that could be helpful, is its data reveal: the good brief offers facts that give perspective to the features, mechanisms, or logistics of the case and not a tendentious perspective on the case itself. Put flatly: a good brief affects a posture of informational neutrality, whereas a bad one reads like a polemic. An example of a good brief is one filed by General Norman Schwarzkopf in *Grutter v. Bollinger*, in which the general argued that diversity among military officers is important to national security. Many of the justices noted the importance of this brief, since it described the importance of race-conscious programs to create diversity within the military. The factual tone of the general in his description of those programs, his authority as someone who would be in the position to evaluate their effect, and his clarity about the axiomatic good that diversity provides to the establishment of national defense contributed to its persuasive effect on the judges as they waded into the extremely political territory of affirmative action.[7] When it comes to the use value of amicus briefs, judges do not need another opinion to read. They need to know if they have the facts right in order to offer *their* opinion.

All this talk of facts and informational neutrality should not suggest amicus briefs pretend to objectivity. Very few modern-day amici understand themselves as simply neutral friends of the court.[8] Instead they are lobbyists of the court directed in the genre to extend their expertise or demonstrate their expertise by way of their symbolic authority relative to the case. Court observers have noted with some concern the increased number of amicus briefs submitted over the last half century, and they connect this increase to the expanding attention to court activities as well as the politicization of the court.[9] According to a comprehensive review of amicus advocacy in the Supreme Court, in the first century of American high-court cases, amicus briefs were rare and, from

1900 to 1950, were filed in only about 10 percent of cases. "This pattern has now completely reversed," this review notes. By 2000, one or more briefs were filed in 85 percent of US Supreme Court cases.[10]

What effect on the case do these amicus briefs have? The answer is disputed. Some studies suggest amicus briefs in general make little difference in the outcome of a case.[11] Some critics suggest this is because of their preponderance: briefs have become so "commonplace" that they have been "rendered meaningless."[12] One of the more prominent critics of amicus briefs, former Seventh Circuit Court of Appeals judge Richard Posner, argued that their impact is limited in part because the motivations behind their preparation are often suspect.[13] Posner's position is often cited in legal considerations of the amicus brief because he highlights an issue under heavy dispute, namely, the question of bias. Bias among the amici, bias among the jurists: wherever you look in the literature on court decision-making, the question of how to discern facts from opinion is central. And Posner says: amicus briefs can't be trusted because they are, finally, more about opinions than facts.

Yet there are many amicus briefs cited in Supreme Court cases. Whose briefs get cited? Statistical studies suggest that amicus briefs by institutional litigants and experienced lawyers are the most effective because those amici are the most focused on imparting new information to the case. The least effective briefs are those that seek to adjust the jurist's attitude toward a case. The assumption of these briefs is that the jurist doesn't need a lot of data to decide a case, since they have already effectively decided every case on the basis of their ideological assumptions. These briefs, based on the "attitudinal model" of court decision-making, assume that court cases are decided finally less because of points of contested data and more because of abstract opinions about government and society. Although these briefs rarely succeed, they dominate the amicus filings.[14]

This may seem odd. Why are there so many briefs filed that are not apparently useful to the court? Because the audience of the amicus brief is no longer just the court; the audience for the amicus brief is also the expanding public that observes the court. In *Courting Peril: The Political Transformation of the American Judiciary* (2016), legal scholar Charles Gardner Geyh argues that a combination of events that were generations in the making has turned the American judiciary into a much more publicized, and therefore much more political, place, in which the observing public is increasingly skeptical of judges and their motives. Geyh argues that this began in earnest in 1987 with the Senate's rejection of Robert Bork's nomination to the Supreme Court and can be seen in the way that traditional media now explain Supreme Court decisions with reference to the court's ideological voting blocs. At the same time, cable news stations such as Fox and CNBC report on the Supreme Court from decidedly partisan perspectives, and a new breed of citizen journalists offer a critique of the courts in a host of online venues that are unconstrained by the norms of traditional journalism. All of these observers assume, unconsciously and consciously, the attitudinal model: they assume that everyone is motivated less by the facts of the case than by their predetermined political outlook. By the reasoning of this model, to watch a court case isn't to observe a group of people deliberate individually over the contours of a problem. Rather, it's watching partisan teams order and reorder themselves relative to the political issues at hand.

In this perceived landscape of political brinksmanship, anyone who is a player in a Supreme Court decision, or might be affected by one, needs to think about how they will be cast in an increasingly mediatized court of political "gotcha." Amicus briefs become not mere tools of factual rehearsal, but advance public relations agenda. Consider, for example, legal lobbying organizations' increased use of corporate endorsements. In March 2017, fifty-three for-profit companies signed onto an amicus brief filed by the Human Rights Campaign (HRC), a nonprofit legal lobbying organization, in the Supreme Court case *Gloucester County School Board v. Gavin Grimm*, supporting a transgender student's challenge to his school's gender-conforming bathroom rule as violating federal law. For-profit companies had little to do with the facts of the case, but the increasing public attention to transgender issues made the case a public spectacle in which nobody (who wanted to make profits, or recruit donations, from those sympathetic to the case) wanted to be on the wrong side.

The HRC brief argued that diversity is good for business and discrimination conflicts with their LGBTQ-friendly corporate policies, harming people and profits. "These companies are sending a powerful message to transgender children and their families that America's leading businesses have their backs," HRC president Chad Griffin explained in a public comment. Those fifty-three corporations together have over 1.3 million employees and generate more than $600 billion in revenue in industries ranging from tech to insurance to cosmetics. In other words, the corporations used the brief like a press release, stating positions not only to inform the court but also to influence public perception. General Schwarzkopf testified in his amicus brief to the value of race-conscious programs; these companies testified to their support for transgender people. The difference to the court is a difference of factual authority. None of the for-profit companies that signed onto the HRC's brief had a specific program for LGBTQ inclusion that they argued had increased their profits or innovation. Many of the companies mentioned that they had single-occupancy bathrooms, but none testified to grappling with the issue of gender-neutral bathrooms in their company facilities. They were simply arguing that they are LGBTQ friendly and that this has long-term positive effects on their business community. Being friendly to different people is undoubtedly good business practice, but this does not add to the factual interpretation of a case involving public bathrooms in a public school. The brief was geared toward a public that might boycott their products, not a court deliberating this case.

Likewise, a month before the HRC filed the brief, nearly one hundred companies signed onto a brief opposing President Donald Trump's executive order banning travel from seven Muslim-majority nations. The filing states that the executive order "inflicts significant harm on American business, innovation, and growth" and "makes it more difficult and expensive for US companies to recruit, hire, and retain some of the world's best employees." With this brief, which was widely reported in the media, the companies also told the world where they stood on the wildly controversial ban, associating their brands with justice for the underdog.[15] This corporate virtue signaling did nothing to affect the outcome of either Supreme Court decision. The amicus contained no information useful for the court's decision, but their public positioning could influence their bottom lines as they sought to represent their political position to the consumer republic.

This could make us all very cynical about the increase in amicus brief filings and their use generally by amici seeking public approval. But that is to be distracted by the chaos of the public sphere and therefore miss how it is importantly undergirded by democratic routes to juridical engagement. Because it is rooted in the right to petition, amicus participation is an integral part of social movements.[16] For every hundred amicus briefs that offer no information of use, there may be one that intercedes with a fact that had not been considered. And in a democracy, we seek to maintain routes for every citizen to offer their testimony, their facts, and their experience to the adjudication of the law that organizes their citizenship. Any vexatious filings are balanced by the overall benefit of making possible democratic participation in the court system.[17] As Helen Anderson has written, "Amicus curiae participation is defended as democratic input into what is otherwise not a democratic branch of government."[18] No matter their content, amicus briefs might be seen as a way to dilute the elite authority of the courts. It creates a platform for anyone to join the critical interpretive conversation about the rule of law that governs them.

Still, though, very few briefs submitted will be cited by the court, and the purpose of this essay is to think about whether scholars of religion could ever offer briefs that might be helpful to the court. Within the genre of the amicus brief there are ways to increase the rare possibility that your information might be used in a court decision. In its guidance to lawyers on the appropriate approach to amicus filings, the American Bar Association warns lawyers who write these briefs on behalf of corporations and organizations against appearing biased, noting, "Although an amicus acts as an advocate, an amicus brief is most effective if not obviously compelled by self-interest, but rather drafted to assist the court from the amicus' special perspective."[19] Recall the amicus brief submitted by General Schwarzkopf: it was a helpful brief not because it seemed to benefit him as a military leader but because it sought to explain something about the military and the advantages of diversity to it, not to him.

According to Supreme Court law clerks, they can discern from the minute they look at a brief whether it will be useful. This is decided as much by the brevity, font, and authorship of the brief as anything else. If an amicus brief *is* then used, it is because it brought something new and interesting to the case from a source respected as an authority on the relevant point. What has been offered might be better research, an explanation of the connection between this specific case and other pending cases, an improved discussion of industry practices or economic conditions, a more penetrating analysis of the regulatory landscape, or a convincing demonstration of the impact of the case on segments of society other than the immediate parties. Justices are understood to be working in a state of relative isolation and have only a small amount of time for research in a particular case. An amicus brief must try to overcome that isolation by providing the information they need to declare legal rules of nationwide applicability. Justice Breyer has said that these briefs "play an important role in educating judges on potentially relevant technical matters, helping to make us not experts but educated lay persons and thereby helping to improve the quality of our decisions." Justice Alito concurs, observing that "even when a party is very well represented, an amicus may provide important assistance to the court . . . [by] collect[ing] background or factual references that merit judicial notice." And former Supreme Court law clerks have remarked that it is the *nonlegal* information provided by amici that is the most useful, since clerks and the jurists they serve possess the requisite legal expertise to decide a case.[20]

Into this frame enters the scholar with nonlegal information. Scholars have found routes to consequence as amici. Although social scientists had been contributing amici successfully since the early twentieth century, in the 1980s, historians began to author briefs.[21] In *Lawrence v. Texas* (2003) and *Parents Involved in Community Schools v. Seattle School District No. 1* (2007), historians offered specific legal histories in order to show how specific district plans and state laws violated the equal protection clause of the Fourteenth Amendment. Historians explained historical facts in these briefs, namely, that the laws that sought to regulate race and sexuality had changed over time and thus the law could (and, these briefs asserted, *should*) change again. For instance, in his examination of the historians' brief for *Lawrence v. Texas*, Daniel Hurwitz explains that the brief had two simple points: first, the Texas law against homosexuals lacked a significant historical pedigree because the history of antigay discrimination was, actually, short and, second, that US sex laws had only recently been used by states to target homosexual activity. The historians' brief in *Lawrence v. Texas* worked because it showed how short the history of an antigay law was.[22] When the justices went to decide whether the criminal convictions of John Lawrence and Tyron Garner under the Texas "Homosexual Conduct" violated their vital interests in liberty and privacy, the majority said "yes," because it violated the

Fourteenth Amendment's due process clause. Citing the amicus curiae through the majority opinion, Justice Kennedy repeatedly reiterated the historical contingency of the "homosexual" as a suspect class. (i.e., "In academic writings, and in many of the scholarly amicus briefs filed to assist the court in this case, there are fundamental criticisms of the historical premises relied upon by the majority and concurring opinions in Bowers.") The majority opinion focused on whether, as consenting adults, Lawrence and Garner were free to engage in the private conduct in the exercise of their liberty under the due process clause, and Kennedy used historical mutability as the term of judgment:

> Had those who drew and ratified the Due Process Clauses of the Fifth Amendment or the Fourteenth Amendment known the components of liberty in its manifold possibilities, they might have been more specific. They did not presume to have this insight. They knew times can blind us to certain truths and later generations can see that laws once thought necessary and proper in fact serve only to oppress. As the Constitution endures, persons in every generation can invoke its principles in their own search for greater freedom.

Kennedy's opinion evinces the effect of historical thinking: he refers to his own sense that laws emerge from specific moments in time, and that the authors of the Constitution knew themselves that times would change. The job of jurists is to think about whether the principle of a law continues to create greater freedom and minimize oppression. In the decision for *Lawrence*, the court argued that Lawrence and Garner were free as adults to engage in private conduct in the exercise of their liberty under the due process clause. "The Texas statute furthers no legitimate state interest which can justify its intrusion into the personal and private life of the individual," continued Justice Kennedy. He came to this resolution in part because he could interpret state interest in this private conduct differently than its interest might have been in the century when the Constitution was authored.

Yet scholars of religion have yet to have such success in the authorship of amicus briefs. I cannot identify a single amicus brief filed by scholars of religion cited by the court in the last several decades.[23] Why might this be? Let us compare the success of scholarly intervention into

Lawrence v. Texas with two unsuccessful amicus briefs filed by scholars of religion to prominent cases, namely, *Boy Scouts of America et al. v. Dale* (2000) and *Elk Grove Unified School District v. Newdow* (2004). Here, "unsuccessful" is defined in two ways: first, the court did not rule as the authors of the briefs hoped; second, in its rulings, the court did not cite these amicus briefs. There are other forms of success—perhaps the court clerks read a brief and were inspired to read something else because of it; maybe a jurist was influenced but left no citation of that influence. The point is that "unsuccessful" here focuses on the available record: the amici wanted a case to be ruled a certain way, and the court's decision did not serve that hope nor indicate in its notes why the brief's information wasn't useful to the ruling.

The amici in these cases were deans of divinity schools, biblical scholars, and historians of religion who offered briefs that worked to offer contextual information to argue, in turn, against the Boy Scouts' ban on homosexuals and against the practice of reciting the Pledge of Allegiance in US public schools. In *Boys Scouts of America*, the amici sought to make two points: first, that there is no consensus among religious scholars that homosexuality is immoral and, second, that a number of major American religious institutions have moved toward acceptance, not condemnation, of homosexuals. The amici hoped to convince the justices to think differently about homosexuals. However admirable a project this attitudinal adjustment might be, such arguments do not provide what an amicus brief needs to provide to be deemed useful. Saying that scholars haven't agreed on the immorality of homosexuality or that most institutions have moved toward acceptance of homosexuals are fair scholarly and sociological observations, but they are not an explanation of a technical point.

As it happened, such observations from the amici did nothing to help the Supreme Court render their decision in *Boys Scouts of America*. Their focus was on whether the application of New Jersey's public accommodations law violated the Boy Scouts' First Amendment right of expressive association to bar homosexuals from serving as troop leaders. The case was not about whether homosexuality was moral; the case was about whether a state law could infringe on a constitutional right. The court was clear: it could not. The Supreme Court decided that the public accommodations law violated the Boy Scouts' First Amendment rights.

This decision was determined by the jurisdiction of constitutional law and not attitudes toward homosexuality.

As did the *Boy Scouts* amici, the three amicus briefs filed by scholars in *Newdow* offered varieties of scholarly common sense. By referring to their contents as "common sense," I mean to suggest that these amicus briefs conveyed ideas about religion that might be taught in an introductory historical survey on religion in America or that might represent the deduction of a great deal of scholarly energy. These briefs argued the following:

- For its first sixty years, the Pledge of Allegiance was wholly secular.
- The 1954 Act infused the Pledge with religion.
- The 1954 Act endorsed monotheism.
- The word "God" is not generic and is not a shared value or unifying concept.
- The founders embraced pluralism, which is the shared value and unifying principle of the nation.
- Asking students in public schools to pledge allegiance to "one nation, under God" violates the establishment clause.

Depending on how much time you have spent studying religion in America, such comments might seem intriguing or banal. For the long-time scholar of religion, these comments reiterated how recently the Pledge of Allegiance emerged as a ritual practice and its problematic theological assumptions. Rather than seeing the Pledge of Allegiance as a unifying, generic testimony to a common national purpose, these comments underlined that it is divisive and sectarian. Each of these "facts" (the pledge was initially secular; it *became* religious; when it became religious, it became monotheistic) bore the hallmarks of the study of religion: grounded in historical research, studious about comparative hierarchy and the exclusions such hierarchies produce, and fiercely committed to a concept of pluralism that recognizes impediments to its public fulfillment. Even more, the scholars hoped to link this concept of pluralism to the authors of the Constitution and to mark later incursions on this principle as a faulty overlay of twentieth-century politics. See this observation from the amici: "In other words, contrary to the impression generally given about the founding era in church/state debates today, expansion of American pluralism well beyond Christianity and Judaism was contemplated and, even though there were dissenters, pluralism was embraced in the founding era." The amici wanted the justices to know that the Pledge of Allegiance as we presently know it is the result of present Christian politics and not the founders' intended pluralist ideal. This is historical thinking with an emphasis on religious issues. Why then was this information unhelpful to the case?

I want to underline that these observations represent scholarly consensus. These are the sorts of things that scholars of US religion say when evaluating the history, ritual function, or theological substance of the Pledge of Allegiance.[24] However, none of these claims bore on the technical issue at the heart of *Newdow*, which did not hinge on the content of the Pledge of Allegiance but on whether Newdow had the standing as a parental figure to bring suit. Because he did not have sufficient custody over his daughter, the Supreme Court decided that he did not have the parental standing to bring suit. Yet not a single sentence of the briefs prepared by scholars of religion reflected on this issue of parental standing. It could be that they—and the lawyers that helped them prepare their briefs—did not predict that this would be the issue on which the case would be decided.

Many briefs focus on themes that don't end up being relevant to court deliberations; it is possible that having the briefs helps jurists determine what issues are at stake, even if they are not cited. But because scholars of religion have *never* been cited in court deliberations, could this instance be more pattern than exception? It begs a moment of reflection. What if the scholars who authored the brief chose not to think about the historical trajectory of the Pledge and the monotheistic incursion of the 1954 Act? What if they had chosen instead to think about the concept of the parent in the history of religions? Considering that personage and its mutable history might have made their information more technically assistive. For example, scholars plumbing scriptures would find ample evidence to support the significance of the noncustodial parent in human growth and development. Yet this is not the interpretive direction in which the scholars traveled. Instead, they explained how unconstitutional the Pledge was and ignored altogether the hinge of familial relation.

In *Boys Scouts of America* and *Newdow*, scholars of religion exerted great intellectual, professional, and writerly effort to develop collaborative amicus briefs explaining biblical tradition and US religious history to no useful end. Perhaps this can be chalked up to a basic misunderstanding of how Supreme Court decisions function. If so, let this chapter be a small note to future amici from the study of religion: those writing amicus briefs should do their best to consider the specifics of a case and, in particular, how their expertise could be used to explain the mutability of specific roles and social identities in human society.

But there is perhaps a stronger lesson to learn. Reviewing the amicus briefs filed by scholars of religion, I am struck by how often they do exactly as the *Newdow* amici did: they try to show how wrongly Christian is the presumptive public norm in American jurisprudence and in American public life. The scholar of religion is thus almost always in a corrective posture toward the jurist, seeking to show how those jurists possess an exclusionary morality underwritten by Judeo-Christian monotheism. These scholars ride into legal cases hoping to correct the apparently clumsily and barely veiled Protestant norms of judicial discernment. There is something oddly overconfident about the scholar of religion in this guise. Despite the fact that few scholars of religion (Sally Gordon and Winnifred Sullivan being important exceptions) are experts in the law, many scholars of religion think of themselves as experts in the court's Protestant prejudice. As I have found, they are rarely quite right. Maybe there is Protestant prejudice, but it doesn't seem to impact the case as the scholar of religion imagines.

One telling footnote: where scholars of religion fail to provide something useful to the court, religious organizations frequently succeed.[25] Religious organizations often file briefs with the Supreme Court—they do so with far greater frequency than scholars of religion, weighing in on a wide variety of moral and political issues. The top filers are the conservative Christian lobbyist organizations Family Research Council and Focus on the Family, although the Unitarian Universalist Association, the US Conference of Catholic Bishops, the United Church of Christ and the Evangelical Lutheran Church in America also frequently submit briefs.[26] A review of briefs submitted by religious organizations reveals that the vast majority offers ethical and legal arguments on religious grounds. Most of these briefs, like those from scholars of religion, end up bearing little consequence on the decisions themselves. However, in the rare instances when a religious organization has consequence—and, again, this is notable because by contrast scholars of religion *never* have sway—they do because they talk about religious doctrine and practical experience.[27] In *Santa Fe Independent School District v. Doe* (2000) and *Little Sisters of the Poor Home for the Aged v. Burwell* (2016), the court decisively used briefs filed by religious organizations to decide in favor of what the majority of religious amici argued. It is apparent from the jurisprudence that courts dislike having to decide what a religious group believes, but they do so constantly. Any definitive brief by a religious organization explaining the technical facets of belief, or the nature of religious belief itself, can be influential.

The Little Sisters of the Poor, a Roman Catholic religious order, runs homes for low-income elderly and therefore was not automatically exempt from the contraceptive mandate, a regulation adopted by the US Department of Health and Human Services under the Affordable Care Act (ACA) that requires nonchurch employers to cover certain contraceptives for their female employees. The Little Sisters of the Poor objected to filing Form 700 (the form required organizations to claim an exemption) because they believed that doing so would make their order complicit in providing contraception, a sin under Roman Catholic doctrine. On the day before the filing requirement was to come into effect, Justice Sotomayor granted a temporary injunction to the Little Sisters of the Poor, allowing them to simply inform the Secretary of Health and Human Services of their objections, pending resolution of the case. Other religious institutions filed similar objections, resulting in *Zubik v. Burwell*, which remanded to the lower courts the work of determining an approach that would accommodate the employers' religious exercise.

To review the many briefs included in *Zubik v. Burwell* is to find a series of voices saying that their beliefs are so specific and complicated that they suggest the Supreme Court get out of the business of pretending to know those beliefs or to have the capacity to judge them in relation to a bureaucratic requirement. Here we see the Orthodox rabbis reminding the court how much difficulty it would wade into if it endeavored to parse what is and is not free exercise:

> Numerous everyday activities such as writing, cooking, or driving a car constitute a desecration of the Sabbath according to Orthodox Jewish practice. In fact, picking flowers, removing bones from fish, and gather-

ing sticks in an open field may each qualify as a violation of the fourth of the Ten Commandments. In biblical times, such a violation merited the death penalty. Numbers 15:32–36. It is unreasonable to ask judges who are unlikely to share, or even be aware of, these beliefs to weigh the substantiality of the burdens placed upon sincere religious believers.

The Society of Krishna Consciousness likewise warned the courts away from getting involved in adjudicating religion. "It is far outside the competence of federal courts—or indeed any government official—to determine whether a person's religion deems him morally complicit in sin if he does certain acts. Nor may courts reweigh whether even an easy 'paperwork' task carries grave religious implications. Those are exclusively theological questions, not legal ones." Scholars of religion might debate the distinction the Society of Krishna Consciousness draws between theological questions and legal questions, but for the Supreme Court, there is no question: *they don't want to get involved in this morass.* Not because they don't like morasses, but because the technicalities of doctrine are indeed not theirs to parse. The courts seek this information about religion: the kind that religious organizations are currently more than happy to provide in order to persuade the court of their posited constituency's right to free exercise.

When amicus briefs about religion are cited in Supreme Court cases, it is from those organizations the court can recognize as legibly "religious" and *not* from those they recognize as scholars of religion. Scholars supply opinions irrelevant to the facts of the case, whereas religious organizations volunteer technical facts about the relevant religion. If scholars of religion want to enter the present culture of providing religious information on juridical matters, they will have to contest the authority of religious organizations. In order for scholars to be understood as authoritatively informational on religion, rather than explaining the history of religions, scholars would do better to contest the nature of religious authority as embodied by the litigants or other amici in Supreme Court jurisprudence. What if scholars of religion offered a definition for what constitutes a "parent" in *Newdow* or what constitutes a legitimate "association" in *Boy Scouts of America*? The history of religions includes more data about the definition of authorities and the organization of distinguishing groups than almost any other documentary archive. Rather than show how the history of religions in America is biased toward Christians—a piece of data that, while true, seems to be unimportant to the court—the scholar might show how the subjects of the state (parents and children, associations and individuals) have been religiously determined and historically mutable. This is information the court does not have, since the litigants are often unconscious of their own remnant religious histories, and many religions are unconscious of their own authoritarian incongruities. Scholars that assembled as amici to provide such information might not end up being a friend to religion, but they might be a friend to the court.

NOTES

1 Scholars look to the number of times amicus briefs are cited in court opinions as evidence of a brief's influence, although the extent of this influence is impossible to determine merely by citation; a brief could be read but not cited. That said, according to one recent study of signed Supreme Court opinions issued in the 2014–2015 term, the justices cited amicus briefs in 55 percent of the cases. This would suggest that at least some justices are highly receptive to the involvement of amici in Supreme Court proceedings. Yet that number is misleading because many of those citations were to amicus briefs filed by the Solicitor General's office, not so-called green briefs (nongovernment amicus briefs) such as those filed by scholars of religion. Closer inspection by this author into the last twenty years of Supreme Court jurisprudence found not a single instance in which a brief filed by scholars of religion was cited in a Supreme Court decision. Anthony J. Franze and R. Reeves Anderson, "Record Breaking Term for Amicus Curiae in Supreme Court Reflects New Norm," *National Law Journal*, August 19, 2015.

2 Jonathan Z. Smith, "God Save This Honorable Court: Religion and Civic Discourse," in *Relating Religion: Essays in the Study of Religion* (Chicago: University of Chicago Press, 2004), 375–90; Winnifred Fallers Sullivan, *The Impossibility of Religious Freedom* (Princeton, NJ: Princeton University Press, 2005).

3 Within the study of religion in America, many works have considered the impact of Christian authority in American life. Two standout texts are Tracy Fessenden, *Culture and Redemption: Religion, the Secular, and American Literature* (Princeton, NJ: Princeton University Press, 2006) and Amanda Porterfield, *Conceived in Doubt: Religion and Politics in the New American Nation* (Chicago: University of Chicago Press, 2012).

4 Garrett Epps, *Peyote vs. the State: Religious Freedom on Trial* (Norman: University of Oklahoma Press, 2009); Greg Johnson, *Sacred Claims: Repatriation and Living Tradition* (Charlottesville: University of Virginia Press, 2007); Thomas C. Maroukis, *The Peyote Road: Religious Freedom and the Native American Church* (Norman: University of Oklahoma Press, 2010); Winnifred Fallers Sullivan, *The*

Impossibility of Religious Freedom (Princeton, NJ: Princeton University Press, 2007); Tisa Wenger, *We Have a Religion: The 1920s Pueblo Indian Dance Controversy and American Religious Freedom* (Chapel Hill: University of North Carolina Press, 2009).

5   Although dated, the best history of amicus curiae briefs in the Supreme Court remains Samuel Krislov, "The Amicus Curiae Brief: From Friendship to Advocacy," *Yale Law Journal* 72, no. 4 (1963): 694–721. The first recorded appearance of an amicus brief in the Supreme Court occurred in 1821. See Green v. Biddle, 21 U.S. (8 Wheat.) 1 (1823), which perhaps not coincidentally was the first year the court accepted written briefs for filing.

6   Kelly J. Lynch, "Best Friends—Supreme Court Law Clerks on Effective Amicus Curiae Briefs," *Journal of Law & Politics* 20, no. 1 (Winter 2004): 33–76.

7   The Schwarzkopf brief is highlighted in Reagan W. Simpson and Mary Vasaly, *The Amicus Brief: How to Write It and Use It Effectively*, 3rd ed. (Chicago: American Bar Association, 2011), 8. It is further discussed in Mary Wood, "Grutter Litigators Explain Strategies Used to Win Affirmative Action Case," *University of Virginia School of Law: News and Media* (April 2004), https://content.law.virginia.edu.

8   Luther T. Munford, "When Does the Curiae Need an Amicus?," *Journal of Appellate Practice and Process* 1, no. 2 (1999): 279–84.

9   A study found that during the ten years between 1946 and 1955, approximately 531 briefs were filed; in contrast, between the years of 1986 and 1995, 4,907 briefs were filed. Joseph D. Kearney and Thomas W. Merrill, "Influence of Amicus Curiae Briefs on the Supreme Court," *University of Pennsylvania Law Review* 148, no. 3 (January 2000): 752. See also Paul M. Collins Jr., "Friends of the Court: Examining the Influence of *Amicus Curiae* Participation in US Supreme Court Litigation," *Law & Society Review* 38, no. 4 (2004): 807–32. See also Ryan Salzman, Christopher J. Williams, and Bryan T. Calvin, "The Determinants of the Number of Amicus Briefs Filed before the US Supreme Court, 1953–2001," *Justice System Journal* 32, no. 3 (2011): 293–313; David Paul Kuhn, "The Incredible Polarization and Politicization of the Supreme Court," *Atlantic*, June 29, 2012, www.theatlantic.com.

10 Kearney and Merrill, "Influence of Amicus Curiae," 744.

11 Ruth Colker and Kevin M. Scott, "Dissing States: Invalidation of State Action during the Rehnquist Era," *Virginia Law Review* 88, no. 6 (October 2002): 1301–86; Donald R. Songer and Reginald S. Sheehan, "Interest Group Success in the Courts: Amicus Participation in the Supreme Court," *Political Research Quarterly* 46, no. 2 (June 1993): 339–54; Collins, "Friends of the Court."

12 Colker and Scott, "Dissing States," 1338.

13 Kearney and Merrill, "Influence of Amicus Curiae," 745–46; Karen O'Connor, "The Amicus Curiae Role of the US Solicitor General in Supreme Court Litigation," *Judicature* 66, no. 5 (December–January 1983): 256–64; Helen A. Anderson, "Frenemies of the Court: The Many Faces of Amicus Curiae," *University of Richmond Law Review* 49 (2015): 361–416. Posner's critique of amicus briefs can be found in Voices for Choices v. Ill. Bell Tel. Co., http://caselaw.findlaw.com.

14 Kearney and Merrill, "Influence of Amicus Curiae," 750, 779–81, 813, 830.

15 Ephrat Livni, "The Amicus Brief Is the New Press Release," March 8, 2017, https://qz.com.

16 Ruben J. Garcia, "A Democratic Theory of Amicus Advocacy," *Florida State University Law Review* 35 no. 2 (2008): 320, makes reference to Richard A. Posner, *Law, Pragmatism, and Democracy* (Cambridge, MA: Harvard University Press, 2003).

17 Garcia, "A Democratic Theory," 333, 344.

18 Anderson, "Frenemies of the Court," 361.

19 "A Business Perspective: The Role of Amicus Briefing in Appellate Advocacy" (presented by the Committee on Business and Corporate Litigation at the 2004 Annual Meeting of the American Bar Association in Atlanta), republished in *eSource for Business Law* 3, no. 5 (October 2004): 2, http://apps.americanbar.org.

20 Alli Orr Larsen, "The Trouble with Amicus Facts," *Virginia Law Review* 100 (2014): 1761.

21 Ronald Roesch, Stephen L. Golding, Valerie P. Hans, and N. Dickon Reppucci, "Social Science and the Courts: The Role of Amicus Curiae Briefs," *Law and Human Behavior* 15, no. 1 (1991): 1–11; Daniel Hurewitz, "Sexuality Scholarship as Foundation for Change: *Lawrence v. Texas* and the Impact of the Historians' Brief," *Health and Human Rights* 7 no. 2 (2004): 205–16; Michael Grossberg, "Friends of the Court: A New Role for Historians," *Perspectives on History* (November 2010), www.historians.org.

22 Hurewitz, "Sexuality Scholarship as Foundation for Change," 209.

23 I define "scholars of religion" as they self-identify in the standard section of the amicus brief titled "Interest of the Amicus/Amici Curiae," which typically explains why the author(s) of the brief have relevant expertise for the fact of the case. We can find many briefs filed since the year 2000 with the phrases "religion scholar," "professors and scholars in the fields of religion and theology," or "theologians and scholars of religion from a variety of traditions." They further introduce themselves as persons who have studied, taught, and written about the role of religion in the US and who are therefore demonstrably recognized as experts on the history of religion in American society.

24 For the most recent articulation of this argument, see Kevin M. Kruse, *One Nation under God: How Corporate America Invented Christian America* (New York: Basic Books, 2016). See also Grace Y. Kao and Jerome E. Copulsky, "The Pledge of Allegiance and the Meanings and Limits of Civil Religion," *Journal of the American Academy of Religion* 75, no. 1 (2007): 121–49; Cecilia O'Leary and Tony Platt, "Pledging Allegiance: The Revival of Prescriptive Patriotism," *Social Justice* 28, no. 3 (2001): 41–44.

25 Andrew S. Mansfield, "Religious Arguments and the United States Supreme Court: A Review of Amicus Curiae Briefs Filed by Religious Organizations," *Cardozo Public Law, Policy, and Ethics Journal* 7, no. 2 (Spring 2009): 343–94; Leo

Pfeffer, "Amici in Church-State Litigation," *Law and Contemporary Problems* 44 (Spring 1981): 83–110.

26 Other frequently participating groups include the Episcopal Church, the American Jewish Committee, Agudath Israel, American Friends (Quakers), Lutheran Church Missouri Synod, the National Association of Evangelicals, the Presbyterian Church (USA), and the United Methodist Church.

27 Paul M. Collins Jr., Pamela C. Corley, and Jesse Hamner, "The Influence of Amicus Curiae Briefs on US Supreme Court Opinion Content," *Law & Society Review* 49, no. 4 (2015): 917–44.

13

Personhood

SYLVESTER A. JOHNSON

In July 2016, the Dallas Police Department set a precedent when officers deployed a Remotec robot to detonate one pound of C-4 explosive in order to kill an African American suspect, Micah Johnson, who was wanted in the shooting deaths of five police officers. Two months earlier, a white driver, Joshua Brown, died in a Florida traffic collision while his Tesla sedan was employing the semiautonomous, assistive Autopilot driving technology that has become a hallmark of the manufacturer. For decades, science fiction films and books have conjured futuristic scenarios of robots and other intelligent machines killing humans and running amok. So these events of 2016 came as a shock to many casual observers accustomed to associating intelligent machines with fiction. For those who have been following the dizzying pace of developing artificial intelligence (AI) robots and other machine intelligence, however, things are less surprising. For everyone, the fact that intelligent machines have now begun to play a role in matters of life and death opens a new chapter in the history of relations between humans and technology. It exposes the fragility of common assumptions about moral agency. And it implies that the domain of religion and ethics will have to be theorized anew in an age of intelligent machines.[1]

The robotic killing of Micah Johnson echoes the historical and enduring pattern of racial disparity in policing that experts have repeatedly demonstrated as a continuing form of lethal violence that US law enforcement personnel use to engage black civilians. (Consider, by contrast, that municipal police pursuing the white shooting suspect Dylann Roof swaddled him in a bullet-proof vest for protection after Roof murdered en masse a group of black parishioners in South Carolina.) Johnson, furthermore, was by no means the first suspect to create a violent standoff with municipal police, but he will now stand in memory as the first US citizen on domestic soil to be targeted and killed by means of a state-powered robot.[2]

In many ways, Johnson's experience has little in common with that of Joshua Brown, a technologist and Tesla enthusiast whose death is not contextualized by racial politics or criminality. Despite their many differences, however, these two cases share overwhelming significance for understanding human-machine relations within the context of life and death. We must consider issues of responsibility, culpability, and restitution. Beyond this, these deaths raise a fundamental question about agency: Who actually caused the deaths of these men? Intelligent machines? Humans exerting agency through machines?

These deaths also raise questions about the law. More specifically, legal frameworks about personhood and the related concepts of agency and rights will increasingly appear at the center of debates over new and emerging technology. This is because the ever-increasing capacity of AI technology and existing legal paradigms are experiencing growing incoherence. US laws do not currently recognize any legal subjecthood in machines, so presently a machine cannot be held legally responsible for a human death, regardless of how intelligent and agential it might actually be. One should not take this to mean that legal doctrine cannot be adapted to recognize legal personhood in nonhuman entities. Corporations, after all, have long enjoyed legal subjecthood as artificial, fictive persons in US law, a tradition that has reached so far as to assert that for-profit corporations have a constitutionally protected right to religious freedom. If corporations have been recognized as such, must we not reckon with the prospect that AI entities might come to occupy such a status and the consequences of such?

In what follows, I explain the designation of corporations as legal persons in the United States, after which I compare the legal and cultural legibility of corporations as people with the future *prospect* that AIs might be designated as such. I then explain how Christian theology has complicated the imagination of personhood in nonhuman things or objects. I end by explaining how race has factored into the quandaries of personhood to suggest that personhood must be engaged as an especially political category, even if not reductively so. This understanding, I conclude, must guide any future deployment of the concept in relationship to AI and human-machine relations.

Corporations as Artificial Persons

We begin by considering the history and legal rationality behind corporate personhood. It is fair to say that the exclusively white men who framed the US Constitution had in mind biological humans (white males, preeminently) when they inscribed recognizing the rights of persons. Since at least the early 1800s, corporations have enjoyed recognition as persons to some appreciable degree. Separate and apart from any biological humans, corporations have been treated by law as possessing some of the rights enjoyed more broadly by humans. This recognition has encompassed such rights as entering into contracts, asserting property rights, and being a plaintiff or defendant in legal suits. *Burwell v. Hobby Lobby Stores, Inc.* (2014), for instance, recognized the right of corporations (specifically those "closely held" by owners) to enjoy freedom of religious exercise, which presumes that corporations can indeed have religious beliefs that merit protection.[3]

The legal inscription of corporate personhood did not originate with religious mysticism. Rather, the pragmatic need for biological humans to enjoy the rights of individuals when acting collectively (typically for business purposes) led to a number of practices that treated human collectives as persons. The colonial history of corporations such as the Dutch East India Company (Verenigde Oost-Indische Compagnie), the Royal African Company, and the Hudson Bay Company all evidence such practices long before the beginnings of US law.[4]

The rise of corporate personhood may have been governed by pragmatic imperatives, but that doesn't mean that religious concepts had no influence. To take but one example, those jurists who rationalized the creation and chartering of colonial corporations emphasized that the individuals undertaking collective action were one "body politic," a foundational concept that has relied extensively on theological reasoning about membership in a collective entity. For centuries, Christians have claimed that their messiah is a resurrected divine figure who incorporates into his mystical body individual members of a universal church. The African bishop Augustine famously termed this doctrine the *totus Christus*—the total and totalizing messiah, whose collective body encompassed all Christians. As Christian empires and polities forged political theologies of Christendom, membership in the mystical community of the Christian church became inseparable from membership in the political community of a Christian state ruled by Christian princes. This same theological tradition furnished the Christian empires of Europe with legitimacy and a slate of governing tactics. These empires deployed a densely structured and exclusive Christian identity to rationalize seizing the lands of Indigenous peoples, enslaving and torturing Africans, and killing entire towns of Indigenous people, whose only offense was dignity in their own sovereignty.[5]

The most important constitutional basis for corporate personhood is the Fourteenth Amendment. This amendment was passed in 1868 to defend one of the most victimized and vulnerable of populations—newly manumitted blacks who had survived the formal regime of racial slavery. Along with free blacks, they had long been denied national belonging by whites. Manumission meant they immediately faced a new reign of white mob terror, state practices of antiblack racism, and an increasingly monetized carceral system that targeted them and reiterated some of slavery's worst tendencies. In one of the nation's grandest ironies, this Fourteenth Amendment was quickly repurposed to secure the rights of corporations at the very time white politicians of the post-Reconstruction era were advancing "white redemption" to systematically reverse the meager civil rights gains that followed the Civil War.[6]

Corporate attorneys and the judges sympathetic to them began emphasizing that corporations were people too and merited the "equal protection" that the nation's Reconstruction Congress had stipulated for blacks. That such equal protection had been meticulously defined in relation to the privileges enjoyed by white men ensured in theory the highest standard for recognizing corporate rights. Such extreme irony raised some dissent from at least a few jurists, even decades after becoming an established legal norm. In the case of *Wheeling Steel Corp. v. Glander* (1949), for instance, the presiding judge acknowledged frankly that the Fourteenth Amendment was crafted to protect the rights of formerly enslaved blacks, and he expressed skepticism that the amendment's authors had in mind corporations when they were crafting the amendment.[7]

In *Santa Clara v. Southern Pacific* (1886), Chief Justice Morrison Waite instructed the attorneys to interpret the Fourteenth Amendment as applicable to corporations and not only natural persons. This approach brought a practical solution to a historic problem: How could the liability of individual investors be limited in order to encourage them to pursue significant business ventures? This limited liability has remained fundamental to commercialism. Treating corporations as persons also obviated individual shareholders bringing individual lawsuits to address their collective interests and instead allowed a single entity (the corporation) to act as the legal subject on behalf of the individual shareholders. It was the subsequent *Pembina Consolidated Silver Mining Co. v. Pennsylvania* (1888) case, however, that produced the first judgment explicitly stating that the Fourteenth Amendment applied to corporations as "persons." This ruling quoted an earlier opinion by Chief Justice John Marshall, who had asserted in *Providence Bank v. Billings* (1830) that "the great purpose of a corporation is to bestow the character and properties of individuality on a collective and changing body of men."[8] Marshall's approach to claiming the personhood of corporations was clearly functionalist. Put simply, it sought to ensure that a collective of individuals enjoyed the same rights as a proprietary business owner might. As the corporation was a changing body of "men," it seemed plausible enough in the 1888 ruling to regard that the Fourteenth Amendment rights of equal protection for "all persons" applied to corporations. In *Minneapolis and St. Louis Railway Company v. Beckwith* (1889), the court went further to recognize that protection of property rights under the Fourteenth Amendment applied to corporations, thus guaranteeing corporate entities the rights of due process.

As a result of these and other developments in US jurisprudence, the personhood of corporations garnered a growing web of recognized rights. Over time, as publicly traded shareholder companies increased in both number and size, they gained legibility in both legal and cultural terms as entities separate and apart from the individual humans who participated in owning their stock.

Corporate Personhood versus AI Personhood

Just how does corporate personhood compare to the prospect of AI personhood? Several common features come instantly to mind. Most importantly, both are nonhuman entities. Also of primary relevance is the fact that corporations and AIs are regarded by law as means for exerting the agency of the biological humans who create, design, and control them. So, when the British Petroleum Corporation was under litigation for the April 2010 Deepwater Horizon oil spill in the Gulf of Mexico, no legal experts or public observers imagined that some artificial entity, instead of biological humans, was responsible for the relevant decision making. This was true despite the long history of jurisprudence already described. The legal tradition of corporate personhood, in other words, did not elide the reality of biological humans creating safety standards, adhering or not to federal guidelines, and implementing (or failing to implement) redundancy systems to mitigate potential for the type of disaster that ensued. In the context of corporate law, agency and fault are nevertheless viewed as the actual consequences of biological humans. This is why it is still possible that human corporate executives may be criminally prosecuted and sentenced to prison. That is, corporate law may limit but does not erase the liability of individual human actors. In the case of unethical behavior by corporations, moreover, it is still a cultural norm for the public to view individual human actors as culpable agents.

So, how might AI differ or correspond to the legibility of fault and agency for corporations? To be clear, US law does not currently recognize fault or agency in machines. What concerns us here is the prospect that legal and cultural norms might change considerably as AI becomes more advanced and more highly autonomous. One significant distinction lies with the fact that an AI exists as a physical, material entity. By contrast, a corporation is an immaterial, fictive entity. It is precisely the physical, material reality of AIs that raises distinct challenges for theorizing agency and personhood beyond the model provided by corporate personhood. Recall Chief Justice Marshall's rationale for corporations: they are instruments for the collective commercial activity of human beings. AIs, by contrast, are increasingly being engineered to think and reason, to observe data and decide how to respond to that data, and to act autonomously, even to the point of overriding human agency—cars that avoid collisions by overriding a human driver's attempt to change lanes are already commercially available and operating on US streets and highways. This means one should not confuse machine-learning algorithms with the older generation of AI machines that merely executed a fixed set of instructions. The new generation of AIs, based on neural networks, are engineered to rewrite their own code by learning from past experience in order to behave differently in the future. They have been designed for cognitive agency.

Those skeptical of recognizing any agency in intelligent machines are quick to point out that these machines are merely following a program. But this only sidesteps the issue. Intelligent machines are programmed to think, to interpret their environment, and to act on the external world by relying on their own faculties. To pretend these machines are not agents is to cling to an antiquated, humanistic notion of the agent.

In response to this skepticism, humanities scholars have increasingly emphasized an assemblage approach to agency and personhood, underscoring the variety of entities that make possible what is experienced as consciousness, decisions, and desire. Given this, it seems clear enough that no one should assume the future of legal and cultural norms in place today will endure the rapid escalation of AI technology. It is more likely that such changes in AI will force a shift in the legal and broadly cultural imagination of agency and personhood.

Autonomous Machines, Ethics, and Agency

This probable shift is evident when we consider further the accidental death of Joshua Brown, as it raises troubling quandaries for traditional approaches to agency and ethical responsibility. Immediately following Brown's death, numerous critics questioned the Tesla Motor Corporation's decision to commercially deploy its Autopilot technology, suggesting that the technology was not sufficiently developed. It would be naïve not to recognize, however, that even the most highly refined and rigorously perfected autonomous driving technology will be marred by at least occasional human deaths. The best technology will never create a perfect universe free of all accidents.

Autonomous driving technology, however, promises to create a driving experience that makes for a better and safer world. In September 2015, the *Atlantic* reported that autonomous cars, once widely adopted, are projected to eliminate 90 percent of traffic fatalities—that is an average three hundred thousand human lives saved per decade.[9] The money saved by avoiding property damage would be equally staggering. However, as the *New York Times* recently reported, any widespread adoption of autonomous cars will require these intelligent machines to make critical, complex decisions, which sometimes might result in death and destruction.[10] For example, if a child chasing a ball were suddenly to enter the car's path, the car would have to decide instantly how to minimize injuries and fatalities. Should it hit the child and save the human passengers? (Given a greater number of passengers, this might seem favorable.) Should the car swerve into a tree to avoid killing the child, thus risking the lives of the passengers? As there would be no time to consult a human decision maker, the car would have to be engineered to decide.

Is this not agency? Does this not mean that, in the event the car hits and kills the child, the autonomous car should be treated as an agent or person in a court of law? And if these intelligent machines were to become legal persons (in this case, the driver who killed the child), would this mean the manufacturers could not be held legally accountable? This is a novel problem, as it combines the qualities of a driver (making decisions and controlling a vehicle) with the status of a manufactured product, which makes this machine driver different from a human driver. Human drivers are not manufactured by companies, and machine systems could not previously make ethical decisions. Such a scenario could upend a long history of holding manufacturers responsible for deaths ensuing from the design of their products.

Federal regulatory agencies are already making decisions that could lead to such novel quandaries. In this regard, of greater significance than the 2016 Tesla accident are recent developments with Waymo. Waymo is the subsidiary of the Alphabet Company (formerly known as Google) in charge of developing autonomous driving technology. In the fall of 2015, Google queried the National Highway Traffic Safety Administration (NHTSA), requesting that the federal government agree to recognize autonomous cars as drivers. Their rationale was straightforward. Traditional vehicles have been required to make driving controls easily accessible to the human driver. The fully autonomous vehicle technology that Google is developing, by contrast, is self-driving and controls braking, acceleration, turn signals, and all driving decisions and actions without human intervention. In February 2016, the federal government responded unequivocally: yes, the NHTSA was willing to recognize an autonomous vehicle as a driver. In the safety administration's own words, "It is more reasonable to identify the driver as whatever (as opposed to whoever) *is* doing the driving. In this instance . . . the [Self-Driving System] is actually driving the vehicle."[11] And just like that, with virtually no fanfare, the United States government granted status to a machine that had always been reserved for only humans.

Beyond this, the emergence of military systems that combine the skills of humans and machines poses a considerable challenge for discerning the locus and constitution of personhood. This problem has already attracted important analytical attention from humanities scholars. In her examination of drone warfare, Kathryn Hayles observes the vast network of command centers, human operators, machines sensors, and so forth that links dozens of humans and multiple machine entities. Given this reality, Hayles argues, agency cannot be accurately understood through solitary, reductive models. Rather, the agency and personhood that emerge through this network obtains through a "cognitive assemblage"; there is no lone human subject or isolated machine entity in this complex system of knowing and acting.[12]

If Hayles's analysis is correct, the legal implications will be profound and fundamentally unsettling. In the case of a human soldier who has been combined with a machine neural system committing a war crime—or doing anything for that matter—it might become impossible to distinguish machine agency from human agency. Such an enhanced supersoldier seems to render impractical any putative distinction between the agential personhood of a biological human soldier and the cognitive and kinetic agency of the machine system that constitutes the person's neural system. This does not preclude the possibility that many people may assert a distinction without regard for human-machine combining and hybrid neural architectures. In a similar vein, it is also possible that new legal norms may simply operate on the basis of practical measures, functioning as blunt instruments that are incommensurate with a highly complex reality.

The Religious Factor

Though but a faint trace remains, the category of personhood legible in and essential to Western legal subjecthood is rooted in religious conceptions that claim that the nature of material objects differs fundamentally from the nature of live human beings. The role of religion becomes evident when we consider the history of conflicts over materialities—the distinction between people and things—and conventions around recognizing persons. What has been termed "fetishism" is among the clearest demonstrations of this. This cultural conflict emerged within the context of Afro-European commercialism and Atlantic slavery. The seismic impact on the epistemological world of Atlantic peoples produced an elaborate system of cultural theory and social-scientific paradigms that lasted roughly four hundred years. This is what the author William Pietz has theorized as a historic "problem of the fetish." The English term "fetish" derives from the Portuguese *feitiço*, which is germane to the Christian theological concept of *feitiçaria*, the juridico-political category of "witchcraft" by which Christian jurists regularly prosecuted suspect Christians for using spiritual power attributed to Satan, Christian cosmology's archvillain. Within the context of Afro-European market systems, however, the term took on a decidedly different meaning. It came to refer to the quintessential religion of Africans. Fetish religion, in other words, was a concept—albeit a fatally flawed one rooted in the unbridled prejudices and misconceptions of European observers—that embodied a racial system of knowledge and classification. African merchants required their European counterparts to interact with material entities in ways that defied the comprehension of Christian Europeans. Business agreements were witnessed not only by human agents and the Christian deity to which Europeans were accustomed; fetishes were also present in the trade agreements of Atlantic commerce. African merchants insisted that parties involved in business transactions take a so-called fetish oath ("take fetish"), often effected by drinking a material substance. These various measures were designed to ensure that the material entities could surveil the commercial parties and punish them if they violated their business agreements.[13]

The human, as the Christian imagined it, seemed woefully at odds with the human as imagined by West-Central African merchants. The latter's interaction with material entities presumed a type of personhood in things that for Christians was—or should have been—limited to people—human people, that is. This also applied to celestial beings such as Christian deities or saints and angels. But among the merchants of the Kongo Empire, in Cape Coast, along the Ivory Coast, a different epistemology seemed to order the day. Rather than asserting a definitive

ontological divide between humans and things, the humans of these societies had no trouble recognizing in material objects—"mere things" as
the Christians saw them—the capacities for affect, agency, and informational tendencies. If not *personhood per se*, fetishes possessed something
with a strong family resemblance.

As Europeans developed the colonial system of race against Africans
to advance their political project of asymmetric rule, they simultaneously employed fetishism with great utility to structure a comprehensive
body of social theory. Drawing on narratives of colonial encounters, in
1760 the French author Charles de Brosses published his *Du culte des
dieux fétiches* ("Cult of the Fetish Gods"), in which he asserted the essential nature of blacks to be delusion. His evidence? Their quintessential
religion of the fetish. De Brosses was not introducing an assertion so
much as he was systematizing a racist interpretation of history, culture,
and causation. Western agents of colonialism did not limit the interpretive category of fetishism to Africans. Fetishism, rather, became a means
of interpreting culture broadly. Karl Marx employed it in his critique of
capital, as he encountered it through reading de Brosses, to assert that
capitalism propagated a delusion, attributing sovereignty to commodi-
ties and thereby eliding the role of labor exploitation. Anthropologists
and Victorian-era scholars of religion made a field day of fetish theory,
employing it to develop the racial category of the primitive: early peoples who existed as if in a time warp, present in the so-called modern era
yet embodying the childlike psychology of primordial human ancestors.
Western psychological theory would not be the same, moreover, without
the concept of fetishistic behavior as a pathology and without primitivism as a baseline for judging the so-called Western mind versus that of
the savage. None of this was narrowly limited to the realm of ideas, of
course. The fetish was also a means of administering social systems of
power, and fetishism became a rationale for colonial rule over Indigenous populations on a global scale. Thus, it concerned not just concepts
but grave, material consequences for millions of people.

By the late nineteenth century, this complex Atlantic history of material philosophies seemed to yield among Western Christian elites an ideological consensus: the earthly realm consisted of people and things. The
only people in that order were humans, to the degree personhood was
indicative of the capacity for intersubjectivity, agency, and will. Chris-

tian theology emphasized the divide of spirit versus matter—people had both, whereas mere things were confined to the realm of matter. Even early secular forms of scientific inquiry regarded thinking as an activity ultimately performed not by things but by some immaterial substance: the mind. The essence of the person, furthermore, lay not in material entities but in the immaterial realm, typically the soul. Think here of René Descartes's famous maxim—*Je pense, donc je suis. Cogito, ergo sum*—"I think, therefore I am." Given the influence of Western Christian theology, any concern with the capacity of things to be conative or informational was derided as a vestige of primitivism, remnants of the psychology that continued to thrive in so-called inferior races.[14]

Is an AI a Person?

The theological concepts of personhood and agency have shaped legal norms that remain relevant today. We can pinpoint the theoretical interests at stake by focusing on the US legal tradition of artificial personhood, which has been shaped by three major cultural themes. The first is the history of necropolitics, slavery, and race governance that whites deployed against the population of men, women, and children of African descent who were enslaved in North America. The personhood of corporations constitutes the second theme. The third concerns the legal status of a human fetus, as crystallized by *Roe v. Wade* (1973). I conclude this discussion by attending to how this first domain (race governance and slavery) functioned to shape the early history of legal subjecthood in the United States.

Slavery in the United States thrived by forcing black people to face a constant assault on their status as human persons, as the majority of whites colluded to rationalize the brutal system of race governance that undergirded slavery. Abduction, sexual assault, torture, incest, and murder were the staples of white slaveholding. White political architects such as Thomas Jefferson went so far as to enslave their own biological offspring. White Americans treated all of these acts as violations of US law in the case of white victims while asserting no breach of law in the case of black victims. What if a white man or woman were abducted from their family to be raped, impregnated, tortured (e.g., by periodically employing a scourge to strip away skin and flesh from their bodies, salting the exposed tissue, or placing burning tobacco in their vaginal orifice to slowly cook their viscera), and forced into servitude at the whim of their abductor? In such an instance, magistrates would have deployed every instrument of the law—the posse, the court, the marshal, the prison—to remedy the situation and restore the white abductee to their "natural state" of liberty.[15] Yet, this was precisely the type of brutality that whites routinely meted out against blacks in order to dominate them into slavery's subjection and to enforce the apartheid system of the white settler state. So, how did white Americans reconcile such extreme and routinized brutality against black people with the laws of the land that guaranteed and protected the constitutional rights of "all persons"?

The legal rituals of American jurisprudence upheld the sanctity of law and the Constitution's authority by investing in the logic of white supremacy—insisting, for instance, that citizenship, liberty, and property ownership were racial capacities exclusive to whites. This was an attempt to naturalize the social origins of inequality. With this came the presumption that every white person possessed the right to deny any black person the right to have rights. Structuring race in this manner was essential to the history of the United States. In other words, antiblack racism was constitutionally protected by structuring whiteness itself as a legal property. Being recognized as a rights-bearing subject was an exclusively held possession of white people. In slightly different language, it is fair to say that the social contract in this white settler society was a racial contract.[16]

This should not be taken to mean that white jurists and their collaborators uniformly claimed that blacks were no different at all from an object such as a chair or desk or even a cow or dog. On the contrary, the tradition of jurisprudence is rooted not in cynicism but in the fine distinctions among exceptional categories. Freedom is one of these categories—arguably the most important in the tradition of political liberalism. Personhood is another. The result was a hybridized conception of black people—their personhood was not on the scale of white persons, but they were no mere things, either. This is why the legal reasoning of even the most venomous antiblack racists can be found either lamenting the ineluctable conclusion that black people were not truly persons or, alternatively, asserting the personhood of blacks but only as part of a larger strategy that denied blacks the constitutional protections that personhood ostensibly entailed.

United States v. Amy (1859) is a telling and striking example of this pattern. The court tried the case of Amy, an enslaved black youth charged with stealing from a post office. Amy was being prosecuted under the provisions of a federal law stipulating that "if any person shall steal a letter from the mail," they would be subject to imprisonment. In a shrewd attempt at her own defense, Amy asserted that she could not be held accountable or receive punishment for her crimes because the law applied to only persons, and as a slave, she lacked any such legal standing. Just two years earlier Chief Justice Roger Taney had ruled that black people possessed "no rights which the white man was bound to respect." In a white settler state, that is to say, the legal coherence of black citizenship was effectively denied. Taney wrote those words in a decision concerning a black man who had fled racial slavery—*Dred Scott v. Sanford* (1857). His ruling applied to all blacks, however, whether or not they were enslaved. Blacks could be "justly and lawfully reduced to slavery," Taney elaborated, and to suit the commercial interests of white people, they could be "bought and sold and treated as an ordinary article of merchandise and traffic." When faced, however, with the prospect of a young African-descended girl escaping punishment for the putative theft of postal property, Taney reiterated the prosecution's argument: Amy was indeed a person, something plainly and visibly evident from the simple fact that she was a human. As was true of any other (white) human, the laws of the United States applied to Amy as well, at least insofar as she was guilty of a crime.[17]

Conclusion

As the history of jurisprudence demonstrates, personhood has not been constituted biologically or empirically but rather has been deployed primarily as a political category. The Fourteenth Amendment, after all, was a political act that emerged in the wake of the bloodiest war fought on US soil. It was the effort by white legislators to protect black women, men, and children from mobs of white terrorists attempting to destroy the political possibilities of multiracial democracy. To no less a degree, the repeated judgments that denied blacks personhood were matters of politics. In this way, personhood is similar to what some experts have begun to identify in reference to "being alive" and being susceptible to death.[18] Rather than focusing on the material structures that constitute being alive, we must instead reckon with the social dynamics that have compelled historical actors to recognize personhood in various populations of biological humans and nonhuman, artificially structured entities.

How does treating personhood as chiefly a political category change the problem and refocus possible resolutions? Approaching personhood in this way foregrounds the need to understand the architecture of social power that contextualizes each problem of personhood. This includes matters of life and death. White jurists of the nineteenth century understood that recognizing the personhood of blacks would determine whether the United States was to remain a nation whose body politic was racially only white. What mattered was whether the privileges and protections inscribed in the US Constitution were for only whites. The answer to this proposition then determined how or whether legal personhood was to be affirmed or denied.

Beyond this, we can discern how personhood has functioned as a legal instrument for securing obligations and mutual recognition among multiple parties. Legislating personhood enables or constrains the possibilities of collective identities and societies. Maintaining a slave society during the nineteenth century required multiple genres of institutions to perpetuate a formidable binary—those who were citizens and those who were alien to the nation's political community. To draw on the argument that Orlando Patterson has advanced concerning slavery, the language of personhood was a respectable "idiom of power" that functioned in relationship to "property."[19] Deploying personhood and property in this way allowed millions of biological humans to be forced into suffering brutality in a manner that was oddly harmonious with liberal structures of freedom and equality. Such structural brutality anchored the legal sanctum and police power of the United States. Those who shared in the legal recognition of personhood enjoyed a common privilege that underscored the value of their status vis-à-vis others for whom personhood was placed out of legal reach. Instrumentalizing personhood in this way lent a civil rationality to the order that bequeathed property to white settlers and meted out unrestrained acts of horror to their black victims.

The future of personhood within the context of AI and under the burden of religious traditions about subjecthood will certainly not be immune from political interests. Given the cultural history of personhood and the distinctions between things and people, we should expect that new formations of subjectivity must be approached using a critical lens of culture theory. It would be a mistake to naturalize the distinctions shaping the imagination of people and things. Rather, we must look for signs that indicate whether we are repeating previous patterns of power or are open to new and different frameworks that might help us avoid perpetuating inequities and abuses of power witnessed in the past.

NOTES

1   Rachel Abrams and Annalyn Kurtz, "Joshua Brown, Who Died in Self-Driving Accident, Tested Limits of His Tesla," *New York Times*, July 1, 2016, www.nytimes.com; Kevin Sullivan, Tom Jackman, and Brian Fung, "Dallas Police Used a Robot to Kill. What Does That Mean for the Future of Police Robots?" *Washington Post*, July 21, 2016, www.washingtonpost.com.

2   Racialized practices of policing and incarceration have been repeatedly documented by expert studies since the 1800s. (Ida B. Wells Barnett produced multiple exposés of such.) The perduring practice of state racism in law enforcement is a major factor for understanding the necropolitical implications of using AI designed for warfare in the context of domestic policing. Representative studies include Khalil Muhammad, *The Condemnation of Blackness: Race, Crime, and the Making of Modern Urban America* (Cambridge, MA: Harvard University Press, 2010); Michelle Alexander, *The New Jim Crow: Mass Incarceration in the Age of Colorblindness* (New York: New Press, 2012); Paul Butler, *Chokehold: Policing Black Men* (New York: New Press, 2017); Andrea Ritchie, *Invisible No More: Police Violence against Black Women and Women of Color* (Boston: Beacon Press, 2017). In 2011 the US military used a drone to kill Anwar al-Awlaki, a US citizen residing in Yemen at the time. Al-Awlaki became the first US citizen to be targeted and killed in an extrajudicial assassination, as he was classified as a terrorist and thus denied due process. See H. Jefferson Powell, *Targeting Americans: The Constitutionality of the U.S. Drone War* (New York: Oxford University Press, 2016).

3   The human owners of Hobby Lobby were seeking exemption from the Affordable Care Act to avoid providing health insurance that covered contraception. The ruling was in their favor.

4   Philip J. Stern, *The Company-State: Corporate Sovereignty and the Early Modern Foundation of the British Empire in India* (New York: Oxford University Press, 2011).

5   Ernst Kantorowicz, *The King's Two Bodies: A Study in Medieval Political Theology* (Princeton, NJ: Princeton University Press, 2016).

6 Douglas A. Blackmon, *Slavery by Another Name: The Re-Enslavement of Black Americans from the Civil War to World War II* (New York: Doubleday, 2008); Saidiya Hartman, *Scenes of Subjection: Terror, Slavery, and Self-Making in Nineteenth-Century America* (New York: Oxford University Press, 1997).

7 "What We Talk about When We Talk about Persons: The Language of a Legal Fiction," *Harvard Law Review* 114, no. 6 (April 2001): 1745–68.

8 *Providence Bank v. Billings* (1830). Also see John W. Johnson, ed., *Historic US Court Cases: An Encyclopedia* (New York: Routledge, 2001), 491.

9 Adrienne Lafrance, "Self-Driving Cars Could Save 300,000 Lives Per Decade in America," *Atlantic*, September 29, 2015, www.theatlantic.com.

10 Robin Marantz Henig, "Death by Robot," *New York Times*, January 9, 2015, www.nytimes.com.

11 Paul A. Hemmersbaugh, chief counsel for NHTSA, to Chris Urmson, director of Self-Driving Project at Google, February 4, 2016, http://isearch.nhtsa.gov.

12 N. Kathrine Hayles, "Cognitive Assemblages: Technical Agency and Human Interactions," *Critical Inquiry* 43 (Autumn 2016): 32–55.

13 William Pietz, "The Problem of the Fetish, II: The Origin of the Fetish," *Res: Anthropology and Aesthetics* 13 (Spring 1987): 23–45; Sylvester A. Johnson, *African American Religions 1500–2000: Colonialism, Democracy, and Freedom* (New York: Cambridge University Press, 2015).

14 Denise Ferreira da Silva, *Toward a Global Idea of Race* (Minneapolis: University of Minnesota Press, 2007).

15 Hartman, *Scenes of Subjection*.

16 Charles W. Mills, *The Racial Contract* (Ithaca, NY: Cornell University Press, 1997); Cheryl Harris, "Whiteness as Property," *Harvard Law Review* 106, no. 8 (June 1993): 1707–91.

17 David W. Hamilton, "Emancipation and Contract Law," in *The Dred Scott Case: Historical and Contemporary Perspectives on Race and Law*, ed. David Thomas Konig et al. (Athens: Ohio University Press, 2010), 100–102.

18 Alex Weheliye, *Habeas Viscus: Racializing Assemblages, Biopolitics, and Black Feminist Theories of the Human* (Durham, NC: Duke University Press, 2014); Giorgio Agamben, *Homo Sacer: Sovereign Power and Bare Life*, trans. Daniel Heller-Roazen (Stanford, CA: Stanford University Press, 1998).

19 Orlando Patterson, *Slavery and Social Death: A Comparative Study* (Cambridge, MA: Harvard University Press, 1982), 17–18.

14

Hope

VINCENT LLOYD

If we desire social justice, law is the wrong place to look. Even the most iconic US Supreme Court decision to seemingly advance social justice, *Brown v. Board*, did not cause meaningful desegregation. It was only after years of widespread grassroots political organizing subsequent to the *Brown* decision that the South saw significant progress toward integration. Political scientist Gerald Rosenberg's study of the *Brown* decision, *The Hollow Hope*, suggests that Americans mistakenly place their hope in law, and he concludes that it is only "if those seeking significant social reform build a mass political base" will "the hope for reform . . . not be hollow."[1]

Yet for years Americans indeed looked hopefully to law, and they continue to do so today. Amid the turmoil caused by the election of Donald Trump in 2016, the political and intellectual establishment spoke of law as an object of hope (and faith and love). From the establishment's perspective, it is because of the strength of the rule of law and its institutions, the court system, lawyers, and administrators, that the American political system will weather the tumult caused by reckless outsiders. Indeed, the establishment's hope is that those outsiders' disregard for the law will ultimately cause them to be ejected from the White House by prosecutors or politicians committed to the law. Exactly the same sentiment was present on the opposite side of the political spectrum as Trump and his supporters threatened to "lock up" Hillary Clinton and restore law and order to urban communities and the immigration system.

Put another way, from the perspective of both left and right, American culture produces injustices; law makes possible hope for an end to injustice. Once, this was articulated in an explicitly theological register. In the background of American law, from the Declaration of Independence, are "the Laws of Nature and of Nature's God." There has long been a tension between the higher ideals implicit in American law and the positivity of law, the sense of law as a closed system of codified rules cut off from abstract, fuzzy ideals.

Such tensions are particularly evident around issues of race. As Justice Roger Taney famously wrote in his *Dred Scott* decision, which affirmed that enslaved Africans and their descendants were ineligible for US citizenship:

> It is not the province of the court to decide upon the justice or injustice, the policy or impolicy of these laws. The decision of that question belonged to the political or lawmaking power . . . The duty of the court is to interpret the instrument they have framed with the best lights we can obtain on the subject, and to administer it as we find it, according to its true intent and meaning when it was adopted.

Courts are not where to turn in search of justice, Taney asserts. It is a place for technical interpretation and administration. Consequently, law would not seem to be a proper site of hope. In contrast, dissenting Justice John McLean thrice cited a lower court: "Slavery is sanctioned by the laws of this State, and the right to hold slaves under our municipal regulations is unquestionable. But we view this as a right existing by positive law of a municipal character, without foundation in the law of nature."[2] For McLean, because law has its foundation in justice, in the law of nature, law becomes a suitable site for hope.

Among abolitionists, a key fault line was whether the law, and the Constitution in particular, made possible the hope for emancipation—or whether the existing law of men ought to be abandoned in favor of a new legal system more in line with God's law.[3] Frederick Douglass would respond to the Supreme Court's "devilish decision" in *Dred Scott* with the surprising declaration, "My hopes were never brighter than now." These hopes were made possible by the conjunction of religious commitment and American law. He intoned, "Such a decision cannot stand. God will be true though every man be a liar. We can appeal from this hell black judgment of the Supreme Court, to the court of common sense and common humanity. We can appeal from man to God." Contrary to secularist expectations, appealing to God's law did not mean waiting

until the afterlife for justice. It did not mean that our hopes must be oth-
erworldly. Because "the very groundwork of this government is a good
repository of Christian civilization," Douglass had hope that the legal
system would eventually come closer to God's law, that slavery would
sooner or later be illegal in the United States. For Douglass, the Constitution gives hope because of its grounding in the divine even as "the
wicked pride, love of power, and selfish perverseness of the American
people" corrupt what is best in the American system of laws.[4]

In this chapter I explore how hopes are invested in law and how hope
motivates those tasked with interpreting law, starting with landmark
civil rights decisions. I do this mindful of hope's location not only in
the American cultural landscape but in the American religious imagination. Hope may be characteristic of Americans, a recognizable part of
the American personality, but it is also part of American civil religion—
and of the American liberal Protestant ethos that continues to shape, to
some extent, all religion in this nation. In a sense, the ambivalence about
locating hope in law is part of a much broader ambivalence about locating hope in the world. If the only proper object of hope is God, with any
other hope derivative or analogous, as more orthodox Christian thinkers
would have it, then hoping rightly requires purging false hopes. Hoping
rightly involves cleaving hopes aimed at worldly objects in themselves
from hopes aimed beyond the world—and capable of transforming the
world. Cultural critics such as Christopher Lasch and Cornel West have
translated this theological distinction for secular American cultural
criticism. For each, it is imperative that we distinguish between hope—
which is desirable and represents the best in America—and optimism—
which is undesirable and represents the worst in America.[5] Believing
that things will inevitably improve, optimism is delusional and necessarily distorts judgment and action, whereas hope is aimed at a world of
justice wholly different from the current world. Can a similar distinction
between hope and optimism be made in the context of law?

Hope and Law

Frederick Douglass may direct his hope at law, but what about jurists?
Do legal decision-makers tap into hope when they pen paradigm-
shifting decisions? At first, imagining a judge hoping appears to buy

into a precritical, junior high civics-class-level understanding of how the judicial process works: that judges base their rulings on their feelings. Surely we grown-ups know that decisions are based on precedent, or on material interest masked as precedent. Neither appeals to precedent nor material interest leaves any room for hope. An account of natural law that would claim that judicial decisions ought to be informed by moral principles, and stresses therefore the just discernment of those principles, also leaves no room for hope. Although philosophers debate the details, hope would seem to have little role in practical reasoning; if anything, it distorts practical reasoning.

Imagine the nine justices of the United States Supreme Court confronted with a practice each feels, personally, to be despicable. Imagine that this practice is well established in statutory law and is protected by a series of court rulings. Imagine further that public opinion is divided on this practice. It seems possible that, in ruling against the practice, the court could have its credibility drastically undermined and could foment division in the nation. It also seems possible that, in ruling against the practice, the court could affect a change in public opinion and could, in the long term, strengthen its own moral authority. The probability of each of these two outcomes is impossible to calculate. If the court chooses to rule against the practice, it might seem as if the best explanation were hope. This would not be ordinary, anodyne hope, and not optimism, but hope for a totally different world, a world in which the practice in question is broadly considered a moral horror. There is no clear path from the present world to that future world. In a sense, the justices must despair at the tragic circumstances that face them: compromise their own moral values or compromise the rule of law, based on (at least the veneer of) authoritative precedent.[6]

It is important to distinguish the necessary from the contingent features of this scenario. Necessarily, there is a desired state of affairs in the future and uncertainty about whether that state of affairs will come about (and even *how* it might be brought about). There is also an action, a decision, that is motivated by that desired state of affairs and cannot be justified according to present circumstances: there is insufficient reason (or precedent) to make the decision and it does not reflect an existing public consensus. Because of this, the decision will certainly be criticized. When judicial hope works, a ruling is eventually accepted and treated as authoritative even though it is not obviously supported by precedent and even though it does not reflect the existing public consensus. There is something like a leap of faith involved here, a leap that sometimes works and sometimes fails. There is an array of available options for the court to take, but the court refuses them all, acting as if the law is something it is not—and so, potentially, making the law something new.[7]

A hopeful ruling need not explicitly appeal to morality that would trump precedent. In order to potentially "catch," judicial hope is expressed not by abandoning precedent but by engaging with precedent and framing its conclusion as flowing from precedent just as any other decision would, even though there necessarily remains a gap between what is justified by precedent and the court's ruling. That gap is not flagged explicitly in a hopeful decision, but careful reading of such decisions reveals an appeal to the rhetoric of hope, in some guise, to fill the gap. In *Brown*, as is typical, children function as a rhetorical figure of hope, the vessel of an as-yet-unrealized future used to justify a decision that precedent, on its face, would not support.

Hope in *Brown*

Landmark court decisions often take on a life of their own in the popular, and even scholarly, imagination. A few sentences summarizing their effects and import stand in for rich legal texts. Bruce Ackerman rightly observed, "There is something very curious about *Brown*'s current [early twenty-first century] status: none of the protagonists take Chief Justice Warren's opinion seriously. Whatever else they disagree about, lawyers and judges all fail to study Warren's words with care, choosing instead to see the opinion as a way station on the route to some far more glorious principle."[8] I will look for judicial hope in the rhetoric of decisions, not in a moral principle or a feeling motivating the decisions. To seek judicial hope, then, we must read decisions closely. Even about a text as canonical and well worn as the *Brown* decision, there is still more to be said.

The *Brown* decision is frequently understood as having used the equal protection clause of the Fourteenth Amendment to invalidate laws that treat racial groups unequally. More recently, conservatives, including those on the court, have treated *Brown* as ensuring that individuals *not* be treated on the basis of race, for example, in the context of affirmative action policies.[9] The second round of oral arguments in *Brown* did, indeed, focus on the intention of the authors of the Fourteenth Amendment. Yet on these grounds the arguments of segregationists were the strongest because segregated education had been part of the social landscape before the Fourteenth Amendment was ratified, and the amendment's passage did not prompt school integration. Chief Justice Earl Warren begins the substantive portion of his decision by recalling this debate over the meaning of the Fourteenth Amendment and states that, despite looking "exhaustively," the results were not decisive. "This discussion and our own investigation convince us that, although these sources cast some light, it is not enough to resolve the problem with which we are faced. At best, they are inconclusive."[10] In Warren's assessment, some of the amendment's authors supported segregation and others did not. Moreover, as he points out, nineteenth-century education was organized much differently from education in the 1950s: most education of whites was private, and few educational opportunities for blacks existed; sometimes, educating blacks was illegal. In short, "We cannot turn the clock back to 1868 when the Amendment was adopted, or even to 1896 when *Plessy* v *Ferguson* was written."[11] History is inconclusive; an additional ingredient is necessary.

Plessy v. Ferguson, which infamously established the "separate but equal" principle that *Brown* would eventually repudiate, itself cites the long history of segregation laws found to be consistent with the Fourteenth Amendment. While *Plessy* was about segregated trains in particular, the segregation laws that the court cites include intermarriage laws and laws segregating theaters, inns, and schools (including in the North, where there was a longer tradition of free public education). The crucial distinction drawn in *Plessy* is between "social equality" and "political equality." Finding this distinction in the amendment itself, the court affirmed the latter but not the former:

> The object of the amendment was undoubtedly to enforce the absolute equality of the two races before the law, but, in the nature of things, it could not have been intended to abolish distinctions based upon color,

or to enforce social, as distinguished from political, equality, or a commingling of the two races upon terms unsatisfactory to either.[12]

For the *Plessy* court, this distinction meant that, for example, jury membership could not be restricted based on the basis of race because a fair
trial is central to political equality, but marriage, schools, and transportation could be segregated because they had to do with social equality.

The astounding fact about the *Brown* decision that has been largely
forgotten is that it does not contest *Plessy*'s foundation: the distinction
between social and political equality. Rather than attacking this distinction, *Brown* reclassifies schools as political rather than social institutions.[13] While education at the time of the adoption of the Fourteenth
Amendment was largely private and, where public, uneven and unsys-
tematic, by 1954, reasoned the court, education had become "perhaps the
most important function of state and local governments."[14] School had
become universal and mandatory. For Warren, this fact demonstrated
the central importance of education to political life: "It is the very foundation of good citizenship."[15] In the specific case of schools, Warren
demonstrates how what seemed like the social sphere is actually part
of the political sphere. Left shockingly untouched, however, were state
segregation laws that affected only the social sphere—or so it seemed.

The southern states contended that their schools were equal, that the
same financial resources were offered to both black and white schools,
and that these schools used the same curricula. In rejecting this argument, Warren famously appealed to the "intangible" factors that reduce
the quality of black education in segregated schools. "To separate [school
children] from others of similar age and qualifications solely because of
their race generates a feeling of inferiority as to their status in the community that may affect their hearts and minds in a way unlikely ever to
be undone."[16] Here, Warren cites psychology experiments purporting
to demonstrate the detrimental effects of segregation on children. According to Michael Klarman, it was social science that bridged the gap
between the law as it stood and the decision the court reached.[17] Indeed,
Warren describes the social scientific research he cites as "modern authority" that may not have been available at the time *Plessy* was decided.
Rather than explicitly taking on *Plessy*, immediately after citing the so-

cial science research Warren writes: "Any language in *Plessy* v. *Ferguson* contrary to this finding is rejected" (494–5). In other words, law must be read in light of science, and science has changed. *Plessy* was not overruled; it was updated. Warren maintained the basic logic of *Plessy* but found space within that logic to obtain the outcome he desired.

The gap between established law and the *Brown* decision, which for Klarman and Warren himself is bridged by social scientific evidence, is rather, as I see it, bridged by hope. Hope is not a feeling invoked by Warren in the text. Rather, hope arrives in the figure of the child. By conjuring the "hearts and minds" of children, the decision taps into a social imaginary that views children as representing a better, brighter future. Indeed, Warren sets aside the "tangible" equality of funding and facilities to focus on these hearts and minds that will, in a future to be averted, be irreparably damaged by segregation. The justices themselves desire a dramatically different world, a world without segregation. They are not sure how that world might be achieved; they have no illusions that one ruling of the court will achieve it. Yet they hope. To express this hope, to use it as a principle guiding their interpretation of the law, they need a figure of hope. The child is the paradigmatic figure of hope, which is why Warren places the hearts and minds of children at the center of the majority opinion.

Additionally, children are effective as a wedge for moving from an attack on political segregation to an attack on social segregation. Warren describes the rapid changes in public education as effectively justifying the switch of education from the social to the political domain, but he makes an argument that is broader than necessary for those purposes. Education, he writes, "is a principal instrument in awakening the child to cultural values, in preparing him for later professional training, and in helping him to adjust normally to his environment."[18] This description goes far beyond the domain of the political. It gestures toward the values of a future society, the society of the next generation and generations to come. Current practices stymy the possibility of a different, better future. This is rhetoric; it is above and beyond the line of argument needed for Warren to make the point that education has come into the political domain. It opens the door to incorporating other segregation laws into the political domain. Surely it is difficult to transmit cultural values to black children and to help them adjust normally to their environment when their families are not permitted to live in the same neighborhoods as whites, when they are not permitted to sit in the same theater seats as whites, and even when they are not permitted to sit in the same train cars as whites. When we think of the children, the social becomes thoroughly political. And when we think of the world of our children, we can hope for a world dramatically different from the present.

For judges, the authority of hope is dependent on the disavowal of hope, the pretense that a judicial decision is strictly clearheaded and rational. This is how Warren later represents the *Brown* deliberations in his memoirs: "We discussed all sides dispassionately week after week, testing arguments of counsel, suggesting various approaches, and at times acting as 'devil's advocates.'"[19] Warren insists that the justices were always unanimous in their decision and the five months it took to produce a decision was spent not on building consensus but on considering the decision's various possible arguments and the implications of these different routes. "In my entire public career," Warren writes, "I have never seen a group of men more conscious of the seriousness of a situation, more intent upon resolving it with as little disruption as possible, or with a greater desire for unanimity."[20]

In fact, unanimity in *Brown* was an achievement rather than a given. By 1954, the strongest voices on the court against integration were justices who saw the case strictly in the terms of a debate between positive law (exclusive reliance on human-made law) and natural law (reliance on principles derived from nature or God), in which they fancied themselves proponents of positive law. Felix Frankfurter, for example, was vehemently opposed to segregation personally, but he was equally vehement in his belief that it was "the compulsions of governing legal principles" that must guide the judge, not "the idiosyncrasies of merely personal judgment."[21] Such commitments had prevented the court from ruling for integration earlier. However, when Warren was appointed chief justice and signaled his support for an integration decision, Frankfurter and those aligned with him found themselves in the minority. As Klarman argues, opinions based on the notion that a narrow reading of precedent should trump justices' own moral ideals are produced most frequently when the court is nearly evenly split.[22] When it gets down to one or two justices potentially dissenting contrary to their own personal convictions, those convictions are more often allowed to have the day.

Thus, in Klarman's view, the result in *Brown* was ultimately unanimous not, as Warren would have it, because careful deliberation brought the best arguments to the fore but because the justices tempted to dissent did not want to place themselves in such an unseemly position, one that ran counter to their personal convictions.

Rather than viewing such choices in terms of personal convictions, as Klarman does, I am proposing that they ought to be viewed in terms of judicial hope. Frankfurter did not set aside "the compulsions of governing legal principles"; rather, he counted hope as one of those governing legal principles, as a principle of interpretation. By reading the Fourteenth Amendment and the laws before the court motivated by hope, Frankfurter was able to sign on to Warren's unanimous decision. Instead of tension between a moral ideal and a narrow reading of precedent, resolved in favor of the former, hope involves entertaining the possibility of a world quite different from ours without having a sense of how to move from here to there.

Warren's discussion of *Brown* constructs a division between the dispassionate court and the passionate public. The chapter of his memoirs in which he describes *Brown* is titled "A Case of Emotional Impact," but the emotional impact of the case was certainly not experienced by Earl Warren. He describes a "wave of emotion" that "swept the room" when he stated that the court's decision was unanimous.[23] He describes the "emotional opposition to the Decision" in the South.[24] At the interface between the passionate public and the staid court, according to Warren, was his decision. "It was not a long opinion, for I had written it so it could be published in the daily press throughout the nation without taking too much space. This enabled the public to have our entire reasoning instead of a few excerpts from a lengthier document."[25] Warren saw himself as communicating to a divided and emotional public, and he wanted to communicate directly. If the public could access the cool reasoning of the court, passions would be less inflamed. But here Warren is also acknowledging that the decision was a rhetorical document, aimed at particular publics. In a sense, Warren is admitting that the decision *performs* dispassion in the hope that dispassion will foster acceptance.

Curiously, rather than using his memoir to defend the legal reasoning of *Brown*, Warren presents himself as a consistent opponent of segregation.[26] To demonstrate, Warren brings the reader back to his California

childhood, where he attended integrated public schools and the integrated University of California. He "sat in classrooms with blacks and
members of almost every minority group" and "never gave it a second
thought."[27] It is the memory of the young Warren, the child, that justifies *Brown* in this text, not reasoning from precedent. Communicating
directly with the public, in a decision he imagined would be published in
"the daily press," Warren appealed to the same hopeful figure, the child,
that he himself once was. He remembered his hopeful youth, his youth
as a figure of hope, integrated, and he projected it into the centerpiece of
the *Brown* decision. This marks both the possibility and the limitation of
hope, which is to say the precariousness of hope, the ever-present threat
that hope is really just bloated optimism.

Hope and Children

Kenneth Karst has documented the way children are often at the center
of legal conflicts over cultural values. As Karst argues, concern for children, or for the figure of the child, is due to "the hope that a child will
continue to self-identify as one of Us, or at least not as one of Them."
In other words, "the hope that children will act in accordance with Our
values, and the fear that they may not."[28] We ostensibly hope for the
well-being of children, but what we are really expressing is hope as such:
hope for a future in which we ourselves will continue, and continually
improve, even after our deaths. Karst's worry is that this politicized image
of the child, and hope for the child, may have destructive effects when
it enters law. As I have already suggested, we can appreciate another,
less conservative dimension of hope for the well-being of children when
hope is understood as part of the vocabulary of a religious tradition,
especially Christianity. Hope can aim at the world, with all its social
hierarchies and divisions, to preserve the way the world is, or hope can
aim for a different, better world. But when hope aims at another world
by means of the image of the child, that rhetoric would seemingly aim at
a brighter future for a quite specific "Us."

Queer theorist Lee Edelman launched a broadside attack on the rhetorical figure of the child in his book *No Future*.[29] The child, Edelman
argues, secures the interests of the powers that be. Orienting us toward a
future secure for the child makes us act in essentially conservative ways,

perpetuating the status quo and with it the interests of the powerful. The child is essentially innocent and in need of protection—by parents, by society, and by laws. For Edelman, queers fundamentally threaten the status quo by their refusal to organize their lives around the child, by their embrace of pleasure in the moment rather than pleasure deferred into the indefinite future, into generations to come.

The *Brown* court relies on hope, but its hope is tethered to the world by its reliance on the figure of the child. Hope for the generations to come is this-worldly, not other-worldly. This hope does not exploit the transformative, justice-seeking capacity of the American religious imagination. This hope does not grow out of despair nor is it cultivated in communities of the marginalized. The sort of hope employed by the court is secular (really secularist) hope, not theological hope.[30] It appears to take great moral courage—to think of the children even if it causes difficulties for us in the present—but it actually advances the desires of parents in the name of the children, as so many parents are wont to do. Barack Obama rose to national prominence invoking the "audacity of hope" with a memoir detailing the promise of the multicultural American child, yet in his presidency this audacity manifested in an era not of racial progress but of racial stagnation, perhaps racial regression. It manifested not in leadership that reframed issues and revealed new possibilities but in leadership that was calculating and pragmatic.

Let us speculate: perhaps the sacralization of the child as a figure of hope is a means by which hope is secularized, a process already begun in Christianity with its essential investment of hope in the child of God and completed in modernity.[31] Through this process, rich religious vocabularies for exploring the collective and tragic dimensions of life are repressed. The expansive means of thinking about justice and hoping for its realization that Frederick Douglass and others accessed through their religious words and styles are shut off when religion talk becomes future talk, and future talk is circumscribed by what we deem achievable for our offspring. If a sense of hope distinct from optimism is possible, it must rely on styles of imagining otherwise together, not on personal beliefs about how the world might improve. When collective visions of justice are set aside, decisions like *Brown* open themselves to conservative readings that take them to be about individual opportunity rather than racial domination. The sacralized child cripples arguments for social justice that cannot be expressed in terms of improving the lot of future generations.

The broad consensus today is that *Brown v. Board* was rightly decided, so in a sense the justices' hopes came to fruition even if thoroughgoing racial justice has not been achieved. In contrast, *Roe v. Wade* is an example of hope failed. There is still deep disagreement about whether it was rightly decided, just as there was when the court's decision was announced in 1973.[32] I suspect this has to do with the court's failure to find a substitute figure of hope, given the unavailability of the child. The rhetorical tropes immediately evoked by abortion are the opposite of those evoked by hope: potential life is ended, opportunities are lost, and futures are foreclosed. Justice Harry Blackmun begins his majority decision by acknowledging how emotionally charged abortion is and offering assurances that the court will "resolve the issue by constitutional measurement, free of emotion and of predilection" (116).[33] Precedent does not offer sufficient reason to reach the court's decision, and the gap is filled by hope. Blackmun expends considerable effort in showing the complicated history of abortion laws and then lists the sequence of cases developing the right to privacy from the due process clause, before stating, "This right of privacy . . . is broad enough to encompass a woman's decision whether or not to terminate her pregnancy" (153). Adverse consequences of prohibiting abortion, he continues, include medical problems, psychological harm, and the stigma attached to unwed mothers. There is no explanation of how these effects are connected to the right to privacy, or how the right to privacy is related to Blackmun's earlier history of abortion regulation. In a sense, the adverse consequences and legal history function as rhetorical flourish similar to the function of the image of the child in *Brown*. In *Roe*, however, the child is hopeless, unwanted: "There is the problem of bringing a child into a family already unable, psychologically and otherwise, to care for it" (153). The mother, too, becomes another figure of hopelessness: "Maternity, or additional offspring, may force upon a woman a distressful life and future" (153). Even when, later in the decision, Blackmun is justifying limits on abortion, he leans on cold science: "At some point the state interests as to the protection of health, medical standards, and prenatal life, become dominant" (155).

Justice Blackmun and six of his colleagues hoped that, eventually, somehow, a consensus would develop in support of the court's decision in *Roe*. The ruling failed to achieve their hopes in part because the hopeless language of the decision misaligned with the justices' hopes. Even more than specific wording, the decision's failure to appeal to figures of hope limited its ability to gain traction in the broader cultural imagination. The justices envisioned a dramatically different world, but Blackmun was not able to conjure this world in the language of his decision. He appealed to science, and he appealed to images of destitution and unhappiness. The court's decision in *Brown* increased social discord around segregation for two decades before ultimately prevailing into a national consensus.[34] In the case of *Roe*, by contrast, the dramatic transformation in the social world that judges hoped for has never materialized. Of course, in important senses *Brown* has also been a failure: American schools remain nearly as segregated as they were before the ruling, and myriad other forms of antiblack racism persist, most dramatically in the imprisonment today of nearly a million black men and women, girls and boys. Is there any way to retrieve a sense of hope that taps into the religious imagination to advance justice? I do not think there is when we are considering court opinions. Hope's power resides outside the domain of formal law.[35]

That leading light of critical race theory, Derrick Bell, agrees, and his work is characterized by a deep ambivalence toward hope. The epilogue to Bell's *Faces at the Bottom of the Well* is titled "Beyond Despair." To move beyond despair, Bell argues, we must reject the anodyne optimism found in narratives of American progress, narratives that ignore the marginalized. To move beyond despair, we must turn to the marginalized: "Knowing there was no escape, no way out, the slaves nonetheless continued to engage themselves. To carve out a humanity. To defy the murder of selfhood." Here, Bell tells us, we find "hope rather than despair."[36] Bell limns the intractable racial injustices of American life and law, but he also describes his own commitment to struggle as more than fatalistic rebellion. Often employing religious idioms and citations, Bell narrates "psalms of survival" that appeal to African American religious traditions and their characteristic virtue, hope.[37] Like slave spirituals, Bell's profound and provocative writings subtly join together bitter despair and a better world to come. For him, despair purges false hopes, worldly hopes, and only after grappling with the depths of this despair does genuine hope become possible.[38] In other words, hope is genuine

not only because it is described in religious texts but also more importantly, because it rejects worldly objects. Yet the practices and affects
that characterize hope persist. Bell's writings inspire, but their audience
is activists, not judges.[39]

With critical race theory institutionalized, or at least part of institutional memory, do new possibilities for hope in law open up? Might
Bell's lessons provide means for a younger generation of lawyers and
judges to bring hope cultivated at the margins into the courtroom? One
Supreme Court justice in particular, of that younger generation, offers
a tantalizing response. Sonia Sotomayor's memoir is animated by two
questions: "How is it that adversity has spurred me on instead of knock-
ing me down? What are the sources of my own hope and optimism?"[40]
Her book is a coming-of-age story, tracking both the depths of despair
she faced (because of an alcoholic father, a distant single mother, un-
supportive teachers, and cultural alienation) and her resilient spirit that
led her from housing projects to the Supreme Court. On the one hand,
Sotomayor's narrative finds hope in despair, even in the experiences of
those at the bottom of the well, as it were. On the other hand, Sotomayor
closely associates hope and optimism, and she finds both in the privileged image of the child (herself) coming of age. This is still secularist
hope, hope invested in stories of American progress (that Bell would
reject), deaf to hope's religious resonances.

In the US academy there is a writerly imperative to end hopefully,
or rather optimistically—to tell the reader where justice can *really* be
found, how the relationship between religion and law can *rightly* be
conceptualized. But not in the courts, then should we turn our hope to
legislatures, or to social movements that will precipitate legal change, or
to critical theorists who interrogate legal concepts, or to religious communities built around figures of law incommensurable with those of the
secular world? The legal expert is imagined as a judge who must decide,
with hope. In short, the desire for hope so deeply determines how we
approach law that this desire must, in some sense, in some modality of
secularization, be religious.

NOTES

1 Gerald Rosenberg, *The Hollow Hope: Can Courts Bring about Social Change?*
   (Chicago: University of Chicago Press, 1991), 431.

2   Dred Scott v. Sandford, 60 U.S. 393, 536, 549, 624 (1857).

3   See, for example, John Stauffer, *The Black Hearts of Men: Radical Abolitionists and the Transformation of Race* (Cambridge, MA: Harvard University Press, 2004).

4   Frederick Douglass, "Speech on the Dred Scott Decision," in *The Portable Frederick Douglass*, ed. John Stauffer and Henry Louis Gates, Jr. (New York: Penguin, 2016), 252, 253, 257, 258. See Vincent Lloyd, *Black Natural Law* (New York: Oxford University Press, 2016).

5   Christopher Lasch, *The True and Only Heaven: Progress and Its Critics* (New York: W. W. Norton, 1991); Cornel West, *Hope on a Tightrope: Words and Wisdom* (New York: SmileyBooks, 2011).

6   This is imagining laboratory conditions, as it were—the sort of conditions assumed in the literature on jurisprudence (as opposed to the literature on law and culture). The real world is more complex, of course, with shifts in public opinion affecting what is possible for the court, for example. It strikes me as productive to move back and forth between laboratory conditions and the world itself in order to sharpen our conceptual tools while remaining accountable to the complexities of culture.

7   It is tempting to read this scenario, perhaps something like the scenario of *Brown v. Board*, as a classic conflict between positive law jurisprudence and natural law jurisprudence. The justices have moral views that conflict with the law; the justices change the law to match morality. Morality, however, introduces a contingent, not necessary, element into this scenario. It is simply necessary for the court, or for a justice, to desire a certain future state of affairs; what motivates that desire is not important. Cases such as *Bush v. Gore* (about the 2000 election) and *National Federation of Independent Business v. Sebelius* (about the Affordable Care Act) can be read as relying on a desire that is not moral but political or pragmatic. These cases may belong to a lesser class of judicial hope because the desired state of affairs is not so different from the current world, a hope more secular than theological.

8   Bruce Ackerman, *The Civil Rights Revolution: We the People* (Cambridge, MA: Harvard University Press, 2014), 3:128.

9   Reva B. Siegel, "Equality Talk: Antisubordination and Anticlassification Values in Constitutional Struggles over *Brown*," *Harvard Law Review* 117 (2004): 1470–1547.

10 Brown v. Board of Education of Topeka, 347 U.S. 483, 489 (1954).

11 Ibid., 492.

12 Plessy v. Ferguson, 163 U.S. 537, 544 (1896).

13 On the specificity of educational institutions in *Brown*, see Risa Gobuloff, *The Lost Promise of Civil Rights* (Cambridge, MA: Harvard University Press, 2007), chap. 9.

14 *Brown v. Board of Education.*

15 Ibid.

16 Ibid., 494.

17 Michael J. Klarman, *From Jim Crow to Civil Rights: The Supreme Court and the Struggle for Racial Equality* (New York: Oxford University Press, 2006), 303.

18 *Brown v. Board of Education.*

19 Earl Warren, *The Memoirs of Earl Warren* (Garden City, NY: Doubleday, 1977), 2.

20 Ibid., 2–3.

21 Klarman, *Supreme Court and Civil Rights*, 303. Klarman further argues that politics enters when the law is indeterminate (308), though this would seem to be true for every case that reaches the Supreme Court.

22 Ibid., 303.

23 Warren, *Memoirs*, 3.

24 Ibid., 4.

25 Ibid., 3.

26 The memoir was published posthumously. Warren worked on and nearly completed it after his retirement from the court. Most of the text concerns his political rather than judicial career, and it does not offer much insight into his ideological transformation, presenting its protagonist with little emotional or psychological complexity.

27 Ibid., 4.

28 Kenneth L. Karst, "Law, Cultural Conflict, and the Socialization of Children," *California Law Review* 91, no. 4 (2003): 970.

29 Lee Edelman, *No Future: Queer Theory and the Death Drive* (Durham, NC: Duke University Press, 2004). See also Rebekah Sheldon, *The Child to Come: Life after the Human Catastrophe* (Minneapolis: University of Minnesota Press, 2016).

30 Though the Jewish tradition develops the theme of hope in future generations, the secular context of the 1950s US is secular in the sense of being post-Christian.

31 See Marcel Gauchet, *The Disenchantment of the World: A Political History of Religion* (Princeton, NJ: Princeton University Press, 1997).

32 For a detailed account of the complex political debate in *Roe*'s wake, see Mary Ziegler, *After Roe: The Lost History of the Abortion Debate* (Cambridge, MA: Harvard University Press, 2015). See also Robert Post and Reva Siegel, "Roe Rage: Democratic Constitutionalism and Backlash," *Harvard Civil Rights—Civil Liberties Law Review* 42 (2007): 373–433.

33 Roe v. Wade, 410 U.S. 113 (1973).

34 Klarman, in *From Jim Crow to Civil Rights*, argues that the polarization effected by *Brown* fueled the social movements that would lead to the federal civil rights legislation that ultimately settled the issue; in short, *Brown* was the indirect cause of a consensus for integration. I do not think such a causal story is necessary or helpful: hope is defined by uncertainty. See also Rosenberg, *Hollow Hope*.

35 More precisely, my worry here is about hope in judicial processes as opposed to hope in political or social processes that might result in creating or eliminating laws.

36 Derrick Bell, *Faces at the Bottom of the Well* (New York: Basic Books, 1992), 197.

37 For an overview of Bell's use of religion, see George H. Taylor, "Racism as 'the National Crucial Sin': Theology and Derrick Bell," *Michigan Journal of Race and Law* 9 (2004): 269–322.

38 See especially Soren Kierkegaard, *The Sickness unto Death: A Christian Psychological Exposition for Upbuilding and Awakening* (Princeton, NJ: Princeton University Press, 1980).

39 Perhaps lawyers in their role as activists as well, but not in their professional roles in the courtroom.

40 Sonia Sotomayor, *My Beloved World* (New York: Alfred A. Knopf, 2013), viii.

Afterword

WINNIFRED FALLERS SULLIVAN

US religious studies has got law! That is the message of this rich and useful volume. In the introductory essay and in the fourteen focused chapters that investigate specific terms, scholars of US religion show us myriad ways in which religion in the US shapes and is shaped by law. Gathered together in this way, the editors present for those new to this idea a valuable introduction to the postseparationist and postsecularist understanding of the conjunction of religion and law, as seen from US religious studies. The contained, mostly deferential—and antinomian— creativity of US religion is on display—often seen seeking permission for its activities. And law—understood as the positive law of the state—is seen to mostly get religion wrong—at least, religion as we in religious studies understand it. On this account, we must, as Ashon Crawley and Vincent Lloyd suggest, find our hope elsewhere than in law.

But we must also complicate our understanding of law.

Before the 1980s, the study of religion in the US was largely the story of white Protestantism. We began with the Puritans, traced the fragmenting of the colonial churches, the growth of evangelical religion, and then the division at the end of the nineteenth century between liberals and fundamentalists. The twentieth century was a story mostly of decline. My own view is that this story was not exactly wrong but that it had become such a depressing and boring story we were compelled to discover Catholics, Jews, Mormons, and others to liven it up. Now the story of American religion is the story of "here comes everyone." It is the vital and vibrant blooming buzzing confusion of voices and bodies that we see displayed here.

With respect to the study of religion and law in the US, I think we may be at a turning point similar to the one just described. We now know the story, and it is ably told here. We can see much more clearly the failure of US law to get religion right. But we may know it a little too well. We have learned how to do close reading of judicial opinions. Judicial opinions are very seductive as texts—short and self-contained and almost irresistible to the critical cultural eye. We can connect the story of religion in rough ways to the founding documents and to an outline of US legal history. But we have mostly accepted law's account of itself as the business of the state. And we have mostly accepted the exceptionalism of US law. What we need to do now is see that law is as radically messy and unstable as religion—and that the two are always intertwined in often unnoticed ways. We need to widen our lenses and work comparatively, seeing how other folks do religion and law. The editors of this volume asked in their prompt to contributors, "How might a scholar of American religion approach the study of religion and law differently?" They meant, I take it, differently from the way judges do it. I want to read the question to mean "differently from the way we do it now."

I am grateful to this volume's editors for their attention to my past work and for inviting me to look ahead. I write to offer some thoughts about studying US law and religion generally, a challenge of sorts, as we go forward, myself included. I will not comment on the essays in this volume individually. They are interesting and together offer a stimulating portrait of religion under law in the US. In my view, as I said, we in US religious studies are getting better at understanding the ways in which religion in the US is legal. We are still failing mostly, however, to engage seriously with the study of law and with socio-legal studies: legal sociology and legal anthropology, philosophy of law, law and humanities, as well as critical legal studies in its various forms. And political theology. What is law? How does law work? Is law about rules or processes? What are the alternatives to rights' talk? What makes law successful? What has law become in late capitalism? What is religious about law? How can we better articulate the law-religion project that is the US?

Interdisciplinary work is not easy. Being faithful to two very different scholarly communities and conversations, both of which mostly conceal their historical ties, requires a kind of hopping from one foot to the other, which can sometimes produce clownish behavior. Let me suggest several ongoing avenues for complicating our story.

Law

The best scholarship on law—by both those in the humanities and those in the social sciences—begins with the assumption that law is everywhere. Just as we in religious studies can always find a religion story, legal scholars can always find a law story. Law, like religion, is something people do. We find law in all societies. It is found not just in courtrooms and statute books but in the supermarket queue and the lynching mob, in commercial life and in the life of families. As Robert Cover argued in 1982 in his now classic article, "Nomos and Narrative":

> We inhabit a nomos—a normative universe. We constantly create and maintain a world of right and wrong, of lawful and unlawful, of valid and void. The student of law may come to identify the normative world with the professional paraphernalia of social control. The rules and principles of justice, the formal institutions of the law, and the conventions of a social order are, indeed, important to that world; they are, however, but a small part of the normative universe that ought to claim our attention.

To see the constant production of law and law's rituals and narratives and the competition among them radically expands the field that should capture the attention of scholars of law, perhaps particularly of law and religion. We need to not just attend to the ways in which formal state law shapes religion but also consider the religiousness of law, law as religion, and religious law. An analysis of law and religion together can enrich our understanding of American life. It can also complicate periodization, regional difference, and our understanding of change over time. It can also address the unfortunate tendency of much of this work to hew to a liberal-left political perspective.

We need to see that law should not be reduced to politics: it is a distinct cultural product. But it is also as messy and unstable as religion. Law is not more foundational than religion, as the editors suggest, except in the imagination of statist liberals who reverence the rule of law. "Not law" is something that is baked into American religion in a strong antinomian strain, as Maria Ashe explains in her feminist critique of Cover. Love rather than law is one version of Paul's message. We should avoid separationist thinking.

Comparison

Another fruitful avenue for the study of law and religion in the US would be to widen the lens to consider the US case comparatively. What is most distinctive about the US constitutional order with respect to religion is the effort to disestablish religion. It is a very specific project, different from separation efforts in Europe and elsewhere. Disestablishment—US style—is a never-ending project of retreat from definition. In other places, government does not pretend not to know religion. There are ministries of religious affairs and other bureaucracies assigned the role of managing religion. Establishment—as Americans would name these arrangements—does not make the law-religion project more or less just, but it does locate and stabilize the field somewhat. Seeing how US disestablishment is differentially modulated across diverse populations both at home and abroad, in domestic and foreign policy, can help us better understand religion in the US. Seeing the distinctiveness of disestablishment can also help bring into focus the pathologies of the law-religion project in the US.

Disestablishment has an intellectual component as well as an institutional one. Americans are deeply skeptical of expertise on religion. A form of anticlericalism, sometimes shading into anti-intellectualism, makes knowledge about religion inherently suspect—Catholic perhaps—destructive of piety and morality. The legal management of religion is made more difficult by this antipathy, on the right and the left, to expert religious knowledge. Yet, in my view, scholars of religion should resist the temptation to close this gap, focusing rather on educating future judges and legislators and voters on how to think better about religion with a view to their general task, which is to govern religion by, for, and of the people.

All governments today guarantee religious freedom. Most also do that under the umbrella of transnational and international legal instruments. Not recognizing international law means that the US basically goes it alone in these matters. How to protect religion without establishing it? That is the constitutional task. But there is no reason that scholars of US religion should submit to that ideology and ignore the rest of the world. Doing so makes it more difficult to understand American religion law.

Legal Subjectivity

An important task today in the study of law is the study of legal subjectivity. If one considers any individual or group on the planet today, one can see the multiple jurisdictions that she/they is/are subject to. Public and private. Local, national, and transnational. Overlapping and competing normative orders, religious and nonreligious, compete to direct her/their thoughts and activities. Recognizing that the natural state of affairs is one of legal pluralism helps the resistance to the wannabe monopoly of sovereignty desired by the nation-state, but it also shows how law works and makes a natural partner with the multiplicity of religious subjectivity. The classic article on legal pluralism is by Sally Merry (see Works Referenced, below).

Conclusion

Successful US religion law, then, should not cast judges as social scientists. Faulting judges for not being religious studies scholars might be to miss the point. The political theology of religious studies today is mostly one of liberalism's religion, an ideology on display in such works as that of political philosopher Cécile Laborde. The political theology of the religion clauses is arguably not that of religious studies. It might be more radical. It might aspire to do something different—that is, not manage religion via ministries of religious affairs and expert pandits but rather enable "we the people" to govern ourselves. What that has meant legally has evolved from the early nineteenth-century world Sarah Barringer Gordon shows us, in which religious groupings were legally limited to small local religious societies, to a late nineteenth-century affirmation of national and transnational churches, and finally to the realization of religious life through commercial life—as described by Kathryn Lofton and others. Always, of course, there were and are plenty of dissenters from these dominant trends.

In my view the US religion cases are most usefully seen over time as diagnostic of unfinished political and social business in a kind of displacement and denial. Obscuring this unfinished business, the impossibility and opacity of the religion clauses might be turned to a different use—that is, one of highlighting the legal and political challenges of achieving a fair and just society through, among other things, universal health care, quality public education, economic justice, and mutual respect. There is a sense in which these cases are not actually about religion. Reimagining religion law itself will require us to look elsewhere.

WORKS REFERENCED

Ashe, Marie. "Beyond Nomos and Narrative: Unconverted Antinomianism in the Work of Susan Howe." *Yale Journal of Law & Feminism* 18, no. 1 (2006): 1–59.

Cover, Robert. "Nomos and Narrative." *Harvard Law Review* 97, no. 4 (1983): 4–66.

Gordon, Sarah Barringer. "The First Disestablishment: Limits on Church Power and Property before the Civil War." *University of Pennsylvania Law Review* 162 (2014): 307–72.

Laborde, Cécile. *Liberalism's Religion*. Cambridge, MA: Harvard University Press, 2017.

Lofton, Kathryn. *Consuming Religion*. Chicago: University of Chicago Press, 2017.

Merry, Sally Engle. "Legal Pluralism." *Law and Society Review* 22 (1988): 869–96.

ACKNOWLEDGMENTS

Together, we offer our earnest thanks to Jennifer Hammer and Amy Klopfenstein at NYU Press for making this book happen, to the anonymous readers whose comments made our work stronger, and to the series editors, Tracy Fessenden, Laura Levitt, and David Harrington Watt. We are grateful as well to the Humanities Project at the University of Rochester for funding our May 2017 symposium and to Caleb Rood for his administrative assistance, which enabled us all to do in person what we never could have done in isolation. Joshua Dubler offers thanks, too, to the Carnegie Corporation of New York and to Bard College Berlin for their generous support during the editing process. Of course, none are more supportive than our partners, Lisa Cerami and Rayna Weiner, for whom each of us is eternally grateful.

Finally, we wish to express our indebtedness to all of our contributors for the seriousness and care they brought to this project. We are fortunate to find ourselves in this community of scholars.

ABOUT THE EDITORS

Joshua Dubler is Assistant Professor of Religion at the University of Rochester, where he also directs the Rochester Prison Education Project. He is the author of *Down in the Chapel: Religious Life in an American Prison* (2013).

Isaac Weiner is Associate Professor of Religious Studies in the Department of Comparative Studies at Ohio State University. He is the author of *Religion Out Loud: Religious Sound, Public Space, and American Pluralism* (NYU, 2014) and a co-director of the American Religious Sounds Project.

ABOUT THE CONTRIBUTORS

Jason C. Bivins is Professor of Religion at North Carolina State University. He is the author of *Spirits Rejoice!: Jazz and American Religion* (2015), *Religion of Fear: The Politics of Horror in Conservative Evangelicalism* (2008), and *The Fracture of Good Order: Christian Antiliberalism and the Challenge to American Politics* (2003).

Rosemary R. Corbett is Faculty Fellow with the Bard Prison Initiative. She is the author of *Making Moderate Islam: Sufism, Service, and the "Ground Zero Mosque" Controversy* (2016) and the co-editor, with Katherine Pratt Ewing, of *Sufi Politics: Rethinking Islam, Scholarship, and the State in South Asia and Beyond* (forthcoming).

Ashon Crawley, Assistant Professor of Religious Studies and African American and African Studies at the University of Virginia, is the author of *Blackpentecostal Breath: The Aesthetics of Possibility* (2016), an investigation of aesthetics and performance as modes of collective, social imagination and *The Lonely Letters* (forthcoming), an exploration of the interrelation of blackness, mysticism, quantum mechanics, and love. All his work is about otherwise possibility.

Finbarr Curtis is Associate Professor in the Department of Philosophy and Religious Studies at Georgia Southern University and the author of *The Production of American Religious Freedom* (2016).

Spencer Dew is Visiting Assistant Professor at Denison University and the author of *"I Am a Citizen of the USA": Law, Race, and Citizenship in Aliite Religion* (2019).

Kathleen Holscher is Associate Professor of American Studies and Endowed Chair of Roman Catholic Studies in the Religious Studies program at the

University of New Mexico. She is the author of *Religious Lessons: Catholic Sisters, Public Education and the Law in Mid-Century New Mexico* (2012).

Sarah Imhoff is Associate Professor of Religious Studies and Jewish Studies at the University of Indiana. She is the author of *Masculinity and the Making of American Judaism* (2017).

Sylvester A. Johnson is Assistant Vice Provost for the Humanities and Professor of Religion and Culture at Virginia Tech, where he directs the Center for Humanities. He is the author of *African American Religions, 1500–2000* (2015) and *The Myth of Ham in Nineteenth-Century American Christianity* (2004) and a co-editor of *The FBI and Religion* (2017).

Vincent Lloyd is Associate Professor at Villanova University, affiliated with the Africana Studies Program and the Department of Theology and Religious Studies. His books include *Black Natural Law* (2016) and *In Defense of Charisma* (2018). He co-edits the journal *Political Theology*.

Kathryn Lofton is Professor of Religious Studies, American Studies, and History at Yale University. She is the author of *Consuming Religion* (2017) and *Oprah: The Gospel of an Icon* (2011).

Ronit Y. Stahl is Assistant Professor of History at the University of California, Berkeley, and the author of *Enlisting Faith: How the Military Chaplaincy Shaped Religion and State in Modern America* (2017). She held postdoctoral fellowships in the Department of Medical Ethics and Health Policy at the University of Pennsylvania and in the Danforth Center on Religion and Politics at Washington University in St. Louis.

Anna Su is Assistant Professor in the University of Toronto Faculty of Law. She is the author of *Exporting Freedom: Religious Liberty and American Power* (2016).

Winnifred Fallers Sullivan is a professor in the Department of Religious Studies at Indiana University, where she is also Affiliate Professor of Law in the Maurer School of Law. She is the author of *Paying the Words Extra: Religious Discourse in the Supreme Court of the United States* (1994), *The*

Impossibility of Religious Freedom (2005), *Prison Religion: Faith-based Reform and the Constitution* (2009), and *A Ministry of Presence: Chaplaincy, Spiritual Care, and the Law* (2014).

Tisa Wenger is Associate Professor of American Religious History at Yale Divinity School. She is the author of *Religious Freedom: The Contested History of an American Ideal* (2017) and *We Have a Religion: The 1920s Pueblo Indian Dance Controversy and American Religious Freedom* (2009).

Heather R. White is Visiting Assistant Professor in the Religious Studies Department and the Gender and Queer Studies Program at the University of Puget Sound. She is the author of *Reforming Sodom: Protestants and the Rise of Gay Rights* (2015) and a co-editor, with Gillian Frank and Bethany Moreton, of *Devotions and Desires: Histories of Sexuality and Religion in the Twentieth-Century United States* (2018).

INDEX

Printed in the United States
By Bookmasters